YELLOWSTONE JACK

YELLOWSTONE JACK

The Life and Times of Legendary Pioneer Jack Baronett

ROBERT V. GOSS

RIVERBEND
PUBLISHING

RIVERBEND
PUBLISHING
An imprint of The Globe Pequot Publishing Group, Inc.
64 South Main Street
Essex, CT 06426
www.globepequot.com

Copyright © 2025 by Robert V. Goss

All rights reserved. No part of this book may be reproduced in any form or by any electronic or mechanical means, including information storage and retrieval systems, without written permission from the publisher, except by a reviewer who may quote passages in a review.

British Library Cataloguing in Publication Information available

Library of Congress Cataloging-in-Publication Data

ISBN 9781493091829 (paperback)
ISBN 9781493091836 (electronic)

This book is dedicated to all those prospectors and miners of days of yore—a hardy breed indeed. Subject to vagaries of weather, they endured frozen streams; aching frostbitten hands; scorching hot, sunbaked deserts; rugged mountains; and deep, dank holes in the ground, where cave-ins and powder burns always threatened. Yet when the golden gleam appeared in a stream or gold pan, or stringers of gold revealed themselves in a quartz outcrop on a rocky slope, all hardships were forgotten with the promise of riches. But sometimes 'twas merely an illusion.

Nonetheless, hope endured, and the Argonaut trudged on, always keeping an eye on the ground and his surroundings, wary of an unseen danger—hostile locals, grizzly bears, or perhaps outlaws and claim jumpers. Yes, it was a perilous life, but one that he could not give up. When the Golden Seductress beckoned, he could not resist her charms that led him onward into the wildness. You good ole boys, along with your fellow pioneers and explorers, helped settle the West and make it hospitable for us greenhorns to follow in your footsteps. And for that, we all say, *thank you*!

CONTENTS

Introduction 1

CHAPTER 1: Who Was Jack Baronett?. 5
CHAPTER 2: Discovering Yellowstone and Early Prospects,
    1864–1871. 15
CHAPTER 3: Finding Mr. Everts, 1870 27
CHAPTER 4: Jack's Bridge: The Genesis 35
CHAPTER 5: Guiding the Guests 49
CHAPTER 6: Working in Wonderland 75
CHAPTER 7: Prospecting in Paradise. 89
CHAPTER 8: Gold Rush to the Black Hills 101
CHAPTER 9: Nez Perce Burn Jack's Bridge 117
CHAPTER 10: Jack's Bridge: The Exodus. 131
CHAPTER 11: Alaska Beckons and Jack Fades from the Frontier. . . 147

Epilogue 159
Acknowledgments 161
Appendix: Jack's Stories—Truth or Fiction? 163
Bibliography 191
About the Author 203

INTRODUCTION

For once you've panned the speckled sand and seen the bonny dust,
Its peerless brightness blinds you like a spell;
It's little else you care about; you go because you must,
And you feel that you could follow it to hell.
You'd follow it in hunger, and you'd follow it in cold;
You'd follow it in solitude and pain;
And when you're stiff and battened down let someone whisper "Gold,"
You're lief to rise and follow it again.[1]

—Robert W. Service

Life in the sixteenth to eighteenth centuries was one of turmoil and tumult in a world seemingly overrun with explorers, exploiters, and those seeking political power and monetary gain. This turmoil, of course, was not limited to that era but was common ever since humanity began its so-called rise to civilization. However, with the advent of more sophisticated ships and navigation, those exploits reached out to remote places and cultures previously safe from foreign marauders, such as Africa, China, Mexico, and South America. Plundering riches already pulled from the ground and fashioned into precious objects was relatively simple for powerful countries such as Spain, Portugal, and others. However, the situation would soon change.

Those easy pickings had mostly been exhausted by the 1800s. The road to riches was a long and usually unattainable struggle for ordinary men. Their lot was one of toil and travail trying to eke out a living as

---

1. Robert W. Service, "The Prospector," *The Best of Robert Service* (New York: Dodd, Mead & Co., 1953), pp. 56–59.

farmers or tradesmen. In America, hopes began to glimmer when James Marshall discovered gold on January 24, 1848, at John Sutter's mill in northern California. Although word of the find spread relatively quickly in Alta California, news was slower to reach the East Coast, some five or six months distant. However, when it did, hopes began to flicker brightly for riches and a better life.

Stories emerged about men easily picking up gold, swiftly filling their knapsacks, and getting rich quickly. Many of those '48ers who got there first—Euro-Americans, Californios,[2] Mexicans, South Americans, and Australians—did get rich, as the news traveled to them much faster by ship. For those in the East, it was a long, dangerous, and rugged journey across the Great Plains and through the Western mountain wilderness to reach the gold fields. It was not until the spring of 1849 that they could begin their quest. Many tried, and many died in the attempt, littering the trails with horse, mule, and ox bones and graves of numerous poor souls. On arriving at their destination, life continued to be arduous and expensive. Most could pan or dig only enough gold for their beans, rice, daily bread, and grog, all of which were very expensive. Those who mined the miners by providing life's necessities and wants were most often the winners in the race to success.

In the larger picture, though, the gold rush was not limited to California. Prospectors of many nationalities made discoveries in China, Africa, Australia, Mexico, Alaska, and British Columbia. These exotic strikes required a stalwart, fearless, and adventurous personality, one not afraid to face adversity, perils, pitfalls, or failure. One such intrepid explorer was Scotsman John H. "Jack" Baronett. The whisper of the Golden Seductress lured him to countries around the world and across the West in search of her bounty. These countries and America's Western territories were his stomping grounds. Historians have dubbed Baronett[3] a prospector, miner, explorer, adventurer, soldier of fortune, scout, hunter,

---

2. The term *Californio* (historical, regional Spanish for Californian) was originally applied by and to the Spanish-speaking residents of Las Californias during the periods of Spanish California and Mexican California between 1683 and 1848. The first Californios were the children of the early Spanish military expeditions that traveled into the northern reaches of the Californias.

3. His name has been spelled in multiple ways: Baronette, Barronett, Barronnett, with or without an *e* at the end, Barnett, Burnett, and so forth. "Baronett" is how he spelled it on various

INTRODUCTION

guide, frontier fighter, and other monikers befitting his wanderlust life. However, despite all his wanderings, he eventually discovered what would be his true home—southwest Montana and Yellowstone National Park.

While Baronett's life was filled with exciting accomplishments and adventures, he was generally of a quiet and unassuming nature. Nor was he prone to self-aggrandizing promotion, as were other, more well-known characters of his age, such as Buffalo Bill Cody, Gen. George Custer, and Texas Jack Omohundro. If he had acted as the showman and possessed a flair for publicity, he might also have become a public figure and made his life more financially secure. Although literate, he left no known notes or diaries about his life and times, as did other well-known characters. This fact contributed to the various inconsistencies and inaccuracies of his life story, which continue to this day. Those untutored in Yellowstone history who may have heard his name probably know only a few of his acknowledgments: a peak in Yellowstone named after him (albeit incorrectly spelled "Barronette" by the 1871 Hayden Expedition); the "Bridge That Jack Built"[4]—the first in Yellowstone National Park and on the Yellowstone River; and his rescue of Truman Everts, lost from the 1870 Washburn Expedition. But there is so much more . . .

---

communications, and "Baronette" is the most common misspelling. He was also known as Collins Jack Baronett or John H. Baronett.

4. Aubrey L. Haines, "The Bridge That Jack Built," *Yellowstone Nature Notes* 21, no. 1 (January–February 1947). Yellowstone Archives.

CHAPTER ONE

Who Was Jack Baronett?

> *Baronette, or "Jack Baronette," as he is best known, is a celebrated character in this country, and although famous as an Indian fighter and hunter, he is still more celebrated as a guide. From early boyhood, he has lived in the mountains, and his whole life is a chapter replete with adventure and hair-breadth escapes.*[5]
>
> —GEN. W. E. STRONG, 1875

Baronett has been called "Yellowstone Jack" in numerous historical texts, the first of which was Hiram Chittenden's 1895 edition of *The Yellowstone National Park*. In the book, Chittenden described the origin of the name Baronett Peak. He noted that it was named "for C. J. Baronett, 'Yellowstone Jack,' a famous scout and guide, closely connected with the history of the National Park and builder of the first bridge across the Yellowstone River."[6] Baronett sometimes went by the name of Collins Jack. Additionally, Aubrey Haines, in his *Yellowstone National Park: Its Exploration and Establishment*, refers to "the colorful career of Jack Baronett (better known as 'Yellowstone Jack')."[7] Interestingly, the name has not yet appeared in written records earlier than 1895. Online newspapers, magazines, books, and documents do not mention the moniker. Perhaps

---

5. Gen. W. E. Strong, *A Trip to the Yellowstone Park in July, August, and September 1875* (Washington, DC: Government Printing Office, 1876), p. 43.
6. Hiram M. Chittenden, *The Yellowstone National Park: Historical and Descriptive* (Cincinnati, OH: Robert Clarke Co., 1895), p. 291.
7. Aubrey L. Haines, *Yellowstone National Park: Its Exploration and Establishment* (Washington, DC: US Department of the Interior, National Park Service, 1974), p. 134.

Baronett used that name in his correspondence to Chittenden, or maybe Chittenden used "Yellowstone Jack" to give Jack a somewhat larger-than-life image, such as those monikers used by Buffalo Bill, Wild Bill, Texas Jack, Yellowstone Kelly, Billy the Kid, and others. Alternatively, the name may have been used in conversation but not in the written record. An interesting speculation indeed.[8]

According to army engineer and historian Hiram M. Chittenden, who had known Baronett in Yellowstone, John H. "Jack" Baronett was born around 1829 in Glencoe, Argyll, Scotland. A US Census dated June 1, 1880, in Upper Yellowstone Valley listed his age as forty-nine, born around 1831, and his birthplace Scotland, his father as Scottish, and his mother from Spain. Oddly enough, two days later, another census dated June 3, 1880, for the inhabitants of Barronette's Bridge, Wyoming, described his birthplace as England. It noted his age as fifty, which put his birth around 1830. Why the difference? It could have been his mood or temperament that day, or maybe just a transcription error, which was not uncommon. His tombstone in Livingston wrongly reads 1834, while Aubrey Haines claims a date of 1827.[9]

There are several short biographies written about Baronett, but many are derived from Chittenden's tome *The Yellowstone National Park*,[10] in which a chronicle of Jack's life was written with his assistance. Aubrey Haines also penned an informative biography in his *Yellowstone National Park: Its Exploration and Establishment*. Park County, Montana, historian Doris Whithorn profiled Baronett in her book *Twice Told on the Yellowstone*, vol. 2,[11] which relied heavily on local newspapers and a few classic books. Dan Thrapp, in his *Encyclopedia of Frontier Biography*, published a

---

8. Two other "Yellowstone Jacks" appear in old Montana newspapers. One was a horse thief and ne'er-do-well, while another was a hunter, guide, and rancher in western Montana. However, once used by Chittenden, the name stuck to Baronett and was widely used across any number of historical tomes and articles of a later date.

9. Aubrey L. Haines, "Biographical Appendix," *Yellowstone National Park: Its Exploration and Establishment* (Washington, DC: US Department of the Interior, National Park Service, 1974), pp. 134–35.

10. Chittenden, *The Yellowstone National Park*, pp. 291–92; "That Was in the Early Days," *Anaconda Standard*, January 30, 1895, p. 8.

11. Doris Whithorn, "Jack Baronett—A Legend in His Lifetime," *Tales Twice Told on the Yellowstone*, vol. 2 (Livingston, MT: Self-published, 1994), pp. 61–74.

Baronett Historians

Hiram Martin Chittenden served as the building and road engineer during two terms of service at Yellowstone National Park in 1891–1892 and 1899–1906. He would have known Baronett well during his tenure and would have been aware of his long residence and activities related to Yellowstone, and the world.

Doris Whithorn was a prolific local chronicler of Park County, Montana, history. Doris and her husband, Bill, self-published dozens of photo histories of events and people from the annals of Park County history. In 2005, the Friends of the Yellowstone Gateway Museum purchased all publications by Bill and Doris Whithorn and have been republishing many of their books.

Dan Thrapp was a graduate of the University of Missouri School of Journalism, a foreign correspondent for the United Press in Argentina, Greece, Italy, and the United Kingdom, and, for many years, an editor for the *Los Angeles Times*. He wrote extensively on the West, including his four-volume set *The Encyclopedia of Frontier Biography*.

Aubrey L. Haines was a Yellowstone National Park and Mount Rainier National Park ranger and the first park historian of Yellowstone National Park. He wrote numerous books concerning Yellowstone history, including his classic two-volume reference work *The Yellowstone Story: A History of Our First National Park*.

short bio of Jack[12] but repeats much of the information found elsewhere. Other, more obscure newspaper sources have printed articles about Baronett but were often prone to hearsay and would frequently print imaginative speculation to fill in the unknown voids of his life. These and others all have one thing in common: very little detail on his activities from 1850 to the mid-1860s and during the final years of his life.

Jack Baronett embarked on a life of travel and adventure early in life. While his father served in the British naval service, Jack and his mother

---

12. Dan L. Thrapp, *Encyclopedia of Frontier Biography: A–F* (Omaha: University of Nebraska Press, 1988), p. 65.

would frequently accompany him on his journeys and sometimes be left temporarily at ports in Mexico, Cuba, China, and the South Sea Islands while he continued his seafaring duties. Many sources claim Jack was on the coast of China in 1850, and, hearing of the gold rush in California, the twenty-one-year-old jumped ship, found another bound for California, and sailed off to seek his fortune.[13] Philetus W. Norris, the second superintendent of Yellowstone National Park, who became well acquainted with Baronett, wrote that Jack was in the Sandwich Islands (Hawaii) in 1850 and shipped to California from that point.[14]

P. W. Norris

Philetus Walter Norris became the second Yellowstone Park superintendent in 1877, serving for five years. He was known for his explorations of the park and geyser basins, and he wrote extensively of his findings. He established the first written rules and regulations for the park and had them published in local newspapers and posted on signs around the park. He obtained the first congressional appropriations in 1878 and set out to build a road from Mammoth to the Lower Geyser Basin. He continued to build many other roads and trails in the park, but his detractors claimed he was more interested in the number of miles built than the quality of the roads. Unfortunately, funds were limited, and he attempted to stretch them as far as possible. Through his efforts, 234 miles of trails and crude roads had been constructed by 1879. Two years later, he was responsible for completing 104 miles of today's 140-mile Grand Loop road system. He built the first administrative building in the park on Capitol Hill at Mammoth in 1879. Due to the American Indian Wars of 1877–1878, the building was erected more as a protective fort and became known as the Norris Blockhouse. Norris Geyser Basin, Norris Pass, and Mount Norris were named after him. His tenure ended in February 1882, and he died three years later in Kentucky.

---

13. Thrapp, *Encyclopedia of Frontier Biography*, p. 65.
14. P. W. Norris, "Meanderings of a Mountaineer, or, The Journals and Musings of a Rambler over Prairie and Plain," unpublished MS (P. W. Norris Collection, Henry E. Huntington Library, San Marino, CA, 1885), p. 97.

WHO WAS JACK BARONETT?

Both stories could be true, as Hawaii was a common resupply point in ocean crossings. How he fared in the Golden State is unknown, but by 1851 he was off to other strikes, prospecting in Walla Walla (Oregon Territory), Australia, and Africa. The gold rush in New South Wales, Australia, began in 1851, and he spent time prospecting there at least once or twice.[15] During the next few years, Jack reportedly served as second mate on a whaling ship bound for Alaska,[16] perhaps because his finances required steady paid work or he simply needed transportation. However, by 1855, he was back plying the gold fields of California.

A *New York Sun* newspaper reporter interviewed Jack in 1882 and requested the story of his life in the Wild West. Jack proceeded to accommodate him, but, unbeknownst to the reporter, Jack decided to have some fun with him. In a hodge-podge of truth and fiction, Baronett declared, "In 1857, I went down to Fort Garland, did some trading with the Indians, and afterward joined the regular army as a scout under General Sidney Johnston."[17] Although Baronett's timeline for the Utah War is correct, Fort Garland (located in south central Colorado) was not officially established until June 1858. However, construction of the fort began in July 1857 by soldiers and civilian laborers.[18]

Johnston took control of cavalry forces en route to Utah Territory in late November 1857 and led a campaign called the Utah War (sometimes known as the Mormon War) to reestablish federal control over the government of Utah Territory. Arriving too late in the season to try to cross the rugged mountain terrain during the winter, Johnston encamped his troops near Fort Bridger in southwest Wyoming along the Oregon Trail and established Camp Scott.[19] Baronett was likely familiar with the area and would have made an excellent scout crossing the mountains in the spring of 1858, but he never mentioned Utah in his travels and may have gone to Fort Garland after Johnston arrived at Salt Lake City.

---

15. Norris, "Meanderings," p. 97.
16. Chittenden, *The Yellowstone National Park*, pp. 291–92.
17. "Jack Baronett, the Scout," *Cincinnati Enquirer*, January 28, 1882. Originally published in the *New York Sun*.
18. Fort Garland, Colorado—The Army Historical Foundation, accessed August 10, 2024, armyhistory.org.
19. "Utah War," Texas State Historical Society, https://hrc.contentdm.oclc.org/digital/collection/p15878coll71.

In the *Sun* article, Jack spoke of his adventures in Mexico, an account that seems to stray into the realm of an amusing campfire story. In the report, Jack alleged that he "drifted over to Mexico. . . . The Mexicans got hold of me and gave me the choice of joining them or being shot. They were fighting Maximilian. Why, I told them that was just what suited me—just what I came over for. When I say they were fighting Maximilian. I only tell part of their business. They were fighting anything that had money. They called themselves Mexicans, but most of them were Europeans and all of them a bad lot." Jack continued his tale, claiming he was captured by another set of Mexicans, given the same option, and then captured by Maximilian's troops. Baronett was pardoned provided he fought with them, until again being recaptured by yet another band of insurgents and offered the same option.[20] It is an amusing saga with only snippets of truth. Most accounts of Jack's life do mention that he served as a captain with Maximilian in 1863,[21] when Archduke Ferdinand Maximilian Joseph of Austria became emperor of Mexico. Mexican president Benito Juaréz did not welcome Maximilian, whose brief and unstable regime ended in 1867 when he was captured by Republican forces and executed.[22]

Baronett also related to the *Sun* reporter his tale of how, at the request of Governor Thomas F. Meagher in 1865, he raised a small battalion of men at his own expense to help subdue American Indian rebellions occurring in northcentral Montana. He claimed, "All the mounting and equipping and fitting out of that company I did at my own cost, at an expense to me of $16,000—good dollars in gold."[23] In those days, it was a considerable sum of money, and it seems unlikely he would have invested that amount in the cause. Jack did speak knowingly of some events during that period, such as the death of Chief Little Dog, a friend of the white settlers, and the killing of Charles Carson, nephew of Kit

---

20. "An Old Scout's Story," *Butte Miner*, February 22, 1882, p. 1. See the appendix for the complete story.
21. Thrapp, *Encyclopedia of Frontier Biography*, p. 65.
22. "Maximilian, Emperor of Mexico," Harry Ranson Center, University of Texas, https://hrc.contentdm.oclc.org/digital/collection/p15878coll71.
23. "Jack Baronett, the Scout." That amount in gold would be worth some $350,000 these days—hardly an amount Baronett could afford.

WHO WAS JACK BARONETT?

The only known image of Jack Baronett. In 1890, he was described as a powerfully built man of sixty, who looked forty-five, with clear skin, blue eyes, and a gray mustache. (Project Gutenberg eBook of Hiram M. Chittenden's *The Yellowstone National Park: Historical and Descriptive*, p. 293, public domain)

JACK BARONETTE.

Carson, by the Piegan in 1866. These were actual events, but Jack's tales of his heroic efforts to bring the murderers to justice dwell on the dubious side of truth. Research has not yet revealed his name in the numerous accounts of those violent days.[24]

Back in Montana, a wag at the Helena newspaper wryly noted, "Jack Baronett has been spinning forty yarns to the *New York Sun*, and when his old Montana chums read them in that voracious journal, they will be surprised to learn what a holy terror Jack has been."[25] In relating his tales, Jack certainly lived up to the expectations of his "chums." In a similar vein, the *New North-West* newspaper characterized the *Sun* article as follows: "The most prodigious contribution to recent sensational literature concerning Montana is the *New York Sun*'s interview with Jack Baronette, of the Upper Yellowstone, now in New York in the interest of having the Clark's Fork country relinquished by the Indians. Jack spins some yarns that would make Munchausen's hair stand on end and tells

---
24. "Jack Baronett, the Scout." See the appendix for his complete telling of the story.
25. "Virginia City Items," *Helena Weekly Herald*, March 9, 1882, p. 6.

of 'hair-breadthscapes' Othello never whispered in Desdemona's willing ear."[26] It seems Jack roguishly followed in the footsteps of his predecessors, the mountain men, who loved to tell a whopper, the truth being a minor player in those tales. He also enjoyed some good-hearted fibbing at the expense of a greenhorn or Eastern reporter asking dumb questions.

Captain Quinton, probably William Quinton of the Seventh Infantry, commented in 1886 about Jack's storytelling abilities, "The papers speak of him now as Captain John Barronette. I suppose that Jack gets his title of Captain from the fact of being the boss story teller of Montana. When I was acquainted with him, he was simply Jack, and was one of the curiosities of the park. He was then a hunter, guide, trapper, and a first-rate story teller." Then the speaker proceeded to relate one of Jack's "Awful Bear Stories" and a famous serpent story (see appendix).

To backtrack a bit, according to Aubrey Haines, Jack traveled north in early 1859 from Fort Garland to join the new gold rush near Denver, Colorado.[27] The Colorado gold rush, originally known as the Pike's Peak gold rush, was the second-largest mining excitement in the West after the California gold rush ten years earlier. Over a hundred thousand people

Snake in the Grass

A Cinnabar, Montana, special to the *Pioneer Press* says, "Last Monday a stage driver and two tourists, while near Yellowstone Lake, claim to have seen an enormous reptile which, while running through the grass, carried its head ten or fifteen feet above the ground. They think it must have been at least thirty feet long. A party was organized to pursue the reptile. Yesterday a party of gentlemen, among them Colonel Wear, Superintendent of the Park, and his assistant, Captain Barronette, while near the cave of an extinct geyser in the vicinity of the lake heard a hissing and saw the head of the reptile thrust out some fifteen feet, and immediately with[drew]. Parties are watching for another sight of the monster" (*Brooklyn Daily Eagle*, July 30, 1886, p. 3).

---

26. See "An Old Scout's Story," *Butte Miner* (MT), February 22, 1882, p. 1.
27. Haines, "Biographical Appendix," *Yellowstone National Park*, p. 442.

WHO WAS JACK BARONETT?

participated in this rush and were known as Fifty-Niners, a reference to 1859, when the rush to Colorado peaked.[28] Once again, details of his life during that time may exist, but I have not found any.

By 1862, the American Civil War was raging, and, being sympathetic to the South, Baronett joined the First Texas Cavalry. The regiment had formed in November 1862 under the command of Edmund J. Davis, later a brigadier general.[29] At some point in 1863, Jack became disenchanted with the South's chances of success and left what he believed was a lost cause.[30] Livingston historian Ellery Christian inquired to the National Archives in 1966 about Baronett's Confederate Army service. Their reply was inconclusive at best:

> We are unable to confirm Baronett's service in the 1st Texas Cavalry, Confederate States Army. Record Group 109, the War Department Collection of Confederate Records, includes the compiled military service records for Confederate volunteers. A check of the index for all Texas troops and the actual documents (for the 1st Regiment of Cavalry-Texas State Troops, McCulloch's 1st Texas Cavalry, and Yager's Texas Cavalry) show no record for any person with the last name of Baronett. The research does not mean Baronett did not serve; Confederate records are not always complete, or he may have served under another name.[31]

Numerous online listings of Confederate soldiers, including the units above, have yet to show a name even close to Baronett. As the archives stated, it does not mean he did not serve.

The various biographies of Baronett mention little of his life during the period between 1867 and early 1870. Hiram Chittenden claimed that after Jack's 1864 travels through Yellowstone, "he was later in the service

---

28. "The Colorado Gold Rush," Western Mining History, https://westernmininghistory.com/4785/the-colorado-gold-rush/.
29. "First Texas Cavalry, USA," Texas State Historical Society, https://www.tshaonline.org/handbook/entries/first-texas-cavalry-usa. Attempts to locate records on Jack's time in the cavalry have been unsuccessful, but he may have used a different name.
30. Thrapp, *Encyclopedia of Frontier Biography*, p. 65.
31. National Archives to Mr. Ellery Christian, letter of June 18, 1996, author's collection.

of Gen. Custer as scout in the Indian territory; then in Mexico and finally back in Montana in 1870."³² Aubrey Haines stated that following Jack's involvement with the 1866 Yellowstone Expedition, he served "as a scout with General Custer's expedition to the Black Hills, and another foray into the Yellowstone country in 1869 increased Baronett's familiarity with the region."³³ Neither historian claimed a specific date for Jack's service with Custer, but both biographies are in chronological sequence, placing his Custer days before 1870. Historian Lee Whittlesey, in his *Yellowstone Place Names*, followed suit and stated Baronett "scouted for George Custer in 1868."³⁴

Custer had been relieved of duty in 1867 and only reinstated in the fall of 1868 to track down warring tribes in southeast Colorado and Kansas. In late November, Custer led his troops in the vicious Washita River Massacre in Oklahoma and slaughtered more than fifty mostly peaceful Cheyenne men, women, and children led by Black Kettle, and as many were taken captive. However, Custer's Black Hills Expedition occurred in 1874, and Dan Thrapp believed Baronett was "a scout with Custer's 1874 Black Hills Expedition."³⁵ This is the likely explanation of the conundrum, so that Jack was not with Custer in 1868. Baronett related his story to Chittenden in the early 1890s, when he was in his sixties and some twenty years after the event. It is easy for old-timers to confuse dates and sequences of events.

Following his foray to Mexico, Jack wound up back in California, still searching for the elusive bane of Midas. Not long afterward, during an adventuresome expedition east to the territories of Montana and Wyoming, he would find his life's calling that would engage him through the rest of his life in an area that would later become Yellowstone National Park.

---

32. Chittenden, *The Yellowstone National Park* (1895), pp. 291–92.
33. Haines, "Biographical Appendix."
34. Lee H. Whittlesey, *Yellowstone Place Names*, 2nd ed. (Gardiner, MT: Wonderland Publishing, 2006), p. 43.
35. Thrapp, *Encyclopedia of Frontier Biography*, p. 65.

CHAPTER TWO

Discovering Yellowstone and Early Prospects: 1864–1871

The first mention I ever heard made of that region [Yellowstone] was by old mountaineers. They told about the experience of a man named Holter [Colter], who was with Lewis and Clark on their famous trip across the continent. . . . In 1864 I went into the park on a gold prospecting tour, going as far as Yellowstone Lake. There were no signs of any white man having preceded me.[36]

—Jack Baronett

Lt. Hiram M. Chittenden of the Army Corps of Engineers was in charge of road design and construction in Yellowstone from 1891 to 1893 and had known Baronett during that period. Chittenden was aware that Baronett had been in and around the park for about thirty years and wrote to Baronett in the early 1890s requesting the park's early history and information about Jack's life. Jack responded to Chittenden's request, and portions of his reply were made available to the *Livingston Post* newspaper. Regarding early exploration of the Yellowstone area, Baronett related, "In 1864 [September] I went into the Park on a gold prospecting tour, going as far as Yellowstone Lake. There were no signs of anyone preceding me. At the east fork of the Yellowstone [Lamar River] I found a camp

---

36. "That Was in the Early Days," *Anaconda Standard,* January 30, 1895, p. 8.

of about 150 lodges of hostile Indians but did not talk to them, as my party was small."³⁷ Chittenden's book relates that account and others.³⁸

Gen. William T. Sherman, traveling through the west with Col. Richard Irving Dodge in 1881, toured Yellowstone with Baronett as a guide. Sherman later recounted the story of Baronett's 1864 epic explorations: "During the ride of the day we had the company of Baronett, or Jack Baronett, as he is better known by, and as he was one of the earliest explorers of this region. I gathered from him what I could of its early history." Baronett explained that "in 1864 he, with a party of miners, prospected from California as far east as Henry's Lake. Here most of the party, becoming discouraged, returned, but he and two or three others continued and entered the Geyser Basins, and saw for the first time the geysers in operation. . . . Baronett upon returning to civilization told of what he had seen, but was only laughed at, and for the time said no more about it."³⁹ He may have thought they were the first to visit the geyser basins, but many other early trappers and explorers had ventured into Yellowstone and the geyser basins in the 1830s through the 1850s;

W. T. Sherman

General William Tecumseh Sherman was an American soldier and businessman who served as a Union Army general during the Civil War. He was known for his command of military strategy and implemented scorched-earth policies against the Confederate States. He became commanding general of the army from 1869 until 1883 and was responsible for the US Army's participation in the American Indian Wars west of the Mississippi River. Sherman avoided political wrangling and, in 1875, published his memoirs and related firsthand accounts of the Civil War.

---

37. "Some Interesting Early History," *Livingston Post*, January 30, 1895, p. 1.
38. Hiram Martin Chittenden, *The Yellowstone National Park: Historical and Descriptive* (Cincinnati, OH: Robert Clarke Co., 1895), p. 292.
39. William T. Sherman, "Report of Journey Made by Gen. W. T. Sherman in the Northwest and Middle Parts of the United States in 1883," in *Annual Reports of the War Department*, vol. 1 (United States War Dept., 1882–1883), p. 211.

DISCOVERING YELLOWSTONE AND EARLY PROSPECTS: 1864-1871

however, they left few written accounts, which were either disbelieved or not published until later years.

Unknown to Baronett at the time, Walter W. de Lacy had ventured through Yellowstone in 1863 with a company of twenty-seven men, all from Colorado and California, who were unfamiliar with this country. Leaving Virginia City, the group traveled to the Snake River in the Tetons, setting up camp early each day to allow time to prospect the area. There seemed to be "color" everywhere but nothing of real significance. They eventually reached the Lower Geyser Basin before journeying out the west entrance and up the Madison and Gallatin Rivers. The trip was a bust, and the men left with empty pockets, but de Lacy later published a map and description of his explorations.[40] His "Map of the Territory of Montana with Portions of the Adjoining Territories" was published in 1865 at the request of the Montana Territory Legislature and was amended and corrected over the next two dozen years.[41]

Baronett also disclosed to Gen. Sherman that he had journeyed to St. Louis in 1869, where he met a gentleman who witnessed geysers in operation in Iceland and was genuinely interested in Jack's experience. According to Sherman, the man was apparently "acquainted with General Henry Dana Washburn, then surveyor-general of Montana, and when he arrived in Montana, he related Baronett's story to Washburn. Washburn undoubtedly heard stories from mountain men such as Jim Bridger, William Hamilton, and perhaps de Lacy. He was also familiar with the accounts from the 1869 Cook-Folsom-Peterson Expedition, the first known documented journey into Yellowstone. Baronett's account definitely interested Washburn, and in the summer of 1870, he organized a party called the Washburn-Langford-Doane Expedition and explored, mapped and described the Yellowstone country in great detail."[42]

Unbeknownst to Baronett, in that same summer of 1864, George Huston, an early prospector, miner, and Yellowstone pioneer, was also

---

40. Walter W. de Lacy, "A Trip Up the Snake River in 1863," *Contributions to the Historical Society of Montana*, vol. 1 (Helena, MT: Rocky Mountain Publishing, 1876), pp. 131–40.

41. Jim Walsh, "The Exploration and Mapping of Yellowstone National Park," *Meridian Journal*, no. 3 (1990): pp. 5–9.

42. General Sherman, "Report of Journey Made by Gen. W. T. Sherman in the Northwest," p. 211.

The only known image of George A. Huston, ca. 1977. He has been described as a man of few words, a natural-born gentleman, and a genial companion. (*Harper's Weekly*, November 17, 1877, public domain)

prospecting in Yellowstone, albeit along the northern section, coming in from the north. Since Baronett entered from the west and likely exited that way, the two parties did not run across each other. According to historian E. S. Topping, in 1864, "prospecting parties were going out in every direction. One of these consisting of thirty men under the leadership of Austin [Huston] went to and up the Yellowstone. When they arrived at the east fork of the Yellowstone, they went up that stream to the first creek coming in from the left above Soda Butte Creek, up which they went." They camped at its head, and early the next morning, a band of Arapahoe drove away all their stock but one jackass. Unable to chase them, they cached their goods, hoofed it on foot, and eventually found their way back to Virginia City.[43] The area was later named Cache Creek. Aubrey Haines related the same story and claimed the party of forty men included Huston, Adam "Horn" Miller, H. W. Wayant, and William Hamilton. Huston mounted another foray into Yellowstone in 1866 with five companions: George Hubbard, Rube Lilly, Soos, Lewis, and an unnamed man from Mexico. They came in by the Madison River

---

43. E. S. Topping, *Chronicles of the Yellowstone* (Minneapolis, MN: Ross & Haines, 1968), p. 16.

DISCOVERING YELLOWSTONE AND EARLY PROSPECTS: 1864–1871

George Huston

George A. Huston was a gold prospector known to have explored the park areas as early as 1864 when he led a party of thirty to forty miners up the Yellowstone River into the Lamar and Clark's Fork drainages. Later in the year, he conducted another party up the Madison and Firehole Rivers. Two years afterward, Huston guided still another small group of miners up the Madison River to the geyser basins; prospected around Yellowstone Lake, Hayden Valley, Mirror Plateau, and Lamar Valley; and returned to Emigrant via the Yellowstone River. He built a cabin in the fall of 1867 near Turkey Pen Creek and the Gardner River, becoming the first permanent white resident in the park. When Truman Everts was lost on the Washburn Expedition of 1870, it was Huston's cabin that Jack Baronett and George Pritchett brought Everts to so he could recuperate. Huston then carried Everts on his horse to the north side of Yankee Jim Canyon, where a wagon could transport Everts to Bozeman. Huston was also heavily involved in the Cooke City mining operation. He died July 4, 1886, in Livingston of typhoid pneumonia and other complications. Huston, like Baronett, left no known written records.

on the west side, up the Nez Perce River to Hayden Valley, and thoroughly explored the park. Striking the Lamar River, they followed it to the Yellowstone River and left through the north entrance. Once again, they found little of significant worth.[44]

Two years before Baronett's venture, gold was discovered in Montana Territory in the summer of 1862 at Grasshopper Creek, near the future town of Bannock. Gold was discovered at Alder Gulch the following year, where the town of Virginia City soon sprang up. Another rush occurred in Last Chance Gulch, near what is now Helena. Thousands of hopeful prospectors and miners from California and Nevada poured into the territory, and Jack later traveled to those areas to try his luck. Perhaps the best claims had already been taken when he got there, so he set out for southwest Montana and Wyoming in search of less crowded virgin prospects.

---

44. Aubrey L. Haines, *Yellowstone Place Names: Mirrors of History* (Denver: University Press of Colorado, 1996), pp. 45–46.

The Lost Mine of the Yellowstone

According to legend, two years after their original discovery, David Weaver and his friends made an incredibly rich find on the slopes of Emigrant Peak. They worked through the fall, but winter snow and potential trouble with local tribes caused them to leave the area. It was two years before they could return, but the snows, rains, and floods had destroyed all signs of their workings. They searched and searched the rugged mountain but could not locate the original site. Weaver had taken out some samples previously that assayed $5,000 to the ton. They returned periodically to seek the lost riches but failed to locate the mine, and it went down in history as the "Lost Mine of the Yellowstone."

Gold was located on August 30, 1864, at Emigrant Gulch, along the Yellowstone River between the Great Bend, near present Livingston, Montana, and the mouth of the Gardner River by David Weaver, Frank Garrett, and David Shorthill. The fledgling community of Yellowstone City was established nearby, and the Shorthill and Curry mining districts were created.[45] Emigrant Peak, Emigrant Gulch, and Emigrant Creek were named around that time. In reporting the Emigrant strike, *The Montana Post* exclaimed, "Stampede to the Yellowstone. The news of the discovery of a rich gulch on the Yellowstone spread through our town like wildfire, and a very extensive stampede has been the consequence. We counted twenty packers in one group. Verily, this is a marvelous country, and its riches are guessed at."[46]

The problem with the Emigrant area, as Jack and others had discovered, was that most of the area was flush with American Indians, and many miners were hesitant to go into those mountains without a large contingent of men. Emigrant, on the west edge of the mountains, was

---

45. David B. Weaver, "Early Days in Emigrant Gulch," *Contributions to the Historical Society of Montana*, vol. 7 (Helena: Montana Historical and Miscellaneous Library, 1910), pp. 73–96. Thomas Curry had prospected in the area the previous winter, but local tribes ran him off. He returned in the summer of 1864. Emigrant Gulch later spawned Yellowstone City, some 30 miles north of Gardiner, Montana.

46. "Stampede to the Yellowstone," *Montana Post*, September 24, 1864, p. 3.

generally safer than farther into the interior but still suffered sporadic horse raiding parties and occasional lethal attacks on the miners. Sometime in August 1874, Harry Horr, while traveling north from Yellowstone, spotted three possible Sioux in the Emigrant area. Baronett and a group of local citizens went down the valley to lay in wait for them, but they did not appear. Reports later declared that nine Sioux had been eyeing Nelson Story's herd of cattle and horses in the valley, but the party was not seen again.[47] So there was definitely cause for caution among the miners and travelers.

Adam Miller

Adam "Horn" Miller was born in Bavaria in October 1839 and moved to St. Louis as a child. He came up the Missouri River in 1854 from St. Louis and settled in Emigrant Gulch as early as 1864. He prospected in Yellowstone that year with John Davis and later prospected with Bart Henderson, Ed Hibbard, James Gourley, Sam Shively, Pike Moore, and Joe Brown. Miller discovered gold in the Cooke City area with Bart Henderson and others in 1869–1870, naming their mine the Shoo Fly Mine. During the next few years, he helped Bart Henderson build the road from Bottler's Ranch to Mammoth. Miller likely assisted Baronett in construction of his bridge. He also acted as a guide for Superintendent Norris in 1877 in the northeastern portion of the park when Norris was looking for another northern approach to the park. Miller was one of the scouts under Gen. Howard during the Nez Perce War of 1877. Miller also guided and hunted out of Cooke City. When asked whether he ever killed any American Indians, he replied, "I never went to see, but I shot a good many." Later, he settled down in a cabin across the Yellowstone River from Yankee Jim. Miller Creek and Miller Mountain were named after him. He died in 1913, and his obituary described him as a "man of sterling character, a man without enemies of any kind, it is said, and a citizen who always had a kind word for everyone."[48]

---

47. "Indians Near Bozeman Again," *The New North-West*, August 15, 1874, p. 3.
48. Mary Margaret Curl, "Me," p. 15, accessed August 29, 2013, www.colorado-west.com.

In 1866, Baronett joined the Yellowstone Expedition led by Jefferson Standifer. They did not prospect in Yellowstone itself but among the Yellowstone River drainages north and east of Yellowstone. The group's lieutenant, Bart Henderson, later discovered gold in the Cooke City area with Adam "Horn" Miller, Ed Hibbard, and James Gourley.[49] Men from various parts of the territory joined Standifer, and the company numbered one hundred when they departed. They crossed the Stillwater River and continued on to Clark's Fork and the Bighorn Basin in Wyoming. At times, the group split up to cover more territory and prospected along the way, finding various amounts of gold in the streams. They engaged in skirmishes with tribes along the route, who killed several of their group. Later in the fall, worried about making it

Bart Henderson

Abel Bartlett Henderson was born in Tennessee in 1832 to Gideon B. and Jane Ritchey Henderson. Bart is believed to have prospected for gold in California and the Far West by at least the 1860s. He began prospecting around Yellowstone Park in 1867, coming up from [Jackson's] Hole over Two Ocean Pass, around the east shore of Yellowstone Lake, and downriver into Montana. Henderson discovered gold in the Cooke City area in 1869–1870 with Adam "Horn" Miller, Ed Hibbard, and James Gourley. He named Soda Butte and Soda Butte Creek during that trip. With help from James Gourley and Horn Miller, he began building a road in 1871 from Bottler's Ranch near Emigrant to Mammoth. The road later passed into the hands of "Yankee Jim" James George. Henderson became the first known user of skis in the park when he skied from Stephens Creek to Bozeman in 1871. Bart and his brother Stokely owned a ranch near Stephens Creek, just north of the northern park border, which came under attack by Nez Perce on August 31, 1877. They burned the ranch, and, after a short battle, Sterling Henderson (son of Stokely), Joe Brown, George Reese, John Werks, and one other man escaped across the Yellowstone River in a small boat. Bart died August 4, 1889, in Nelson, British Columbia.

---

49. Aubrey L. Haines, "Biographical Appendix," *Yellowstone National Park: Its Exploration and Establishment* (Washington, DC: US Department of the Interior, National Park Service, 1974).

DISCOVERING YELLOWSTONE AND EARLY PROSPECTS: 1864–1871

to civilization in the winter, with hostile tribes frequenting the area, many men wintered at the relative safety of Fort C. F. Smith. The fort had been established in August 1866 along the Bighorn River near the current border of Wyoming. It was one of five forts constructed to protect travelers from the Lakota Sioux on the Bozeman Trail. It was not stocked or designed to provide for that many residents, and supplies soon began to run low, and the men suffered greatly.[50]

Finally, at the end of April 1867, Baronett and four others surreptitiously left the fort and, after eleven days, straggled into Fort Ellis near Bozeman, with Baronett reporting, "There were two hundred men there, soldiers and refugees. Since Christmas, they have had no flour; are completely destitute of coffee, sugar, tobacco; in fact, every necessity except corn, bacon and 'hard tack'; and on last Thursday evening the hard bread would be exhausted and the last cracker issued." Occasionally, friendly tribes were allowed to approach the fort to trade food or other necessities. One soldier reportedly bartered his blankets for a pipe full of tobacco, an item almost as important as food. The *Montana Post* reported on May 25 that Col. de Lacy and forty men left on a potentially dangerous but successful mission to accompany a supply train and relieve the beleaguered men.[51]

Meanwhile, back in Yellowstone, Bart Henderson and George Huston had been prospecting along the northern edge of Yellowstone. The country was wide open to prospecting, as the lands were not established as a national park until 1872. Uncle Joe Brown and three other men worked the mouth of Bear Creek over the winter of 1866–1867 and took out $8,000 in gold dust and nuggets. Bear Creek is the first stream flowing into the Yellowstone River above the junction of the Gardner and Yellowstone Rivers. Lou Anderson, A. H. Hubble, George Reese, Caldwell, and Simms ventured up Bear Creek in 1867 and, at the juncture of another creek, discovered gold in a crevice, anointing the area Crevice Gulch.[52] Around that time, George Huston built a cabin on the flat across from the mouth of Bear Creek, becoming the first white

---

50. "The Very Latest," *Montana Post*, May 11, 1867, p. 8.
51. "The Very Latest," *Montana Post*, May 11, 1867.
52. Chittenden, *The Yellowstone National Park* (1895), p. 34.

resident of the future park. He spent his time hunting, providing meat for other miners passing through, and prospecting at the mouth of Bear Creek, Crevice Creek, and other locales.

David Weaver declared that the Bear Gulch Stampeders—perhaps some of the men previously mentioned, specifically Hubble—had trekked out to the lake at the head of the Yellowstone River (Yellowstone Lake) on a prospecting mission. The dispatch does not mention them finding gold, but they discovered a wealth of natural wonders described in devilish phrases: "a volcanic country emitting blue flames, living streams of molten brimstone, and almost every variety of minerals known to chemists.... The steam and blaze was constantly discharging from these subterranean channels in regular evolutions or exhaustions, like the boilers of our steamboats, and gave the same roaring, whistling sound." The prospectors gave it a significant name—"Hell!" They went as far as to declare they had been to that "bad place," and even saw the "Devil's horns," but fortunately their "souls have been delivered." If they survived their escape to civilization, he declared that they would never return.[53]

In July 1870, Bart Henderson, Adam Miller, Ed Hibbard, J. H. Moore, and James Gourley became the first known prospectors to discover gold in the Clark's Fork section of the northeastern corner of the Yellowstone area. However, the group believed that Jack Crandall and Fin Dougherty had previously discovered gold in the same area, but, unfortunately, they never made it back to civilization. They were savagely killed and beheaded by American Indians, with their heads placed on the ends of their picks stuck into the ground. The gruesome spectacle was a grave warning to others who would follow. Henderson noted in his diary on July 2, "Here we found the first gold on the trip—gold in every gulch & sag ... & discovered several quartz lodes in the afternoon." Regrettably, there was too much snow and water to actively prospect and mine, but they vowed to return in the fall when conditions had improved. While following a creek back to the Yellowstone River, they encountered a unique butte, "some 40 feet high, which has been

---

53. "The Upper Yellowstone," *The Montana Post*, August 31, 1867, p. 2.

DISCOVERING YELLOWSTONE AND EARLY PROSPECTS: 1864–1871

formed by soda water. We gave the cone the name of Soda Butte, & the creek the name of Soda Butte Creek."[54]

These men and others returned in the fall and struck claims on what became known as Henderson and Miller Mountains, and "on the 21st of June [1872] the Miller Lode was recorded, being the first in the district. It was staked in 1871." The miners later established the town of Miner's Camp in 1872, the fledgling burg that later became Cooke City. Henderson noted that on June 19 "the camp [came] together for the purpose of making laws to govern the mines. The same to be known as New World District." Henderson and others, likely including Baronett, staked claims around that time.[55]

When Congress and President Ulysses S. Grant created Yellowstone National Park in March 1872, the mines at Bear and Crevice Gulches (including the New World mines) were excluded. The land bordering the northern border of Yellowstone was part of the Crow Indian Reservation, so mining and township claims had no factual legal basis for another decade.[56] Mining continued, nevertheless, and the men continued to register claims locally. Two miners built a four-stamp mill with two arrastras to process the silver ore the following spring. The future was beginning to look profitable for the miners.

---

54. A. Bart Henderson, *Narrative of a Prospecting Expedition to the East Fork & Clarks Fork of Yellowstone*, July 2–15, 1870. Yellowstone Vertical Files, Yellowstone Library, Gardiner, MT.

55. Henderson, *Narrative*, June 18–21, 1872.

56. New World Mining District Report, US Forest Service, pp. 1–4, accessed July 15, 2023, https://www.fs.usda.gov/Internet/FSE_DOCUMENTS/stelprdb5127407.pdf.

CHAPTER THREE

Finding Mr. Everts, 1870

"Are you Mr. Everts?"
"Yes. All that is left of him."
"We have come for you."
"Who sent you?"
"Judge Lawrence and other friends."
"God bless him, and them, and you! I am saved!"[57]
—Jack Baronett

While Jack Baronett and his mining companions were prospecting for gold, a group of Helena businessmen in 1869 resolved to explore for the fabled "spouting fountains" and "boiling lakes" in the Yellowstone country. However, reports of hostilities with local tribes and the failure to secure a military escort effectively whittled down the original troupe to just three daring explorers. In early September, Charles Cook, David Folsom, and William Peterson departed for the Yellowstone region and all three successfully returned to Helena about five weeks later in early October. Their journals and personal accounts produced the first documented exploration of the future Yellowstone Park as well as inspiring a second expedition in 1870 headed by Henry D. Washburn.

Washburn, a former major-general in the Union Army and then surveyor general for Montana territory, assembled a diverse civilian party consisting of former tax collector and bank examiner Nathaniel Langford;

---

57. Truman C. Everts, *Thirty-Seven Days of Peril* (San Francisco, CA: E&R Grabhorn & James McDonald, 1923), p. 54.

Washburn–Langford–Doane Expedition

During their explorations, party members made detailed maps and observations of the Yellowstone region, explored numerous lakes, climbed several mountains, and observed wildlife. The expedition visited both the Upper and the Lower Geyser Basins and, after observing the regularity of eruptions of one geyser, decided to name it Old Faithful since it erupted about once every 74 minutes.

The party named the following geysers: Beehive Geyser, Castle Geyser, Fan Geyser (originally Fantail Geyser), Giant Geyser, Giantess Geyser, Grotto Geyser, and Old Faithful Geyser.

Party members named the following features after themselves: Mount Washburn, Hedges Peak, Langford Cairn, Mount Doane, Mount Langford, and Mount Everts.

the US attorney of Montana Territory, Cornelius Hedges; banker Samuel Hauser; Helena merchants Warren Gillette and Benjamin Stickney; hide and fur merchant Jacob Smith; the son of a US senator, Walter Trumbull; and the hapless former US assessor for Montana Territory, Truman C. Everts. Packers Elwyn Bean and Charles Reynolds and cooks Nute and Johnny provided support for the entourage. Lt. Gustavus Doane, US Army, Second Cavalry, Fort Ellis, Montana, supplied a military escort. While this excursion contributed volumes of information concerning Yellowstone's natural wonders and wilderness, one single event—the disappearance and dramatic rescue of Truman Everts—would make Jack Baronett famous for the rest of his life.

The Washburn Expedition left Fort Ellis on August 22, 1870, and followed the Yellowstone River to Tower Fall, completely bypassing the spectacular Mammoth Hot Springs. After camping near the falls, the group proceeded along a route used by countless visitors after their time—around Mt. Washburn to the Grand Canyon of Yellowstone, through Hayden Valley, and on to Yellowstone Lake; all of these features were, of course, unnamed at the time, except for the lake. By September 9, they had reached the South Arm of Yellowstone Lake. When

FINDING MR. EVERTS, 1870

they were ready to leave, the members discussed finding a proper route back to Fort Ellis.[58]

In many areas, "The trees were thick and the ground strewn with fallen trunks, requiring the men to dismount often to assist the pack horses or pick a better way. As a result, fatigue was great and tempers were short."[59] As the men struggled to find a route through the dense forest, several became separated from the group but were eventually reunited at a night camp. That is, all but the nearsighted Mr. Everts. He floundered around the wilds all day but was unable to locate the group's camp. So he spent the night in the woods, determined to find the right path the next morning.

When Everts failed to show up at camp that night, the group began to worry about him. They set off in search of him the following morning, firing their rifles occasionally to try to attract Everts's attention. After several fruitless days of pursuit, the group gave it up as a lost cause and departed homeward on September 17, assuming Everts would eventually find his way back. Meanwhile, they discovered the geyser basins and named many features while enjoying the incredible sights. They returned to Fort Ellis on September 22 and divulged the sad news of the unfortunate turn of events. Judge Lawrence, a Helena friend of Everts's, offered a $600 reward for his safe recovery.

Meanwhile, Mr. Everts was having a rough time of it. According to a later account by George Pritchett, one of his rescuers, "He lost his mare, saddle, gun, and canteens the first day out, and was left without fishing tackle or matches; but after making his bed over warm holes for several nights, he thought he might produce fire from his opera-glass, and did so. He lost both his knives. During his wanderings, he saw no human beings, neither whites nor Indians, until we found him."[60]

Everts wandered aimlessly in the wilderness for days, making camps near hot springs. While sleeping one night, the crust below him gave way

---

58. Hiram M. Chittenden, *The Yellowstone National Park, Historical and Descriptive* (Cincinnati, OH: Robert Clarke Co., 1895), pp. 75–81.

59. Aubrey L. Haines, *The Yellowstone Story*, vol. 1 (Denver: University Press of Colorado, 1996), p. 124.

60. "The Long-Lost Found," *Helena Weekly Herald*, October 27, 1870, p. 7.

Truman C. Everts

President Abraham Lincoln appointed Everts as assessor of internal revenue for the Montana Territory, a position he held between July 15, 1864, and February 16, 1870. Everts was offered the first superintendent position of the newly established Yellowstone National Park, but he declined since it did not include a salary. Everts later moved to Hyattsville, Maryland, and worked in the US Post Office. He died of pneumonia in his home in 1901.

and the hot water seriously burned his hip. In addition, he was suffering from frostbite on his feet. Some days afterward he unknowingly put his hand into the campfire while sleeping, burning it quite severely. Another night, while in camp asleep, his campfire spread into a raging inferno, burning one of his hands again. Then, while trying to escape, he lost his fishing line, hook, and a knife-type buckle he had sharpened. Suffering from pain and lack of sufficient food, he experienced frightful hallucinations. As his

Truman Everts's nightmares about his imaginary friends. ("Thirty-Seven Days of Peril," in *Scribner's Monthly* 3, no. 1, November 1871)

FINDING MR. EVERTS, 1870

body and mind rapidly deteriorated, he imagined his various body parts were his friends. Whether prone to bad luck or just a klutz, in the end, he was lucky to be rescued alive, though barely, but for now Lady Luck seemed nowhere close to Yellowstone as Everts continued to suffer relentlessly.[61]

After returning from a trip to Mexico, Jack heard about the reward for locating Everts, who had been missing for around a month. Jack, along with George A. Pritchett (an experienced trapper and mountaineer) and a good dog, took on the task. They outfitted themselves with provisions, blankets, arms, and ammunition and headed out to search for Everts,[62] beginning their journey on October 5. They finally located Everts on October 16, "on the summit of the first big mountain beyond Warm Spring Creek," an area known as The Cut.[63] Baronett observed drag marks in the snow, and his dog led him to a spot where he saw a black creature across the hill. Thinking the object was a small bear, he noted, "My first impulse was to shoot him from where I stood, but as he was going so slowly I saw that I should have no difficulty in overtaking him, and crossed over to where he was. When I got near to it I found it was not a bear, and for my life I could not tell what it was. It did not look like an animal that I had ever seen, and it was certainly not a human being. It never occurred to me that it was Evarts." Jack cautiously crept up and realized the figure was indeed Everts, who was "nothing but a shadow! His flesh was all gone; the bones protruded through the skin on the balls of his feet and thighs. His fingers looked like bird's claws. I carried him down to the Gardner River."[64] Pritchett later recounted, "We have found Mr. Everts. He is alive and safe, but very low in flesh. . . . We sent a messenger to this post [Fort Ellis] for a surgeon."[65]

---

61. Truman C. Everts, "Thirty-Seven Days of Peril," *Scribner's Monthly* 3, no. 1 (November 1871).
62. Theodore Gerrish, *Life in the World's Wonderland* (Biddeford, ME: Press of the *Biddeford Journal*, 1887), p. 112. The Rev. Theodore Gerrish of Biddeford, Maine, toured Yellowstone in June 1886 and heard about the Everts story. Desiring to hear more of the story, Gerrish was directed to speak with Jack Baronett, who happened to be at Mammoth Hot Springs at Superintendent Wear's office and was happy to relate his tale. Gerrish described Baronett as "one of the most famous and popular guides at the present time in the Northwest."
63. The Cut is located along the current Blacktail Plateau Drive, just southwest of Crescent Hill, not far from Tower Junction. Mount Everts is opposite Mammoth Hot Springs on the north side of the Gardner River.
64. Gerrish, *Life in the World's Wonderland*, pp. 113–15.
65. "The Long-Lost Found," p. 7.

The Cut

On October 21, 1870, the *Helena Daily Herald* printed a letter from George Pritchett and addressed at Fort Ellis: "To. Messrs. King, Gillette, Langford, Lawrence and other Gentlemen." In the letter Pritchett noted, "We found him on the 16 inst., on the summit of the first big mountain beyond Warm Spring Creek, about seventy-five miles from this fort." Aubrey Haines later revealed that the Hayden Expedition was confused over which Warm Spring Creek Pritchett had noted, as the Gardner River was also called by that name. This resulted in placing the event on the stream Hauser had called "Lost Trail Creek"; thus they changed the name to Rescue Creek, and so it has remained. Rescue Creek is located on the north side of Mount Everts near where George Huston's cabin was located. (Aubrey L. Haines, *Yellowstone National Park: Its Exploration and Establishment* [Washington, DC: US Dept. of the Interior, National Park Service, 1974], p. 175.)

After taking care of Truman Everts for two days at a temporary camp, Baronett and Pritchett took him to George Huston's cabin to recuperate. Baronett carried him much of the way, thinking he could not have weighed more than 40–57 pounds. After four days, Everts had recovered enough to be moved, and Huston placed Everts on his horse in the saddle, climbed on behind, and rode about 18 miles to the north side of Yankee Jim Canyon. A wagon from Fort Ellis awaited them and transported Everts the final 55 miles to Fort Ellis.[66] Everts survived the ordeal and later moved to Maryland, where he died in 1901.

The Hayden Expedition, which ventured into Yellowstone in 1872, stopped at a ranch along the river, likely Bottler's. They heard the story about Everts and how, after his rescue and recovery, Everts continued to believe he was not lost, but the rest of his group was, and he knew the route home.[67] He never accepted the reality of the situation. Baronett

---

66. G. L. Henderson, *Bound Volume 141*, p. 100. Manuscripts, Yellowstone National Park Archives.

67. "From Our Special Correspondent," *Western Home Journal* (Lawrence, KS), August 18, 1872, p. 2.

FINDING MR. EVERTS, 1870

later noted he killed a mountain lion a few days after finding Everts and believed it had been on Everts's trail for several days.[68] Why it did not attack is something of a mystery.

Robert C. Wallace, a Civil War veteran living in Helena since 1869, was touring the park in 1874 with four others and encountered Jack Baronett, who described his adventures with Everts. Jack avowed to Wallace that sometime after the rescue, "he visited New York City and called on Mr. Evarts [sic], who received him so coldly that, as the trapper explained it, he wished he had let the son-of-a-gun roam."[69] To make matters worse, Jack never received the reward for Everts's salvation. Some years later, Baronett complained about not getting his due compensation: "His friends refused to pay me because I found him alive, they saying that it was his place to pay the bills. He would not pay me because he said that if I had left him alone he would have found his own way out."[70] Of course, it was unlikely Everts could have made his way out on his own, as he was probably about as close to death as one can get without actually dying.

A Helena newspaper in 1870 applauded Baronett for his successful rescue: "Too much praise cannot be accorded to Mr. Barnett . . . [to whom] alone belongs the credit of finding Mr. Everts. I would not by this detract from those generous-hearted and whole-souled men who assisted him in various ways after he was found; but it is no doubt owing to Mr. B.'s sagacity and forethought as a mountain man that Mr. Everts was found, and so admirably taken care of afterwards, when the least indiscretion in nursing him might have resulted in his death."[71] This is the event that first brought Jack to the attention of the public, although sadly, at the time, he was given little news coverage. But the episode was prominently recorded in later biographies and stories of his life.

A year later, *Scribner's Monthly* published Everts's written account of his ghastly and ghostly experiences, and his reprieve from death by

---

68. "The Lost and Found," *Montana Record-Herald*, October 28, 1870, p. 1.
69. Robert C. Wallace, *A Few Memories of a Long Life* (Fairfield, WA: Ye Galleon Press, 1988), p. 61.
70. Gerrish, *Life in the World's Wonderland*, p. 240.
71. "The Finding of Hon. T. C. Everts," *Helena Weekly Herald*, October 27, 1870, p. 8.

Baronett, titled "Thirty-Seven Days of Peril." The article is filled with considerable self-praise for his survival in the wilderness, but in the end, he did respectfully note, "I took leave of my kind friends, with a feeling of regret at parting, and gratitude for their kindness as enduring as life."[72] The misadventure has become a classic tome of survival, adventure, and stubbornness in Yellowstone National Park.

---

72. Everts, "Thirty-Seven Days of Peril."

CHAPTER FOUR

Jack's Bridge: The Genesis

The construction of the bridge was followed by the building of a house several hundred yards away on the east bank, then the bearded miners shouldered their broad-axes and went back to the mines.[73]

—Aubrey L. Haines

Prospectors Bart Henderson, Adam "Horn" Miller, Ed Hibbard, J. H. "Pike" Moore, and James Gourley discovered paying amounts of gold near the head of Soda Butte Creek in 1869–1870. Such news traveled fast in the mining world, and men soon rushed into the remote area to stake their claims. Parties leaving Bozeman faced an arduous 150-mile journey. Traveling the usual route from Fort Ellis or Bozeman along Trail Creek to the Yellowstone River, they followed that upriver, past the mouth of Gardner River to the East Fork of the Yellowstone [Lamar] River, trailing that to Soda Butte Creek and on to Clark's Fork. Old maps show an existing trail along the north side of the Yellowstone to the East Fork; however, travel there was problematic due to the rugged mountainous terrain, but crossing the Yellowstone River was not required. The route on the south side was much easier, especially with pack trains, but necessitated navigating the unpredictable and sometimes raging Yellowstone River. The closest spot was the old Bannock Indian Ford near the outlet of Tower Creek, but the terrain was steep and the river could be treacherous during spring runoff and heavy rains.

---

73. Aubrey L. Haines, "The Bridge That Jack Built," *Yellowstone Nature Notes* 21, no. 1 (January–February 1947): pp. 1–4.

Jack Baronett devised what he hoped would be a profitable idea in 1870—build a toll bridge over the Yellowstone River along the route everyone would use. Scouting out the most likely location, he chose a spot just above the mouth of the Lamar River. It was relatively narrow, with rock outcroppings on the north side for support. Jack gathered the tools and ironwork he thought would be required and brought them in from Bozeman by pack train during the winter. Jack, John W. Ponsford, and a few miner cohorts cut trees over the winter and began construction as weather permitted. The bridge was ready for travel in the spring of 1871, and Jack started collecting his two-bit tolls.[74] Jack and the boys also built a one-room log cabin on the flat between the two rivers and perhaps a barn and corral area.[75]

Historian Aubrey Haines described the bridge many years after its demise: "A rocky bank on the east side formed a ready footing for that abutment, and a rocky ledge, just exposed near the west bank at low water, provided a footing for a rock-filled, log-crib pier 20' high. Thus, he bridged the river with two spans, one of 60' and the other of 30'. The superstructure consisted of a 10-foot roadway carried on three stringers,[76] which in turn were supported by a pair of queen-post trusses in each span. The timbers were all of square-hewn pine with a minimum of iron fastenings." The cost of the work, including the house and outbuildings, is given as $4,000,[77] a considerable sum of money in those days. The bridge was unsuitable for wagon travel but adequate for saddle horses and pack trains. People generally called it Jack's Bridge or Miner's Bridge. According to historian Doris Whithorn, "Charles Elliot, who had worked on the original Chittenden Bridge in 1903 at Canyon and Fred Russell, tore down the old Baronett Bridge in 1911. They said it had been put together without a nail, using only wooden plugs and dowel pins."[78]

Early prospectors, hunters, and survey expeditions crossed the Gardner River above where it flows into the Yellowstone River, near

---

74. Some sources mention a 50-cent toll.
75. Haines, "The Bridge That Jack Built."
76. Stringers were the long, parallel wooden beams supporting the bridge decking.
77. Haines, "The Bridge That Jack Built." The queen-post trusses were not added until 1878.
78. Doris Whithorn, "Jack Baronett," *Twice Told on the Upper Yellowstone*, vol. 2 (Livingston, MT: Self-published, 1994), pp. 61–73.

JACK'S BRIDGE: THE GENESIS

Baronett Bridge, soon after construction in 1871. It was designed to support only horse and pack train traffic, not wagons. (William H. Jackson Photo, 1871, Online Photo Collection #14836, Yellowstone National Park, public domain)

current-day Gardiner, Montana, and crossed overland to arrive at the bridge, subsequently following the trail to the Clark's Fork mines or to Tower Fall and the route to the interior of the park. Following a trail along Rescue Creek, they crossed over Blacktail Plateau, passed between Garnet and Crescent Hills, and then into Pleasant Valley, just west of Baronett's Bridge. Pleasant Valley is the location where John F. Yancey settled in 1882. Yancey, an old Kentuckian and veteran of the gold rush and American Indian Wars, built a cabin and mail station to serve the stages and miners en route to the mines of Cooke City. Two years later, he constructed a simple one-and-a-half-story log hotel to house miners, hunters, fishermen, and assorted travelers. He is known to have entertained the likes of writers Owen Wister, Earnest Thompson Seton, world traveler Burton Holmes, President Theodore Roosevelt, and many others. It was an excellent camping area with plenty of water, grass, hunting, and fishing. From there, it was a short jaunt to the bridge and on to Specimen Ridge and the mines at Clark's Fork.

YELLOWSTONE JACK

John F. Yancey

"Uncle John" Yancey was a colorful character born in Barren County, Kentucky, in 1826; he moved with his family to Missouri while he was still a boy. He fought in the Civil War and was in California in 1849 following the gold rush. Yancey built a cabin and mail station at Pleasant Valley in 1882 to accommodate teamsters and mail stages en route to Cooke City. He opened the Pleasant Valley Hotel in 1884 and served the "undiscriminating" tourists until his death. The hotel was one and a half stories and could accommodate twenty guests in the upstairs bedrooms at $2.00/day or $10.00/week. His main business catered to fishermen, hunters, miners, freighters, and prospectors to and from the Cooke City gold mines. He knew all the good fishing holes and had plenty of tall tales to amuse his guests. Supposedly, his whiskey glasses were undefiled by the touch of water. He erected a one-and-a-half-story saloon between 1887 and 1893. His nephew Dan took over the business when Uncle John died on May 7, 1903, at seventy-seven years of age. John Yancey was buried in the Gardiner cemetery at Tinker's Hill, and his tombstone and plot can still be visited. Three years later, his hotel was destroyed by fire.

The first known party to cross the new bridge was the Barlow-Heap Expedition of the Army Corps of Engineers on July 24, 1871. They were conducting a reconnaissance of the upper Yellowstone country in conjunction with the F. V. Hayden Expedition. Capt. John Barlow noted the bridge was "built with a considerable amount of labor and boldness, for the river flows with great rapidity along the narrow, rocky channel ... [and] the first, and only one as yet which has been erected across the Yellowstone River, and may in the future assume some historical importance."[79] It was indeed important, being the only bridge over the Yellowstone River that allowed access to the northeast portion of Yellowstone and the Cooke City mines. It was also the only road bridge crossing the Yellowstone River in Montana until 1881–1882. News reports indicate

---

79. "Lamar River Bridge," *Yellowstone Roads and Bridges*, HAER No. WY-12 (1968), p. 2.

JACK'S BRIDGE: THE GENESIS

that four bridges were built between 1881 and 1884 between Baronett's Bridge and Livingston, Montana. The Main Street bridge was constructed in Livingston around 1882–1884, along with the Harvat Bridge, a mile or two east of town. A bridge erected in 1883 near Emigrant Gulch was washed out and replaced the following year. Reportedly, a bridge was built at Gardiner in 1884 as a private enterprise but was taken out by floods the subsequent year,[80] and a new bridge was erected in 1893.

Ferdinand Hayden crossed the bridge in August 1871, about a month after Barlow, with artist Thomas Moran and photographer William Henry Jackson, who took the first known photograph of the bridge. In the fall, at least part of the expedition was leaving Tower Falls and approaching the East Fork of the Yellowstone, where "[they] crossed the Yellowstone on the first and only bridge ever thrown across its waters. It was built by a trapper in expectation of a rush to the gold diggings of Clarke's Fork."[81]

In 1875, Captain William A. Jones led another government expedition to locate a wagon route between the Union Pacific Railroad in the southern part of the Wyoming Territory and Yellowstone Park. The group also crossed "Miner's Bridge, a substantial structure which spans the torrent not far above the entrance of East Fork," en route to Fort Ellis and back.[82] Photographer L. A. Huffman took photographs of the bridge in 1882 that showed a teepee-style tent near the bridge with twenty or so logs of various lengths nearby, indicating repairs were being made.[83] The tent likely housed the various bridge tenders during Jack's absences.

Reports from 1873 indicate that prospecting in the Clark's Fork region was finally beginning to pan out. Prospectors discovered silver, gold, and lead lodes in numerous locations. The men later constructed small mills to process the ore. Many miners gathered in Bozeman that

---

80. "Jack Baronett, Early Day Scout Was Builder of Initial Span," *Billings Gazette*, January 17, 1932, p. 11.
81. "Yellowstone Expedition," *Chicago Tribune*, October 4, 1871, p. 2.
82. William A. Jones, "Report upon the Reconnaissance of Northwestern Wyoming" (Washington, DC: Government Printing Office, 1875), p. 215.
83. The photo from the Montana Historical Society, titled "Jack's Bridge from South," is dated 1882. See https://www.mtmemory.org/nodes/view/72434?keywords=huffman%20bridge&type=all &highlights=WyJodWZmbWFuIiwiYnJpZGdlIl0=&lsk=068a0faf6f12827baec74ce7c5a0e15f. Repairs could have been made in 1882, assuming the date is correct.

spring, awaiting the snowmelt to obtain access to the claims. One newspaper noted that a dozen men had left for the mines, and another group was preparing to leave.[84] Another paper claimed, "We think we are safe in saying that a camp of several hundred men will be established this summer in that district."[85] The *Avant Courier* (Bozeman, MT) touted Jack's bridge as being in excellent order and awaiting the rush. At the same time, Huston & Werk's pack train, which operated from Mammoth Hot Springs into the park and the Clark's Fork region, would soon be ready

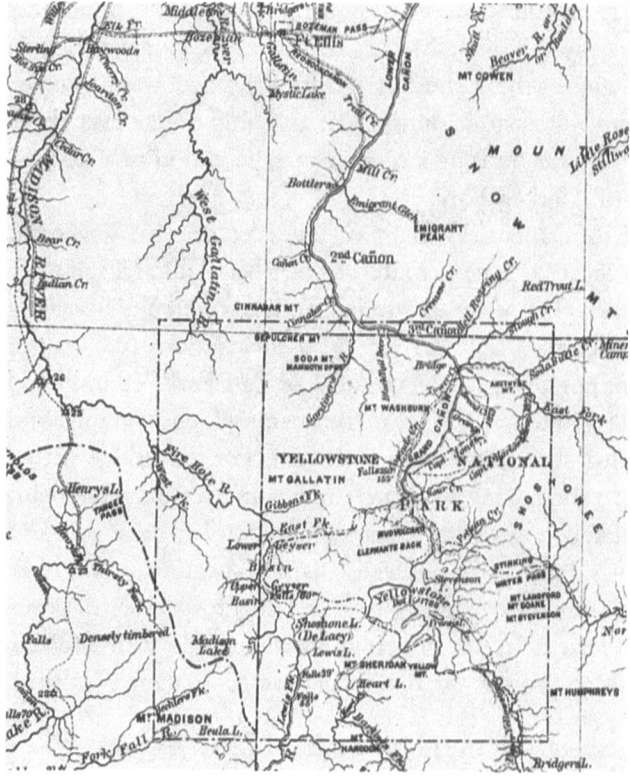

1876 map showing Yellowstone Park, the Madison River, and the Yellowstone River trail from Fort Ellis to Baronett's Bridge. (Capt. W. F. Reynolds, War Department Map of the Yellowstone and Missouri Rivers and Their Tributaries, public domain)

---

84. "For Clark's Fork," *Bozeman Avant Courier*, June 20, 1873, p. 3.
85. *Bozeman Avant Courier*, February 28, 1873, p. 3.

JACK'S BRIDGE: THE GENESIS

for operation.[86] It seemed Baronett might finally obtain a payback in tolls for his investment in "Jack's Bridge."

In the spring of 1874, a group camped near the bridge, and the leader chatted with Baronett to exchange news. The leader, Wyoming surveyor Alonzo V. Richards, later published his account in a newspaper and mentioned that two brothers named Baronett were living at the cabin. One of the men was obviously a cohort of Jack's, perhaps Horn Miller or George Huston. The article claimed the two made a living by "hunting and gathering specimens from the neighboring hills, which they sell to visitors to the Park. Some of these specimens are very rare, and consist of beautiful petrifactions [*sic*] and crystallizations, amethysts, chalcedony, opals, topaz and various other formations of quartz and silica."[87] Collecting artifacts was a common practice among the early pioneers struggling to make a living in the days before park management prohibited the activity. The men at Mammoth Hot Springs, Gardiner, and Cinnabar did likewise, and, no doubt, so did Yankee Jim and John Yancey. The route through Lamar Valley to Cooke City passed Amethyst Mountain and Specimen Mountain or Ridge. Together, they formed what was known as the Petrified Forest.

Jack was actively collecting and selling the crystals and agates from Specimen Ridge and surrounding areas. The *Helena Weekly Herald* reported in 1873 that "Mr. Jack Baronett, the finder of Truman C. Everts, has succeeded in getting together a large collection of these valuable stones, which will, we understand, be offered for sale at Gallatin City during the Fair."[88] The annual fair began on October 13, but, as is typical for Montana, a snowstorm moved in that same day, causing havoc for the planned horse races and visitors alike. Baronett's display, however,

---

86. "From the Yellowstone," *Bozeman Avant Courier*, April 4, 1873, p. 3. George Huston and John Werks began the pack train operation in 1873, carrying mail, freight, and passengers from Bozeman. They operated for several years.

87. "Field Notes," *Cheyenne Daily Leader*, June 30, 1875, p. 2. Alonzo Richards surveyed the southern border of Wyoming with his brother William in 1873. In 1874, he surveyed the rugged western boundary of Wyoming, including Yellowstone. Alonzo constructed monuments at the southwest and northwest corners and erected small markers at every milepost. Almost 150 years later, many of these posts along the west border of Yellowstone still exist. William Richards went on to become Wyoming surveyor-general and governor of Wyoming.

88. "Crystal Specimens," *Helena Weekly Herald*, October 9, 1873, p. 3.

Yellowstone Petrified Forest

Specimen Ridge and adjacent Amethyst Mountain are collectively known as Yellowstone Petrified Forest. Most petrified wood and other plant fossils in Yellowstone come from Eocene deposits, which are about 50 million years old and occur in many northern parts of the park. The fossil forests of Specimen Ridge are best known, where the remains of hundreds of these 50-million-year-old trees stand exposed on a steep hillside, with trunks up to eight feet in diameter and some more than 20 feet tall. The specimens include sequoia, fir, and numerous deciduous species.

The early Hayden Survey parties collected the first fossil plants from Yellowstone. An 1878 report referred to fossil "forests" on Amethyst Mountain opposite the mouth of Soda Butte Creek.

Around 1900, F. H. Knowlton proposed that the petrified trees on Specimen Ridge were forests petrified in place. His theory remained dominant through most of the twentieth century. A more recent theory proposes the trees were uprooted by volcanic debris flows and transported to lower elevations. The 1980 eruption of Mount St. Helens supported this idea. Its mud flows transported trees to lower elevations and deposited some trees upright—similar to what you see on Specimen Ridge. (NPS, "Specimen Ridge Day Hike" brochure, Yell 232, 02/2015.)

---

was impressive, and the *Bozeman Avant Courier* claimed his mineral collection was the center of attraction and that "the magnificent collection ... of beautiful specimens was never before exhibited here or elsewhere." Various private buyers purchased the collection at the show's end. The author lamented that the collection should have been taken east for additional presentations.[89] As an interesting side note, the Helena article claimed that Hayden Expedition members "realized handsome sums by gathering choice specimens of these purple-hued crystals and selling them to Eastern jewelers." Unfortunately, there are countless stories of similar looting of park artifacts and the sales to Easterners, with the effect

---

89. "The District Fair," *Bozeman Avant Courier*, October 24, 1873, p. 3.

JACK'S BRIDGE: THE GENESIS

that the best specimens soon disappeared from the park. The government banned the practice long ago, and removing any natural or historical objects from the park is also illegal.

Walter Cooper, a prominent Bozeman gunsmith and politician, purchased a portion (if not all) of the Baronett Collection. The *Bozeman Avant Courier* reported in February 1877 that "the valuable Yellowstone and Montana quartz cabinet of Mr. Walter Cooper, a portion of which was known here as the Baronette Collection," was exhibited in Philadelphia in 1876. The collection was no doubt displayed in the 1876 Centennial Philadelphia Exhibition. Professor Frank Smalley, a geology professor at Syracuse University, asserted, "I have seen many collections of far greater range of species, but never one so rich in varieties." Auburn University in New York cataloged the collection in preparation for a sale by Cooper. Both Auburn and Syracuse University were competing for its purchase.[90] The ultimate acquisition of the collection has yet to be discovered.

General William E. Strong, who toured Yellowstone in 1875 with Baronett and a host of others, observed, "[We] moved down to Baronette's cabin, where we stopped for an hour examining the curious and beautiful specimens of fossils, minerals, &c., he has collected from the Wind River range of mountains, Specimen Mountain, and from the entire Valley of the Yellowstone. After purchasing some of these we moved on."[91] That same year, army engineer Captain William Ludlow, during his reconnaissance of Yellowstone in August 1875, also noted that at "Baronet's Ranch there [is] a large collection of specimens from Amethyst Mountain, on the east side of the river, a locality which we had not time to visit. The specimens were mainly impure amethysts and forms of quartz chalcedony, &c." However, Ludlow made no mention of purchasing any of the specimens.[92]

In addition to collecting and peddling crystal formations, Baronett seemed to have a penchant for building bridges, as he reportedly

---

90. "The Cooper Cabinet," *Bozeman Avant Courier*, February 15, 1877, p. 3.
91. W. E. Strong, *A Trip to the Yellowstone National Park in July, August, September 1875* (Washington, DC: Government Printing Office, 1876), p. 89.
92. Kenneth H. Baldwin, *Enchanted Enclosure: The Army Engineers and Yellowstone National Park* (Washington, DC: Office of the Chief of Engineers, US Army, 1976), p. 81.

constructed two other bridges in 1876. Newspapers in February 1876 announced, "Jack Baronett is bridging Gardiner's River, extending the Park Road to Tower Creek Fall."[93] Baronett likely built the bridge near the current Rescue Creek trail bridge. In September 1872, the second Hayden Expedition had passed over the Gardner River near its mouth. A correspondent described crossing "the river on a rude, narrow bridge, constructed by the miners who sometimes travel up the park."[94] By 1876, the bridge may have been washed out by spring floods and was being replaced by Baronett.

The other bridge was on the East Fork of the Yellowstone, today's Lamar River, likely near Soda Butte. One paper announced, "There is to be a toll bridge on the East Fork of the Yellowstone," and "The timbers are already in position for the new bridge across the East Fork of the Yellowstone."[95] Horn Miller and George Huston probably assisted him, as the bridge was another convenience for miners traveling to the Clark's Fork mines. Yellowstone's second superintendent, Philetus W. Norris, referred to it as the "miners' bridge" in his 1878 report.[96] There is no mention of Jack ever collecting tolls at either location. Ultimately, Jack's Bridge was not a big moneymaker, and often men could not pay the toll but were allowed to cross in any case. Being of the wanderlust sort, Jack preferred the life of a prospector and miner and spent many summers guiding tourists through the park. He often found old pensioners who enjoyed the peaceful serenity to manage the bridge for him. Herman Haupt told a fascinating story in his 1883 book about just such a man. He was called Billy and lived in a Sibley tent near the bridge with his dog and a book, collecting the two-bit tolls from occasional passersby. A newspaper remarked that Billy was "a remarkable instance of the pertinacity with which some men cling to life. By the accidental discharge of a blast of Giant Powder in a coal-mine in which he was working, numerous particles of rock and a piece of his felt hat were blown through his forehead and into the fore part of his brain,

---

93. *The New North-West*, "Territorial Items," February 11, 1876, p. 3. See also *Bozeman Times*, February 3 and February 10, 1876.
94. "From Our Special Correspondent," *Western Home Journal*, August 18, 1872, p. 2.
95. *Helena Independent*, "Territorial News," April 14, 1876, p. 3, and "New Eldorado Humbug," April 25, 1876, p. 3.
96. Philetus W. Norris, "Report upon the Yellowstone National Park to the Secretary of Interior, 1878," Washington, DC. Montana Memory, https://www.mtmemory.org/nodes/view/104718.

JACK'S BRIDGE: THE GENESIS

and during the long illness that followed pieces of the bony tables of the skull came away; yet that man recovered, and is now in apparent health of both body and mind—a most remarkable case."[97]

Billy's accident occurred early February 1882 in the Bozeman Pass area in a coal mine owned by Col. Chestnut and Major Pease. Billy and his partner, John E. Smith, had set two explosive charges and retired to a safe distance when one charge went off. After waiting a bit and thinking both explosives had ignited, they cautiously approached, and suddenly the second blast occurred. Smith received a blow to his chest, severe but not fatal. Rock fragments struck Billy in the head, and people believed he could not possibly survive.[98] Although seriously maimed, the men managed to crawl out of the tunnel to a nearby cabin. Several newspapers reported that Billy lost two ounces of his brain in the accident. Remarkably, after receiving extended care at Fort Ellis Hospital, he showed significant improvement by April. Doubtless, part of his recovery later transpired as a bridge tender at Baronett's Bridge.

Billy turned out to be William "Uncle Billy" Langston, who hailed from Georgia and, like many others, forged West during the gold rush days of yore. While on his prospecting travels, he seldom enjoyed profits from the fruits of his labors and, in the process, engaged in numerous skirmishes with the tribes, reportedly twice with Sitting Bull. "The vicissitudes of the roving years have blunted, may be, the finer moral instincts, but he stands today as the living exponent of a man positively without physical fear."[99] He was said to have "gone through hardships on the frontier sufficient to kill half a dozen men."[100] Nevertheless, he was still a courteous man. Once Billy was in a Cooke City saloon boasting about some of his exploits while using the "colorful" language of bars. He suddenly noticed a woman seated nearby. Realizing his faux pas, he immediately apologized, saying, "I always respect a lady and wish to do her honor. I beg your pardon. I had some sisters and a mother once. I don't know much about them now, but I have a memory for the tender

---

97. Herman Haupt, *The Yellowstone National Park* (New York and Philadelphia: J. M. Stoddard, 1883), pp. 157–58.
98. "Montana Melange," *The Madisonian*, February 11, 1882, p. 2.
99. Belle Vinnedge Drake, "Uncle Billy Langston," *Livingston Post*, February 12, 1891, p. 2.
100. "County News," *Red Lodge Picket*, March 19, 1892, p. 1.

associations of other days and, in their name, I ask a thousand pardons."[101] Mrs. Belle Vinnedge Drake of Iowa, who recorded the conversation, was a noted newspaper woman living in Cooke City at the time with relatives who had formed the Vinnedge Mining Company.[102]

French traveler Jules Leclercq related an amusing anecdote about Billy during his journeys in 1883. He included a fascinating account about his group spending the night in Baronett's cabin with Billy as host. He described the cabin as "crude construction made of rough-hewn tree trunks and not draft proofed, admitting the wind through its chinks." He compared it to the simple shepherd houses built in Iceland and noted that the interior was one large room serving as a kitchen, living room, and bedroom. He described the night he and others spent in the cabin:

> *Foul bison skins spread on a floor that has never seen water served us as beds for the night. Not counting the two dogs, we were at least a dozen sleepers in this narrow room, since some miners had also come seeking hospitality. This whole crowd slept scattered about in all the corners. The temperature was suffocating. The candle was blown out at nine o'clock, and the room was lit only by the dying embers of the logs. Before closing their eyes, these "rough people" told a thousand episodes from their adventurous lives in the nasal accent so characteristic of the Yankee. Then profound silence, soon followed by a phenomenal concert of snores.*[103]

As is typical for mountain men and pioneers in the early days, adventuresome tales were bandied around to pass the long nights. A few were true, some imaginative yarns, but most likely a melding of both genres. Even though eyelids closed and sleep ensued, it would turn out to be a sleepless night for Leclercq. At one point, he felt something move under his cheek and, on opening his robe, saw something scurry into the darkness. "Was it a rat? Was it a snake? What did I know? I am not even

---

101. Drake, "Uncle Billy Langston."
102. "Court House Notes," *Helena Independent*, August 22, 1890, p. 8.
103. Jules Leclercq, *Yellowstone: Land of Wonders, Promenade in North America's National Park* (Omaha: University of Nebraska Press, 2013), p. 187. The original was published in France in 1886.

JACK'S BRIDGE: THE GENESIS

mentioning the spiders and other horrible insects that were running over my body," Leclercq reflected.[104] He and the others were happy to see the light of dawn, get outside into the fresh mountain air, and have breakfast.

In 1884, Richard Fuller took over as bridge tender, collecting tolls and living in a tent near the bridge on the east side of the river. When park superintendent Robert Carpenter found out about Fuller, he ordered him to "get a proper lease or leave the area."[105] Of course, he was under the direction of operator John Ponsford, who had earlier purchased an interest in the bridge; Fuller was not responsible for the legalities of the bridge.[106] One might speculate he merely ignored Carpenter. This account, however, does not begin at that point. The rest of the story is that several months prior, Superintendent Conger issued orders that people residing in the Soda Butte area of the park be declared trespassers, as they had no written authority to be there—this order included a man named Tate and his partner Winfield Scott, who settled a ranch up Soda Butte Creek near the park boundary, which at that time was not marked. They believed they were outside the park. George Jackson, Jack Rutherford, and Robert "Buckskin Jim" Cutler had settled just below Soda Butte. Cutler related that he had received verbal permission from Conger to live there.[107]

When Carpenter became superintendent in September 1884, he ordered all those parties to vacate the park within ninety days. When more than eight days had passed the limit, he sent deputies out to evict them all. They burned Tate and Scott's ranch buildings and stored wheat, and they also confiscated supplies en route to the ranch. When they were about to do the same to Cutler, he unwisely pulled a gun on them but was prevented from shooting by his partner. The men were arrested and hauled to Uinta County, Wyoming. Baronett's Bridge was next, but, luckily, the deputies merely warned Fuller to leave or get permission.[108]

New York publisher William H. Wiley related another entertaining bridge story during a trip to Yellowstone in 1886. He and his companions

---

104. Leclercq, *Yellowstone: Land of Wonders*, p. 187.
105. Robert Flather, "Bridges," MSC007_04.01, Yellowstone National Park Archives.
106. See chapter 10, "Jack's Bridge: The Exodus," for additional information about Ponsford.
107. "The Park Arrests," *Livingston Enterprise*, December 20, 1884, p. 3. Also, "Trouble in the National Park," *The Madisonian*, December 20, 1884, p. 3.
108. "The Park Arrests," *Livingston Enterprise*.

desired to visit Soda Butte and Specimen Mountain. After leaving Mammoth Hot Springs, they arrived at Uncle John Yancey's and spent the night. They proceeded across Baronett's Bridge, where there was an unlocked gate at the entrance (something other accounts have yet to mention). With no one in sight, they opened the gate, proceeded across, and headed up the valley. In the Soda Butte area, they arrived at the cabin of a different Uncle Billy, who was described as an "old Missourian" around 6 feet, 3 inches tall and a member of Quantrill's band during the US Civil War.[109] This description would rule out Uncle Billy Hofer, who was from Connecticut and too young to serve in that war. The man was likely Billy Jump, who, in 1882, was authorized by Yellowstone Park superintendent Patrick Conger to establish a mail station at Soda. Jump moved into the old gamekeeper's cabin and established a stage station for traffic between Mammoth Hot Springs and Cooke City.[110]

The travelers apparently persuaded Uncle Billy to let them stay at the cabin for a few days: "We had with us the 'Universal persuader' [whiskey] warranted to suit every man in Montana." Uncle Billy was "not the man to throw good liquor over his shoulder." After exploring the area and catching a passel of fish, the group returned to Baronett's Bridge; "we again let ourselves across and had gone a short distance when we heard a hail and saw a man running towards us with a rifle in his hand. The guide said we had better stop, and we found he only wanted to collect the toll for crossing the bridge, and he charged for both ways, because he argued we must have crossed once to get on the side we were, as he knew we came from the springs. It is no use to argue with a man who carries a rifle unless you shoot first, so we paid and went on."[111] Indeed, it is a wise philosophy to embrace if one desires to live a longer life, especially if unarmed. The man's name was not mentioned, but apparently he was one of Baronett's bridge tenders.

---

109. William H. Wiley, *Yosemite, Alaska and the Yellowstone* (New York: John Wiley & Sons, 1893), pp. 209–12.

110. Aubrey L. Haines, *The Yellowstone Story*, vol. 1 (Denver: University Press of Colorado, 1996), pp. 303–5. Billy Jump later ran saloons in nearby Horr and Cinnabar, Montana.

111. Wiley, *Yosemite, Alaska and the Yellowstone*, pp. 209–12. See also *Engineering: An Illustrated Weekly Journal* 44, July–December 1887 (London: October 14, 1887): 362–63, 373, 415. This journal dates the expedition before 1887.

CHAPTER FIVE
Guiding the Guests

Jack Baronett is our guide, and a most excellent one he is too, having probably had more experience than any other man in this country.[112]
—Major Walker Party, 1873

Ferdinand V. Hayden, an American geologist and physician, headed the US Geological and Geographical Survey of the Territories in 1867, which later became the US Geological Survey. He led America's first federally funded geological survey into the Yellowstone region of northwestern Wyoming in 1871. A party of around fifty men from various scientific specialties, including artist Thomas Moran and frontier photographer William Henry Jackson, accompanied Hayden. The expedition was in conjunction with the Barlow-Heap scientific party, under orders from Gen. Phil Sheridan to explore the Yellowstone region. Hayden returned in the summer of July 1872 to continue his examinations. He was accompanied by numerous notables, including photographer William H. Jackson, N. P. Langford (member of the 1870 Washburn Expedition), scientist James Stevenson, geologist Gustavus R. Bechler, artist and topographer William Henry Holmes, botanist John C. Coulter, and others. In total, sixty-one people were in the expedition, divided into two separate divisions, the Southern and the Northern. English venture capitalist Sir William Blackmore and his wife, Mary, were specially invited guests to the Northern expedition.[113]

---
112. "Wonderland," *Helena Weekly Herald*, September 18, 1873, p. 4.
113. Robert V. Goss, *The Chronology of Wonderland*, 5th ed. (Gardiner, MT: Self-published, 2015), pp. 13–14.

William Henry Blackmore

Born in 1827 in Salisbury, Wiltshire, England, William Blackmore became a lawyer and investment promoter. He married Mary Sidford in 1851, and the couple entertained many prominent people, including Oliver Wendell Holmes Sr., Alfred Lord Tennyson, and Mark Twain. Beginning in 1863, William made several trips to the United States to locate investment opportunities, making compacts with lands in Colorado and New Mexico. He used his fortune for philanthropy, primarily centered on his interest in Native Americans. Sadly, he ended his life in 1878 after a failed investment deal, one that was related to the Denver and Rio Grande Western Railroad.

Prior to Blackmore's arrival in Utah Territory, he boasted, "You see I have carved out an excursion which for interest, novelty, or enjoyment will rival and that can be planned in the Old World. . . . [I] shall hope to return—barring scalping and accidents—to the Old World."[114] Little did he foresee the ill-fated events that would soon play out. Arriving at Corinne, Utah, by rail in mid-July 1872, Sir Blackmore and his party traveled by stagecoach to Bozeman to join the Northern group. Blackmore continued another three miles to Fort Ellis to help prepare for the trip while his wife rested from the arduous journey in a Bozeman hotel. Later at the fort, Blackmore received news on July 18 that his wife had suddenly taken ill, no doubt from the stress of the trip. By the time he arrived, she had passed away. Saddened and disheartened, Sir Blackmore made arrangements for a funeral and burial. He purchased five acres of land on the east end of Bozeman and donated it to the city for a cemetery, still in use as the Sunset Hills Cemetery. A stone pyramid was later erected, engraved with the words, "Mary Blackmore, July 18, 1872, Fide Et Amore" (translated, "By Faith and Love"). Mourning his beloved wife, Blackmore continued his journey to Yellowstone to catch up with the Hayden party, who had already left for the park.[115]

---

114. "An Englishman's Tour," *Mower County Transcript*, July 4, 1872, p. 2.
115. "Personal," *Helena Weekly Herald*, July 18, 1872, p. 7; "Sad News—Sudden Death of Wife of Sir William Blackmore," *Helena Weekly Herald*, July 25, 1872, p. 8; Aubrey L. Haines, *The Yellowstone*

GUIDING THE GUESTS

Jack Baronett, with his eight years of living, exploring, and prospecting in and around northwest Wyoming, along with his hunting and survival skills, was the perfect choice to guide Hayden's party around Yellowstone. Baronett's companions were prospector and mining comrade George Huston and packer, trapper, hunter, and American Indian fighter Jack Bean—all were intrepid men and knew their way around the wilds. The Hayden group traveled up the Yellowstone River to Baronett's Bridge to meet with Baronett, Huston, and Bean. Part of the party made a side trip to the mines of the upper Clark's Fork area. A newspaper correspondent reported, "After we had passed up the river ten or twelve miles, we camped several days in a beautiful valley, so as to give Dr. Hayden and Mr. Blackmore time to visit the new silver mine upon Clarke's Fork, thirty or forty miles up the east fork of the Yellowstone."[116] The men conducted an intense geological and mapping examination of the area and the gold and silver outcroppings before continuing their tour around Yellowstone.[117]

Sir Blackmore recorded one rather amusing event in his journal. He had conversed with Bart Henderson at the mines. He noted Bart referred to the as-yet-unnamed Index and Pilot Peaks as "dog turd" peak. His diary reads, while traversing up the valley, "opposite to us was Index and Pilot Mountain two of their highest and most important in this locality—probably 9,000 to 1,000 [10,000] feet high—called locally dog turd mountain a regular mountain landmark."[118] His proper British etiquette was slightly affronted, but he apparently passed it off as an American backwoods colloquialism. The brown, globular breccia peaks were, of course, later renamed. In another instance, hunter Bill Hamilton[119] had

---

Story, vol. 1 (Denver: University Press of Colorado, 1996), pp. 184–86. The now seventy-three-acre cemetery continues as the Sunset Hills Cemetery. The cemetery website notes Mrs. Blackmore died of peritonitis, but news clippings generally indicated pneumonia.

116. "The Wonders of the Yellowstone," *Western Home Journal*, September 12, 1872, p. 2. They likely camped in Pleasant Valley, near Baronett's Bridge.

117. Haines, *The Yellowstone Story*, p. 186.

118. Haines, *The Yellowstone Story*, p. 186. Also, "Wm Blackmore Diary #6, 1872 Yellowstone Trip," William Blackmore Collection, AC018, Box 3, Folder 6, Fray Angelico Chavez History Library, Santa Fe, NM, p. 88.

119. "Wildcat Bill" Hamilton had explored Yellowstone in 1839 with a group of fur trappers and was a member of the 1864 prospecting expedition.

been regaling Blackmore with his feats of capturing buffalo calves the previous winter in Hayden Valley, claiming he captured seven buffalo calves and seven elk. Blackmore later commented in his diary, "Jack Burnet [Baronett] when [he] met us informed me that he had capital sport in the Spring lassoing yearling buffaloes on the plains."[120] Jack always enjoyed telling a good story, sometimes even true ones. One night Jack sat down at the campfire and recounted one of his bear stories. Unfortunately, Blackmore only briefly described it in his diary: "Treed by grizzly, watched his dog—pursued by bear took refuge with his master—No time to load took to tree Fork and when branch broke & he fell—caught by lowest limbs of tree kept hold of gun—Shot bear."[121] Apparently, Blackmore never spent much time using punctuation in his notes.

One day, the men were partaking of a rather frugal lunch and Blackmore asked mountaineers Baronett, Bill Hamilton, and Jack Bean whether they cared to imbibe some whiskey, as it was the only beverage they had, and all of them refused. "These true mountaineers are remarkedly temperate and rarely touch spirituous or fermented liquors. Bean told me he had never taken as much of a swallow of whisky in his life." Blackmore intimated that drinkers and drunkards were merely a set of rowdies who were generally disliked by the genuine mountain men, "whose course of life & great dangers to which they are constantly exposed necessitates a life of temperance & sobriety." He explained that the men prospected or mined during the summertime and hunted in the fall, when the proceeds from the sale of hides, fur, and meat could last them through the winter.[122]

In August 1873, Baronett was at the helm of a party of greenhorns exploring the park. The author, denoted as A. Spouter, wrote of the journey in the 1874 *Notre Dame Scholastic Journal*. He begins, "On the 17th of August last, I was one of a party of seventeen that left Fort Ellis, M. T., fitted out for a four weeks' trip in Wonderland. . . . Our guide, Mr. Baronett—than whom there is no better in the mountains." Members of the party were not named, but it included at least one woman. Traveling

---

120. Blackmore Diary #6, p. 76.
121. Blackmore Diary #6, p. 79.
122. Blackmore Diary #6, p. 86.

from Bozeman along the Yellowstone River, the group encountered Devil's Slide, an unusual geologic feature around five miles from the park's northern border. Spouter mused, "It was a strange thing to me that his satanic majesty should choose to slide down this; and he would never have done so unless he enjoyed friction—for it is very rough, and does not at all conform with my idea of a slide. But then, he probably has different tastes from mine."[123] Leaving this question behind, they continued up the hill to Mammoth Hot Springs.

While exploring the terraces, Spouter admitted that members of his party (and perhaps himself) were vandals. He described the beauties of the geyserites: "On being broken, they are found to be hollow; the shell varies in thickness, and looks much like a striped cornelian, while on the inner side are most beautiful, delicate crystals of pure sulphur. Dozens were broken by our party, and many others carried away as specimens."[124] While the party was in the Specimen Mountain area, he noted, "Specimen hunters were successful in the evening, and gathered in the neighborhood of the camp amethyst, crystals, cornelians [a translucent red or orange variety of chalcedony], agates, and many curious petrifactions, for their respective cabinets." Spouter also mentioned passing by a petrified tree trunk some thirty feet long and twenty inches in diameter. It was a fine specimen, but he proudly asserted he "let it lie," no doubt only because he had no means of moving the tremendous log.[125] As was all too common in those days, the party was destroying and removing the very sights they had come to view, as well as opportunities for future visitors to enjoy them.

In September 1872, Baronett journeyed with Dr. Monroe and Harry R. Horr to explore and view the majesties of Yellowstone. Monroe was a doctor and occasional miner from Bozeman, while Horr had settled at Mammoth Hot Springs with James McCartney and built a crude hotel. The *Bozeman Avant Courier* remarked, "Rumor hath it that they propose writing up their notes and placing them in the hand of a New York Publisher by the 1st of January. Jack Baronette, the best

---

123. A. Spouter, "Geysers in the Distance," *The Scholastic* 7, no. 29 (March 14, 1874): p. 225.
124. "Geysers in the Distance," *The Scholastic* 7, no. 30 (April 11, 1874): p. 258.
125. "Geysers in the Distance," *The Scholastic* 7, no. 29 (March 21, 1874): p. 233.

guide in the Upper Yellowstone, pilots these 'knights of the quill.' They will not come home until the snow drives them home."[126] It appears their return to civilization was not worthy of press ink, and any works by the men have yet to be uncovered.

Baronett kept busy guiding another large group that September, the Major Walker party, who expected to be touring for a month. "There were twenty in the party—Major R. C. Walker; Mrs. Walker and two daughters; Miss Nellie Galen; E. Blaine Walker, Master Bob Walker, Hon. Geo. G. Symes, Harry Lambert, D. W. Fisk, Jack Baronett, the guide; Hank Wilson, the packer; a sergeant and six soldiers from Fort Ellis, and Sargentine, the cook." It was standard practice in those early years for groups to request a few soldiers to accompany their tour around Yellowstone, as it was a common perception and fear (for the most part unfounded) that American Indians were lurking behind every bush waiting to attack. Men in the parties were usually armed, if for no other reason than to provide game for their victuals and protection from grizzlies, mountain lions, and wolves.

Major Robert Craighead Walker

"Robert C. Walker first entered the military service November 1, 1861, as captain and commissary of substance of volunteers, and served as such until January 1, 1863, when he was appointed major and additional paymaster of volunteers, in which capacity he served till honorably mustered out, November 3d, 1865. He was commissioned major and paymaster, U.S. Army, May 4th, 1866, and resigned September 3d, 1874, where he was stationed at Helena, Montana" ("The Paymaster's Case," *The Madisonian*, August 10, 1878, p. 1). He also cofounded White Sulfur Springs, Montana, and built a 12-foot hot pool and bathhouse at the hot springs. One of the city blocks was named after him. His son-in-law O. J. Salisbury was famed for his Gilmer & Salisbury stagecoach lines. Walker passed away in June 1894 at age seventy-three.

---

126. "Gallatin County News," *Bozeman Avant Courier*, September 5, 1872, p. 8.

GUIDING THE GUESTS

The group left Fort Ellis along the usual route to Mammoth Hot Springs. At one point in the trip, desiring a feast for supper, "Judge [Symes], Blaine Walker, Jack Baronett, and Harry Wilson captured what is known in common parlance among hunters as a 'slow elk.' So we are now provided with meat for the balance of the trip."[127] One day in the Mud Volcano area of Hayden Valley, Baronett guided them to "another boiling spring, about fifty feet deep by forty feet wide. The water, which comes from the mountain above by a subterranean passage, is dark and muddy, and is in constant action. It is the most terrifying, infernal looking thing we have ever encountered. Our guide, Jack Baronett, says it 'throws up' once a year, and from the looks of the surrounding trees and shrubbery we have no reason to doubt Jack's statement." Again, Jack was honored as "our guide, and a most excellent one he is, too, having probably had more experience than any other man in this country." One of the party later declared, "Thus far we have had a most delightful time, and I never enjoyed myself so much in my life. It has been a continual picnic from the day we left the Post until the present time."[128] It was a busy summer, and the Walker party encountered several well-known Montana personages, including Granville Stuart, Col. W. F. Sanders, Major Pease, and photographer Joshua Crisman.

A party of famous military brass toured the park in 1875 after riding the rails of the Union Pacific Railroad to Corinne and Franklin, Utah. They proceeded by stagecoach to Fort Ellis, where they prepared for the trip. They set out for Yellowstone on July 28. The party included Secretary of War William W. Belknap; Gen. Randolph B. Marcy, inspector general of the army; Gen. J. W. Forsyth; Gen. W. E. Strong, Chicago lawyer and businessman; Gen. Sweitzer, commander at Fort Ellis; Dr. R. M. Whitefoot; and a contingent of the Second Cavalry from Fort Ellis. The entire entourage numbered thirty-five. Lt. Doane, of the 1870 Washburn Expedition, was responsible for the pack train.[129] They planned to meet Baronett at Tower Fall.

---

127. As in a "cow," for the Western neophytes.
128. "Wonderland," *Helena Weekly Herald*, September 18, 1873, pp. 3, 5, 7, 8.
129. General W. E. Strong, *A Trip to the Yellowstone National Park in July, August, September 1875* (Norman: University of Oklahoma Press, 1968), pp. x–xix.

YELLOWSTONE JACK

They traveled the standard route from Fort Ellis to Bottler's Ranch on the Yellowstone River and continued upriver to the Tower Falls, where they picked up Baronett as a guide for portions of the trip. Gen. Strong, an avid hunter, fisherman, and sportsman, split off from the group to do some hunting and agreed to meet at a specified location. Being unfamiliar with the area, Strong managed to lose his way but finally reached Baronett's Bridge. There, he met Baronett, who had come from the group's camp above the falls to try to locate Strong. Taking leave of the military party, Baronett said he would meet them at Yellowstone Lake in a week or so. He also promised to take Strong and Marcy for the hunt of their lives up Pelican Creek. After being shown the route to Yellowstone Lake, they would be on their own for a while.[130] Although established as a national park in 1872, protections for park game had yet to be implemented in Yellowstone. Hunting was a routine activity for both sustenance and sport in the park's early years.

Gen. Strong was impressed with Baronett as a man and with his abilities. He provided an excellent description of Jack: "[He] is a celebrated character in this country, and, although famous as an Indian fighter and hunter, he is still more celebrated as a guide. He is highly esteemed by those who know him and his word is as good as gold. He is of medium stature, broad-shouldered, very straight and built like Longfellow's ship, for 'strength and speed.' Eyes black as a panther's and as keen and sharp; complexion quite dark with hair and whiskers almost black. He speaks well, using good English, and his manner is mild, gentle and modest; is proud of his knowledge of the mountains and of his skill with the rifle. I took to him at once."[131] It is a very striking verbal portrait indeed. In the days before photography became commonplace, descriptions of people and places were much more interesting, vivid, and expressive.

After touring the geyser basins and other sights, the group reached Yellowstone Lake. Gen. Marcy had fallen ill, so Baronett could not take the men on the hunt as promised but assured Strong they would get in some shooting around Mt. Washburn. True to his word, Jack and Strong later

---

130. Strong, *A Trip to the Yellowstone National Park* (1876), p. 43.
131. Strong, *A Trip to the Yellowstone National Park* (1876), p. 43.

Gen. William Strong

William Emerson Strong was born in 1840 in New York. He later moved to Wisconsin, and when President Lincoln issued a proclamation calling for 75,000 men in 1861, Strong raised a company of volunteers at Racine called the Belle City Rifles. He had a successful career during the Civil War, attaining the rank of brevetted brigadier-general. He retired honorably in 1866 and entered private enterprise. As a close friend of Gen. Sheridan, they made six trips across the rugged West, sharing many enjoyable hunting and fishing opportunities. Strong passed away in Florence, Italy, at age fifty, on April 10, 1891.

came upon three fine bucks in the timber. Allowing his guest to make the tricky shot, Strong took down a huge black-tail deer, providing a sumptuous feast on reaching Jack's cabin. The group had killed at least one grizzly, six deer, elk, a multitude of grouse, and other birds and small game.[132]

In a bit of ironic and twisted logic, Strong questioned, "How is it that the Commissioner of the Park allows this unlawful killing? The hunters who are doing this cruel and outrageous work are well known. Jack Baronette can point out and name the men who glide up to bands of elk on snow-shoes and shoot them down when too poor and weak to run away, or when the snow lies on the ground to such great depth that they are unable to travel, and fall an easy prey to their pursuers. In the name of humanity let this kind of hunting be stopped." However, in the next paragraph, he paradoxically noted that the group took sixty game birds.[133] Baronett certainly knew who many of these hunters were, likely most of them friends and acquaintances. He was smart enough to realize that if he said anything about the miscreants, it would probably be a death sentence for him, and he would be a marked man. In later years, Norris claimed that in conversations with a few of the mountaineers, they avowed "that with a firm business effort of a superintendent and

---
132. Strong, *A Trip to the Yellowstone National Park* (1876), pp. 80–81.
133. Strong, *A Trip to the Yellowstone National Park* (1876), p. 93.

assistants to protect, all will abstain."[134] Of course, there will always be a few who will be noncompliant; unfortunately, some remain so to this day.

This military junket has been cited in numerous sources as a prime example of the abuses committed on park wildlife, even though there were no laws prohibiting these activities at the time. In 1875, George Huston, with a few companions, was said to have "1,000 elk hides and a number of small furs and skins at the Gardner River bridge. Parties from Bozeman and the Yellowstone Crossing, dealing in furs and skins, have gone up to the bridge for the purpose of relieving the boys of the fruits of their winter's work."[135] Philetus Norris wrote of a conversation with the Bottler brothers, who had assured Norris that "they alone had packed over 2,000 elk skins from the forks of the Yellowstone, besides the vast numbers of other pelts, and other hunters had as least as many more, in the spring of 1875."[136] It was not until 1878 that Superintendent Norris published rules and regulations addressing the wildlife problem and other park issues. The first rule stated, "All hunting, fishing, or trapping within the limits of the Park, except for purposes of recreation, or to supply food for visitors or actual residents, is strictly prohibited; and no sales of fish or game taken within the park shall be made outside of its boundaries."[137] The weak regulation was an attempt to prohibit commercial hunting and fishing while still allowing visitors to provide for their sustenance and enjoyment. Still, at least the new rule was a beginning. Norris had no legal powers of prosecution and could only confiscate game and equipment and escort the parties out of the park. But there was nothing to prevent them from returning.

Finally, in 1883, Secretary Teller gave notice that "in regard to killing game in the Yellowstone National Park [the rules] are amended so as to prohibit absolutely the killing, wounding or capturing at any time, of any

---

134. P. W. Norris, "Meanderings of a Mountaineer, or, The Journals and Musings of a Rambler over Prairie and Plain," 1885.

135. Robert V. Goss, *Pack Trains and Pay Dirt in Yellowstone* (Gardiner, MT: Self-published, 2007), p. 8.

136. Norris, The Great West, Conclusion of Firehole Letter-22, 1870, in "Meanderings of a Mountaineer." Copy courtesy of Lee H. Whittlesey.

137. P. W. Norris, "Report upon the Yellowstone National Park to the Secretary of the Interior, 1878," p. 993, Washington, DC. Montana Memory, https://www.mtmemory.org/nodes/view/104718.

buffalo, bison, moose, elk, black-tailed or white-tailed deer, mountain sheep, Rocky Mountain goat, antelope, beaver, otter, martin, fisher, grouse, prairie chicken, pheasant, fool-hen, partridge, quail, wild goose, duck, robin, meadow-lark, thrush, goldfinch, flicker or yellow hammer, blackbird, oriole, jay, snowbird, or any of the small birds commonly known as singing birds." Fishing regulations were also amended "so as to prohibit the taking of fish by means of seines, nets, traps, or by the use of drugs, or any explosive substances or compounds, or in any other way taken by hook and line."[138] Note that bears, grizzlies, wolves, and coyotes were not on the list and could still appear in the crosshairs of a rifle. It would be another eleven years before the Lacy Act of 1894 actually provided legal means for the arrest, prosecution, and punishment of offenders.

Meanwhile, before he was appointed park superintendent in 1877, Philetus Norris commenced a journey through Yellowstone on August 20, 1875. After examining the Mammoth Hot Springs, he left various pieces of wire work to be "coated" with minerals in the hot springs waters with James McCartney. These were known as "coated specimens" and were very popular with visitors. It was a memento that they could make or purchase that did not destroy the natural features. The vast majority of coated specimens were created at the Coating Terrace and Cleopatra Springs on the lower portion of the Mammoth Terraces. The minerals in the falling waters deposited a beautiful white coating on items left there for four or five days. Commonly coated items included horseshoes, bottles, wire baskets, candle holders, toy cannons, vases, teapots, coffee cups, picture frames, animal figurines, bookends, and pine cones.

Norris enlisted George Huston and C. H. Wyman as guides to Lamar Valley. At Soda Butte, Norris wanted to explore Specimen Ridge and look for crystals and amethysts, while Huston was to return to Mammoth to guide Col. Black's party from Fort Ellis. Huston left "but came charging back soon after shouting, 'Indians!'" The group discerned men and horses "pouring out of a dark canyon in the tall mountain." Evidently, both parties were surprised at seeing each other and made preparations

---

138. Kiki Leigh Rydell and Mary Shivers Culpin, *Managing the Matchless Wonders: A History of Administrative Development in Yellowstone National Park, 1872–1965* (Yellowstone National Park, WY: National Park Service, Yellowstone Center for Resources, 2006), p. 16.

for defense. A "blanket signal"[139] was waved, and the parties cautiously approached each other and made peace. The "Indians" proved to be Jack Baronett, his Bannock wife, children, and friends, returning with their horses from a bison hunt on Clark's Fork. Huston and Baronett were old friends, and they immediately spent a few minutes of "how-how greeting and gossip of Sitting Bull and other news." Meanwhile, a great storm had set in, and everyone headed for Baronett's cabins to ride it out. Being the only lodging in the area, it soon filled "with full breeds, half breeds and mountaineers of every age, nationality, dress and arms. As there was not a drop of 'pizen' [booze] all was song and story, fun and feast, upon every kind of mountain delicacy."[140] Aside from Jack's short-lived marriage in 1884, this is the only mention of his having a spouse and children, and they are not spoken of again. It was common among the fur trappers and mountaineers to take Indigenous wives to assist with the domestic chores, skin animals, and tan the hides.

During this same time, Capt. William Ludlow was on a reconnaissance assignment in the territory between Carroll, Montana, and Yellowstone Park. He was accompanied by his brother Edwin; assistant W. H. Wood; George Bird Grinnell, who would report on paleontology and zoology; and Edward S. Dana, examining the geology of the areas covered. The famed frontiersman and guide Lonesome Charley Reynolds served as hunter and scout while Lt. Thompson of the Sixth Infantry joined them as a topographer and general assistant.[141] While in the park, the Norris and Ludlow parties encountered each other, and Norris, for the first time, met Reynolds, who impressed him deeply.

Reynolds and Norris shared in the festivities at Baronett's cabin the night of the big storm, and the two men "recognized one another as true kindred spirits." They both exulted in the life of rugged outdoorsmen and enjoyed the solitude of the wilderness. "Each soon discovered that

---

139. A blanket signal was made by holding a blanket at the corners and opening it three times, a signal for a friendly invitation to smoke.

140. Norris, "Meanderings of a Mountaineer," letter of August 30, 1875. See also Aubrey L. Haines, *The Yellowstone Story*, vol. 1 (Denver: University Press of Colorado, 1996), p. 357.

141. Capt. William Ludlow, *Report of a Reconnaissance from Carroll, Montana Territory, on the Upper Missouri, to the Yellowstone National Park and Return, Made in the Summer of 1875* (Washington, DC: Government Printing Office, 1876), p. 10.

"Lonesome Charley" Reynolds

Charles Alexander Reynolds was born in Stephensburg, Kentucky, in 1842. In 1860, he was hired to be a Pony Express rider and later served in the 10th Kansas Infantry during the Civil War. After that, he traveled around the West, generally by himself, earning the moniker "Lonesome Charley." He worked as a trader, buffalo hunter, hunter, and guide. Reynolds was noted as an expert marksman, frontiersman, and hunter, and he had been a scout with Buffalo Bill and George Custer during the 1874 Black Hills Expedition. The night before the Battle of the Little Bighorn, Charley reportedly had premonitions and gave away his personal items to the soldiers.

the quiet exterior of the other concealed an unexpected depth of sensitivity, integrity, and honor. That night, a communication more elemental and meaningful than words quickly established a lasting bond between them." The new friends parted ways the following day but not long after were reunited at Carroll, where they spent time hunting before leaving on a boat down the Missouri River.[142] The two spent about two weeks together but never met again. Sadly, less than a year later, as a scout for Gen. George Custer, Charley Reynolds would be counted among the fallen under Custer's luckless command at Little Bighorn.

Later in July 1878, Jack guided Edward G. Westcott, president of the Sharps Rifle Manufacturing Co. of Hartford, Connecticut. Before leaving for the park, Westcott telegraphed an order of Sharps rifles for the Coleman & Co. store in Bozeman.[143] The Sharps company produced about 100,000 rifles between 1851 and its demise in 1881, due to the rising popularity of repeating rifles. Perhaps Jack received one of the rifles for his guiding expertise.

Silas Weir Mitchell, an American physician specializing in medical neurology, was also a scientist, novelist, and poet who journeyed to

---

142. John S. Gray, "Last Rites for Lonesome Charley Reynolds," *Montana: The Magazine of Western History* 13, no. 3 (Summer 1963), p. 46. See chapter 9, "Nez Perce Burn Jack's Bridge," for additional related material on Norris.

143. "Personal," *The New North-West*, July 26, 1878, p. 3.

Montana in 1879 specifically to tour Yellowstone. Arriving at Fort Ellis, he made the acquaintance of Baronett and George Huston. In an article published in *Lippincott's Magazine* in 1880, Mitchell observed, "The personnel of our staff had begun to interest me at Fort Ellis, especially Jack Baronette, with his handsome face, and George Houston [Huston], pleasantest of guides." Huston, in turn, engaged Billy Jump and Zed Daniels[144] as muleskinners for the pack train.[145] It was a large contingent of men, animals, and equipment. According to Mitchell's notes, the group included seven gentlemen, one cavalry major, twenty-two soldiers, Baronett as the guide, Huston as a hunter, four packers, two cooks, fifty-five horses, twenty-one mules, one dog, and four wall tents.[146] It was quite an assemblage to lead, feed, and keep track of in the wilderness.

At the start, the mules were being cantankerous and getting them calmed down and finally on the road was an achievement in itself. Mitchell rode up to Billy Jump and asked "if the mules 'get on well'?" Billy answered with distinct sadness in his tone, "I was a-thinkin', that the first day's mule-packin' is like the first year of gettin' married: thar is allus the devil to pay, and after that it most usually settles."[147] It was a bit of backwoods wisdom to ponder.

They rode into Bottler's Ranch the next day, about midway between Bozeman and Yellowstone. In charge of the household, Mitchell observed "an amazing old woman with a face that looked as if she must have inherited wrinkles, and added to them industriously." Reinvigorated with fresh milk, they continued to Mammoth Hot Springs, where they camped for the night.[148] Mitchell was duly impressed at nature's handiwork in forming the beautiful terraces. He enjoyed soaking in several different pools and being completely relaxed. He was, however, dismayed at all the damage and vandalism committed by other visitors.

---

144. Billy Jump opened a mail station in Harry Yount's old cabin at Soda Butte in 1883. In later years, he bartended at Jardine and Aldridge, Montana. Daniels had mining interests at both Crevice and Cooke City.

145. Silas Weir Mitchell, "Through the Yellowstone Park to Fort Custer," *Lippincott's Magazine* 25 (June 1880): p. 688.

146. Silas Weir Mitchell Papers, MSS 2/241-03, Series 5, Folder 7, Item 1, p. 44. Library of the College of Physicians of Philadelphia.

147. Goss, *Pack Trains*, 40–41.

148. Mitchell, "Through the Yellowstone Park to Fort Custer," p. 690.

GUIDING THE GUESTS

Everyone seemed obsessed with the desire to cart off some of nature's marvelous artwork. He decried the mutilation, exclaiming, "This sort of foolish and reckless destruction of the geyser-mounds and the pools of the three great geyser-basins, goes on constantly during the season of summer, so that some of the loveliest bits of geyserites modeling, which may have taken these industrious waters a century to build, are already hopelessly ruined. I saw over and over again rough men with axes engaged in this vandal work."[149] At the time, Superintendent Norris was woefully understaffed and unable to prevent much of the damage—he and his few assistants could not be everywhere at once. It was not until 1886, when the army took charge of Yellowstone, that these problems began to be resolved.

Once again, on trying to prepare the pack train, the mules put up an awful fuss, kicking up their heels, wanting no part of it. One mule named Molly was particularly obstinate. One member of the peanut gallery, amused at the ongoing circus, remarked, "That 'ar mule 'ud kick a freckle off a girl's nose and she never know it." Finally, marginally under control, the train headed east to Tower Falls, over Mt. Washburn, the Grand Canyon, on to Mud Volcano, and across Mary Mountain to the geyser basins. At one hot pool, an attempt to "boil some beans in a tranquil-looking geyser resulted in their wild and rapid exit into the air; but our commissary had better luck in another place, and 'boiled beans d' la geyser' made part of our carte."[150] The group continued their tour through Yellowstone to their destination at Fort Custer, Montana.

It was an enjoyable trip for Mitchell despite the hardships. At a camp close to the end of their journey, Mitchell commented on an idyllic camp scene: "Not an unpicturesque scene, our campfire, with the rough figures stretched out on the grass.... Jack and George [Houston] good naturedly chaffing, and now and again a howl responsive to the anguish of a burnt boot. He who lived a life and never known a camp-fire is—Well, may he have that joy in the Happy Hunting-grounds!"[151] Anyone who has

---

149. Mitchell, "Through the Yellowstone Park to Fort Custer," p. 693.
150. Mitchell, "Through the Yellowstone Park to Fort Custer," p. 703.
151. Silas Weir Mitchell, "Through the Yellowstone Park to Fort Custer," *Lippincott's Magazine* 26 (July 1880): p. 39.

camped out in the wilds, away from autos and the sounds of civilization, can certainly appreciate this bit of philosophy.

Jack was blessed with meeting a group of thirteen folks from the mining town of Wickes, Montana, located around five miles west of Jefferson City, while tending his bridge in the summer of 1880. The party comprised eight men and five women, including Mrs. Elizabeth D. Wickes. She and her husband, Rev. Thomas Wickes, journeyed to Montana in 1879 via steamboat and wagon train and founded the first Montana Presbyterian church in Wickes. The following year, Mr. Starrett at the Montana Mining Works and Mr. Wickes arranged the trip to Yellowstone, even though their duties at work would not allow them to accompany the group. Mrs. Wickes's account of her journey was first published in an Eastern newspaper and later reprinted in the *Livingston Enterprise* in 1927 and the *Great Falls Tribune* in 1936.[152]

Equipped with horses, wagons, and plenty of camping equipment and rations, the Wickes party traveled along the Yellowstone River, where they met Yankee Jim (James George). They called him "Lankey Jim" (an appropriate description), who gave them some fish for their travels. Arriving at Mammoth, they left the wagons behind and proceeded on horseback to Baronett's Bridge. There they met "Scotty" Baronett, and his heavy Scottish brogue impressed Mrs. Wickes enough that she tried to emulate it in her writings. Learning that they were low on foodstuffs, he generously gave them "of his own tea, bacon, fish, and bread, for which we gladly paid him out of our store of sugar." He seemed genuinely happy to be in their company and asked them to sing him some songs. Someone suggested Gospel hymns, but Scotty declared he was raised on Scottish psalms in his homeland and was tired of them.[153]

Nonetheless, the group proceeded to serenade him with "Ninety and Nine," and at its close, the poor Scotsman dropped his head on his hands, exclaiming, "'Oh, I'm that lost sheep, I am; can ye gie me the buk, and I'll tak one day for the Lord a reading it, the first for mony a year.' He seemed surprised to learn we had entered the month of September,

---

152. "Mrs. Elizabeth Wickes, 88, Came to Montana in 1879," *Great Falls Tribune*, October 16, 1936, p. 12.

153. "Mrs. Elizabeth Wickes, 88, Came to Montana in 1879."

and then, looking pensive again, he urged, 'Sing it again, won't ye? And do ye coll thot church music?'"[154] Although Jack had plenty of friends, he had no family on this side of the world. Despite the traditional macho demeanor of Western men, he occasionally missed that part of life and was sometimes swept up in emotions.

"Ninety and Nine" was composed in 1874 and refers to a shepherd of a hundred sheep bemoaning the loss of one of his flock and his efforts to bring it back into the fold, as the second stanza beseeches:

> "Lord, Thou hast here Thy ninety and nine;
> Are they not enough for Thee?"
> But the Shepherd made answer: "This of Mine
> Has wandered away from Me.
> And although the road be rough and steep,
> I go to the desert to find My sheep."[155]

Later, the weary travelers made their way back to Mammoth to continue their journey with only a few biscuits for their sustenance. Tired and sore, the ladies had to be lifted from their saddles. No doubt "Scotty" was in a pensive mood after they left him and returned to his lonely duties.

On a little-known tour in early September 1880, Baronett led a group of nine persons on an excursion that included the Grand Canyon of the Yellowstone. George Miles, nephew of General Nelson Miles, accompanied Jack, along with six Bozeman women, and a pair of other gentlemen. The tour would not be noteworthy, except that Superintendent Norris's crew of road builders was constructing a wooden bridge across picturesque Cascade Creek and Crystal Falls, and Baronett and his charges were the first to pass over the as-yet-unfinished bridge.[156] A stereoview from the T. W. Ingersoll Co. from the 1880s show a rather primitive log bridge.[157] It was somewhat crude, due to a lack of funds and proper materials.

---

154. Lee H. Whittlesey and Elizabeth A. Watry, *Ho! for Wonderland* (Albuquerque: University of New Mexico Press, 2009), pp. 60–77.

155. "Ninety and Nine," WholesomeWords.org, accessed May 28, 2022. The song has five stanzas, with words by Elizabeth C. Clephane; Ira D. Sankey composed the music.

156. P. W. Norris, *Calumet of the Coteau* (Philadelphia: J. B. Lippincott, 1883), pp. 210–11.

157. T. W. Ingersoll stereoview, "1270—Bridge Across Grotto—Crystal Cascades," ca. 1880s. It was later built in the king post truss style prior to 1882.

YELLOWSTONE JACK

General Philip Sheridan visited Yellowstone twice in the 1880s, each time guided by Jack Baronett. On his first trip, Sheridan toured Yellowstone in 1881 with his brother Mike Sheridan, Gen. W. E. Strong, and others. Strong had been in the park in 1875 with Baronett and knew him well. The group traveled from Fort Kearney through the Bighorn Mountains and into Yellowstone, arriving at Baronett's Bridge around the end of August.[158] The party proceeded into the park and to Hell's Half Acre (now known as Midway Geyser Basin) and witnessed one of the park's most impressive sights—the eruption of the largest geyser crater.

A Helena paper reported, "On Sunday morning, August 26th, the day Gen. Sheridan left the basin with his party, this remarkable geyser spouted up a solid body of water from 60 to 75 feet in diameter to a height closely estimated at 500 feet. The display lasted a number of minutes, and is pronounced by those who witnessed it to have been one of the grandest sights ever witnessed in that Wonderland."[159] This description mimics W. W. Wylie's observation of the geyser, except Wylie claimed it was only 300 feet high, not the 500 feet quoted in the paper.[160] At that time, Baronett believed he had witnessed the first eruption in 1881, and because it passed "from the state of a hot spring to that of a geyser, it was entitled to a new name, and Mr. Baronett, as the discoverer, was entitled to name it, which he did, calling it the 'Sheridan Geyser.'"[161] However, hotelier George Marshall, living on the Firehole River at the junction of Nez Perce Creek in the early 1880s, likely saw the first eruption in February 1881. The name did not last, and by September 1882 it was referred to in newspapers as Excelsior Geyser, a moniker it still retains.[162] Baronett and the group were unaware that Superintendent Norris had previously named it Excelsior Geyser earlier in 1881.[163]

---

158. "Territorial Items," *The New North-West*, September 2, 1881, p. 3.
159. "The Sheridan Geyser," *Helena Weekly Herald*, September 15, 1881, p. 8.
160. William W. Wylie, *Yellowstone National Park, Or, The Great American Wonderland* (Kansas City, MO: Ramsey, Millett & Hudson, 1882), p. 31.
161. Edward Pierrepont, *Fifth Avenue to Alaska* (New York: G. P. Putnam's Sons, 1884), pp. 254–56.
162. "The Yellowstone National Park," *Burlington Free Press* (VT), September 20, 1882, p. 2. "Sheridan Geyser" continued to appear in newspaper reports until at least 1886.
163. P. W. Norris, "Fifth Annual Report of the Superintendent of Yellowstone National Park" (Washington, DC: Government Printing Office, 1881), p. 60.

Gen. Philip H. Sheridan. He was once described by Abraham Lincoln as "a brown, chunky little chap, with a long body, short legs, not enough neck to hang him, and such long arms that if his ankles itch he can scratch them without stooping." (*Harper's Weekly*, November 19, 1883, cover)

Excelsior Geyser in rare eruption, 1888. Baronett named it Sheridan Geyser in honor of Gen. Philip Sheridan, whom he was guiding. (Haynes-Photo postcard #10094, Goss Collection)

Sheridan and others toured Wyoming and Yellowstone in 1882, traveling from Green River over Jack's Bridge and on through the Clark's Fork mining community to Billings, Montana. Sources do not mention whether they encountered or traveled with Baronett. Jack was in the park around that time, as he is mentioned by Mary Bradshaw Richards, who wrote a now-famous and fascinating account of her travels through Yellowstone. She and her husband, Jesse, traveled by rail from New York to Beaver Canyon, a railhead west of the park. They were camped in a lush meadow just southwest of Norris Geyser Basin when they observed two horses galloping toward them from nearby Elk Park. A man running behind them shouted out to stop the horses at the bridge. Two of the party led one of their horses and blocked the bridge. The owner, none other than Jack Baronett, got to the faithless steeds and, according to Mrs. Richards, they rubbed "their noses as if to say, 'this behavior is all a

GUIDING THE GUESTS

joke, we are delighted that you ran all these miles after us.'" Richards had met Baronett the previous evening as he and his horses were headed to Elk Park to camp. She regretted not camping in the same area, as they could have listened to some of his famous stories by the campfire.[164]

Gen. Sheridan escorted President Chester Arthur and a host of dignitaries on a tour of Yellowstone in late August 1883. As Sheridan's favorite guide, Baronett was chosen to have the honor of guiding the presidential party. Arthur's companions included Secretary of War Robert T. Lincoln, Maj. Gen. Stager, Senator George Vest, Montana governor John Crosby, Frank J. Haynes as a photographer, and seventy-five men from the Fifth Cavalry.[165] The group traveled by a Union Pacific train to Green River, Wyoming, where they disembarked on August 6. They traveled by wagon and stage to Fort Washakie on the Shoshone Indian Reservation. Continuing along the east side of Wind River Mountains, they crossed over to Jackson Lake and the Tetons and entered Yellowstone at the south entrance on August 23. Arthur became the first US president to set foot in Yellowstone.[166] The party met Jack Baronett on reaching the Upper Geyser Basin; he would ride at the president's side for the remainder of the trip. Jack definitely would have shown Arthur some of his prime fishing spots, as the president was an ardent follower of Izaak Walton.

Toward the end of August, the group traveled from Canyon, over Mt. Washburn, and down to Baronett's Bridge. The army established Camp Cameron to allow the president and Gen. Sheridan, who had been ailing that day, some rest. Baronett volunteered to show Arthur some of the sights near his homestead. "President Arthur, accompanied by Secretary Lincoln, Surgeon Forbes and the guide Baronette, made a trip from camp to view Tower Falls and the surrounding mountain scenery," escorted by half a dozen armed cavalrymen.[167] The party returned to Mammoth the following day, where all were ready to rest. Physically, the president

---

164. Mary Bradshaw Richards, *Camping Out in the Yellowstone* (Salem, MA: Newcomb & Gauss, 1910), pp. 22, 36.
165. Haines, *The Yellowstone Story*, vol. 1, p. 279.
166. Dick Blust Jr., "The President Arthur Expedition: The Fishing Trip That Helped Save Yellowstone," accessed September 19, 2022, https://www.wyohistory.org/encyclopedia/president-arthur-expedition-fishing-trip-helped-save-yellowstone.
167. "By Telegraph," *Livingston Daily Enterprise*, August 30, 1883, p. 1.

"President Arthur's Journey Through Wyoming." Front row (L to R): John Schuyler Crosby, Philip H. Sheridan, Chester A. Arthur, Robert Todd Lincoln, and George G. Vest, all seated and wearing hats. Back row (L to R): Michael V. Sheridan, Anson Stager, Capt. Clark, George G. Vest, and Col. Gregory, all standing. ("Northern Pacific Views," Cabinet card, F. J. Haynes, Fargo, Wyohistory.org, public domain)

was not in proper condition for such a rugged trip, which showed on his return. A newspaper observed, "The president is by no means indisposed, but, though his cheeks are bronzed and healthy looking, he looks old and worn and stoops as he rides. The long journey has evidently been too fatiguing. The whole party confessed that they will be glad when they reach here and once more enjoy the luxury of a civilized bed after nearly a month of sleeping on the ground under canvas."[168] Despite that, one can be sure Arthur did not regret the trip and would have myriad tales to relate on his return to Washington.

The *Livingston Daily Enterprise* gave Jack a bit of glory at the journey's end by publishing praise for him on page 1 of the August 30 edition: "Jack Baronette who has acted as chief guide for the party

---

168. "By Telegraph," p. 1.

The President Arthur Expedition

Excerpt: Dick Blust Jr., "The President Arthur Expedition: The Fishing Trip That Helped Save Yellowstone," https://www.wyohistory.org/encyclopedia/president-arthur-expedition-fishing-trip-helped-save-yellowstone

By 1883, 11 years after Yellowstone was created as the world's first national park, the US Department of Interior was set to grant a private enterprise more than 4,000 acres of park land for sale and commercial development. Plans of the Yellowstone National Park Improvement Company included allowing private business control of the park's premier locations, building a railroad into the park, and permitting logging, cattle ranching, and even mining. The company was already cutting park forests for wood for a 250-room hotel at Mammoth Hot Springs and hiring local hunters to poach elk and other big game to feed its work crews. Yellowstone was on track to become another Niagara Falls at a time when "Niagarizing"—destructive exploitation of natural wonders for profit—was a term in everyday use.

Arthur's trip and the publicity it generated helped Sheridan and other influential supporters of protection for Yellowstone, particularly Sen. Vest, make their case for conservation, wildlife preservation, and strict control of commercial concessions inside the park. After a hard fight, Vest passed a resolution that obliged the Secretary of Interior to submit concession proposals and contracts to the Senate for approval and oversight. Concessions were sharply curtailed, and no railroad was ever built inside Yellowstone.

through the Park, has every reason to feel proud. President Arthur has ridden by his side during the greater part of the trip, and has listened to Baronette's accounts with the greatest interest when any of the natural curiosities were being examined. Sheridan too has high regard for him, beside having been a western guide during the past nineteen years he was Gen. Sheridan's guide through the Park last year."[169] Baronett was not a publicity hound and may have been a bit embarrassed by all the hoopla.

---

169. "By Telegraph," p. 1.

YELLOWSTONE JACK

Sometime after the trip, Baronett left Montana to travel to Europe, perhaps visiting his old homestead in Scotland. One newspaper commented, "Jack Baronette, the famous guide and scout of the Yellowstone and National Park, after many years sojourn in the western wilds, will rusticate in Europe during this coming winter."[170] If indeed Jack went to Europe, it must have been in December or later, as the *Bozeman Courier* reported on December 6, "he has been quite ill from an attack of heart disease, but at present has so far recovered as to be about again."[171] Nothing else seems to have been reported about his illness or the trip to Europe.

On returning to Yellowstone in 1884, he pursued a different path. Guiding was an essential part of Baronett's life, and part of the task of leading his patrons through the wilderness involved using pack animals and ensuring that the ropes and ties would securely bind the loads. But that year, Jack encountered a different "tie that binds"—that of matrimony.

His once footloose days of freedom now faced a daunting challenge (perhaps even more significant than the quest for his precious bullion)—his betrothal to Marion A. Scott. Little is known of her life, except that she was a niece of Charles R. Glidden, a longtime miner in Chico, Montana, working at the Emigrant Gulch and owner of a rich claim. That was likely where the two met, as it appears she was staying with the family then. Gifted with artistic talents, as a paper reported in 1882, she had recently completed a large painting of the lower canyon of the Yellowstone that was said to be "one of the grandest and most romantic to be found in Montana, and the artist is talented and experienced."[172] The marriage ceremony took place in Bozeman on March 14, 1884,[173] where "the large hearted Jack Baronette [was wed] to the accomplished Miss Scott, of Chico. Rev. F. B. Lewis officiated with the impressive and beautiful ceremony of the Episcopal church, when the guests were regaled with choice refreshments."[174] A wag at the Butte newspaper joked, "During a long career of adventure, Jack has had

---

170. "Montana Mélange," *Helena Daily Miner*, October 13, 1883, p. 4.
171. "Personal," *Bozeman Courier*, December 6, 1883, p. 3.
172. "Territorial," *Helena Weekly Herald*, July 20, 1882, p. 6.
173. Baronett, Marriage Certificate, Montana County Marriages 1865–1950, Familysearch.org.
174. "Wedding Bells," *Bozeman Weekly Chronicle*, March 19, 1884, p. 4.

many hair-breadth escapes; but it couldn't be expected he would always escape Scott free."[175]

After the wedding, the blissful couple traveled to Yellowstone with a team, wagon, and his greyhound. Jack, somewhat amorously distracted, allowed "man's best friend" to lead while he attended to more pleasant business. Nearing Yankee Jim's ranch, the "guide" spied three rabbits off in the brush, and away he bounded with the carriage close behind until it became snowbound in a drift. Jack, perhaps fueled by spirits of the liquid sort, decided it was a good time for a nap. A mail agent soon passed by and woke up the colonel, who no doubt abashedly got down to business, and they got the wagon back on the road again, a bit more observant this time.[176]

Their marital bliss proved to be short-lived. In the fall of 1885, one paper announced, "Jack got married about eighteen months ago; like Othello, he won his Desdemona against the wishes of her relatives by 'the tales he told.'" But the marriage does not seem to have worked out very satisfactorily, "as the lady has been in California during about a year past, and shows no signs of returning, while Jack has deserted the marital roof and resumed his old life in the mountains."[177]

In autumn 1886, Marion returned to accept the position of postmaster at Mammoth Hot Springs. The post office on the north side of Capitol Hill was near what later became the Haynes Photo Shop. A cabin was attached to or near the store where Mrs. Baronett lived. Early in 1888, she received permission from the Department of Interior to operate a small store in conjunction with the post office. She was permitted to sell to tourists "photographic views, stationery, and other small articles, subject to the approval of the Acting Superintendent of the Park." She "conducted her business in a satisfactory manner," according to an official report.[178] But on October 10, 1888, a newspaper divulged

---

175. "Madisonian," *Butte Miner*, March 26, 1884, p. 2.
176. "The Shortcomings of Col. Baronett's Guide," *Bozeman Courier*, March 27, 1884, p. 3.
177. "In Yellowstone Park," *St. Paul Globe*, September 26, 1885, p. 4. Desdemona is a character in William Shakespeare's play *Othello*, a Venetian beauty who enrages and disappoints her father by eloping with Othello.
178. "Report of the Superintendent of the Yellowstone National Park to the Secretary of Interior, 1888" (Washington, DC: Government Printing Office, 1888), p. 10.

that Mrs. M. A. Baronett had successfully divorced Mr. Baronett, and she soon left her job.[179] Nothing more is known about Mrs. Baronett except for occasional and vague references to Mrs. M. Baronett appearing in Butte newspapers. Former husband Jack once again returned to the lifestyle with which he seemed most comfortable, assuredly a wiser man. Prospecting for a partner was a one-time event, it appears.

---

179. "District Court Proceedings," *Bozeman Avant Courier*, October 10, 1888.

CHAPTER SIX
Working in Wonderland

Would you go where the winds of summer
Lull you to sleep with their cool;
Where a story awaits you at every turn,
A mystery lies in each pool,
As onward they dash in their glee,
Where the pine trees chant hymns to the silence?
Then come to the westward with me.[180]

—Jack Cheney

Baronett entered a different profession in November 1875, albeit temporarily—that of law enforcement. He was deputized by the US marshal in Bozeman and tasked with breaking up a horse-thieving operation. A group of men, familiar with the environs of Yellowstone Park, had been running horses back and forth through the park from Bozeman, Jackson's Hole, and Idaho.[181] The *Madisonian* reported that a group headed by "Rocky" Stoner was operating in the vicinity of Fort Hall, Idaho. Thomas Davis and Jack Foster (one of the horse owners) and two soldiers journeyed to the Snake River country near the Tetons to chase down the bronco bandits. Meanwhile, deputies Baronett, Frank Murray, and a squad of soldiers pursued the outlaws through the park in their search. The men pushed on as far as the Upper Geyser

---
180. Jack Cheney, *Foolish Questions—Yellowstone's Best* (Lincoln, NE: Woodruff Press, 1928).
181. Aubrey L. Haines, *The Yellowstone Story*, vol. 2 (Denver: University Press of Colorado, 1977), p. 56.

Basins but were stopped by deep snow. The thieves narrowly escaped south to the Teton River area; however, Baronett's men did manage to recapture seven horses. The soldiers in the Tetons tracked the bandits and engaged in a firefight, with around twenty shots fired. Rocky was wounded but escaped with a cohort and a few horses. The soldiers gathered the rest of the horses, along with the saddles and camp gear.[182] Baronett's appointment as a US deputy gave him the honor of being the first federal law enforcement officer in Yellowstone National Park.[183]

In addition to chasing horse thieves, Baronett strove to prevent the slaughter of park wildlife, even though those duties were probably outside his deputy authority. One newspaper lamented, "Some one, not exhibiting any authority and not known to possess any, has been recently ordering people off the Park. Langford was once Superintendent, and may be yet for aught we know to the contrary." This was in reference to Baronett's assumed deputy duties and park superintendent Nathaniel P. Langford's well-known lack of presence in the park. The writer described Jack as "a live, wide-awake U.S. Deputy Marshal, [who] is at present in charge of the same, but we did not think his duties extend to ordering people off the Park, unless they come there for unlawful purposes."[184] Langford was a bit miffed about Baronett and the publicity that reflected poorly on him. In response to a letter from James McCartney at Mammoth Hot Springs, Langford curtly retorted, "Dear Sir: I have made no appointment of any one as custodian of the Park, except that of yourself and Harry Horr made in the summer of 1874. If Mr. Baronett has been appointed Deputy U.S. Marshal, he doubtless has all the authority that U.S. Marshals have in removing all trespassers from Government reservations, pursuant to law. I have given no one authority to remove trespassers."[185] For better or worse, at least someone was attempting to keep order in Yellowstone.

Langford, appointed the first Yellowstone Park superintendent, could be termed the "ghost" superintendent, since he was rarely seen in Yellow-

---

182. "Horse Thieves," *The Madisonian*, November 13, 1875, p. 2; "Horse Thieves," *Helena Weekly Herald*, November 18, 1875, p. 7.
183. National Park Service, "Chronology of the Ranger Story," http://npshistory.com/publications/ranger/ranger-story-chronology.pdf.
184. "The National Park," *Bozeman Avant Courier*, December 31, 1875, p. 3.
185. "Yellowstone Park," *Bozeman Avant Courier*, February 18, 1876, p. 3.

stone. In November 1873, Harry Horr, co-owner of McCartney's Hotel at Mammoth, wrote to the secretary of the interior complaining hunters were killing deer and elk and taking only the tongues and hide. Knowing that Langford was never around, he suggested that Baronett be placed in charge of protecting wildlife, as, "[b]esides myself . . . he is the only one who will hibernate in this national domain."[186] Indeed, winters at those elevations of 6,000–7,000 feet could be brutally cold, snowy, and intimidating, even in these modern times. But Baronett was never officially elevated to that position.

The superintendent position was unpaid, so Langford spent most of his time making a living in Helena. Aubrey Haines claimed Langford visited Yellowstone only twice during his superintendence, once in 1872 and again in 1874—certainly no way to properly maintain and improve one of America's treasures. It was not until 1877, when Philetus Norris became superintendent, and actually lived in the park, that many protections and worthwhile improvements, including constructing roads, building bridges, and establishing rules and regulations, began to be accomplished.

Unfortunately, Patrick Conger, who replaced Superintendent Norris in 1882, proved ineffective at the job, which alienated him from those

N. P. Langford

Nathaniel Pitt Langford (1832–1911) arrived at the goldfields near Bannack, Montana, in 1862. He was involved with the vigilante movement and later published "Vigilante Days and Ways." He served as the territorial tax collector from 1864 to 1869. Langford was a member of the Washburn Expedition of 1870 and helped promote the idea of preserving Yellowstone as a public park (under the sponsorship of the Northern Pacific Railway) with a series of tours and lectures. While accompanying the Hayden Expedition of 1872, he claimed to have scaled the Grand Teton with James Stevenson. He became the first superintendent of the park in 1872 but served his five years without pay and spent little time in the park.

---

186. Louis C. Cramton, *Early History of Yellowstone National Park and Its Relation to National Park Policies* (Washington, DC: Government Printing Office, 1932), p. 39.

in power and others who could have been helpful. Hiram Chittenden declared that Conger's administration was "characterized by weakness and inefficiency which brought the park to the lowest ebb of its fortunes, and drew forth the severe condemnation of visitors and public alike."[187] A petition was circulated in January 1884 in Bozeman and surrounding areas calling for Jack Baronett to be appointed to the position. Indeed, he was familiar with the park environs, desired its protection, and was an upright, honest man. A newspaper disclosed, "It is understood that Conger is about to have his official head cut off and as Jack is a competent man we think this appointment will meet with satisfaction from the people of Montana, whose interests more [than] that of any other should be consulted."[188] Secretary of the Interior Henry M. Teller requested Conger to resign in July 1884, leaving the position open for Baronett.

A petition was then submitted to Teller that read in part, "Mr. C. J. Baronett is a gentleman who has been a resident of Said Park for a period of fifteen years, and who is thoroughly familiar with the Natural Curiosities, and is most anxious to preserve them uninjured. That we know him to be fitted and competent to fill the position of Superintendent." The document was signed by Bozeman mayor J. V. Bogert, along with dozens of other local luminaries. At least three other petitions were submitted, all worded the same but with different signatories.[189]

Baronett was well liked and a popular choice for the position and was friends with folks in high places, including President Arthur, Generals Sherman and Sheridan, and others. Montanans were tired of old guys from the east who knew very little of local affairs. One article wryly lamented, "There are already enough fossils in the park without sending any more out."[190] Nevertheless, the appointment would not be his despite Jack's popularity and at least four petitions sent to Washington on his behalf. Instead, another "fossil" from the East, Robert Carpenter, was awarded the job due only to the influence of his brother, Governor

---

187. Hiram M. Chittenden, *The Yellowstone National Park: Historical and Descriptive*, 3rd ed. (Cincinnati, OH: Robert Clarke Co., 1900), pp. 131–32.
188. *Bozeman Weekly Chronicle*, January 30, 1884, p. 2.
189. Jack Baronett Files, "Petition for J. C. Baronett for Superintendent," RG48, No. 62, Roll 4, National Archives, copy from Yellowstone National Park Archives (hereafter YNP Archives).
190. "A Scout for Superintendent," *Minneapolis Journal*, February 1, 1884, p. 2.

Cyrus C. Carpenter of Iowa. Chittenden claimed Carpenter believed the park was created as an "instrument of profit for those shrewd enough to grasp the opportunity."[191] This ne'er-do-well was replaced less than a year later. The management of the park was not looking good. But Baronett, seemingly unconcerned with all the brouhaha, carried on with his mining activities and tending his bridge.

Carpenter's reign lasted only until May 1885, when the Interior Department replaced him with Col. D. W. Wear. Among Wear's first decisions was choosing Baronett to be an assistant superintendent. A Bozeman paper announced its approbation of this choice, noting that Baronett "entered and explored Montana wilds when high-toned eastern tourists kept their scalps at a safe distance from that hostile country."[192] Edward Wilson, an experienced mountaineer, was also selected by Wear, who paid Wilson's salary out of his own pocket after Wilson apprehended two poachers in the park.[193] Funds for Yellowstone were always in short supply, and superintendents had to operate as best they could with little financial support.

Most of the previous assistants had been ill suited, both physically and mentally, for the rigors of the job. Jack's extensive backwoods experience made him an excellent choice. In discussing the matter, the *St. Paul Globe* commented, "The dude assistant superintendents who were sent out here from the East two years ago are being dropped one by one. All they ever did was draw their salaries and make money on the side by guiding tourists. Their places are being filled by mountaineers selected from this country who know their business, are accustomed to the nature of their duties, and find it a pleasure to attend to them." The article spoke highly of Baronett, who spent that winter at Soda Butte, where a mail station and stage stop had been established a few years prior.[194]

Soda Butte was an essential location to protect the high density of wildlife, particularly in the winter, as the Lamar Valley generally received

---
191. Chittenden, *The Yellowstone National Park*, 3rd ed. (1900), p. 136.
192. "Baronett's Bridge," *Bozeman Weekly Chronicle*, September 30, 1885, p. 3.
193. "How the US Cavalry Saved Our National Parks," in *The Early Years in Yellowstone*, chap. 4, https://www.nps.gov/parkhistory/online_books/hampton/chap4.htm.
194. "In Yellowstone Park," *St. Paul Globe*, September 26, 1885, p. 4.

Ed Wilson

Edward Montgomery Wilson served as an assistant superintendent in 1885–1886 and was selected as a scout for the army in 1887, serving admirably for several years. He joined Frank Haynes on the winter expedition of 1887 after Lt. Schwatka became ill and returned to Mammoth. Wilson later fell in love with Mary Henderson, daughter of Mammoth hotel owner G. L. Henderson, but she spurned his advances. Disconsolate, he took his life on July 20, 1891, after drinking morphine on the hill above the National Hotel. His remains were not discovered until a year later. He is buried at Mountain View Cemetery in Livingston, Montana.

less snowfall than the rest of the park and many herds of buffalo, elk, and deer wintered there. It was also close to Cooke City, where the locals considered Lamar Valley part of their own personal hunting and fishing preserve, both for sustenance and for sale to others. The men knew Baronett and his reputation as a straight shooter (literally) and wisely tried to avoid him.

In August 1886, the US Cavalry took over the jurisdiction of Yellowstone Park under the leadership of Capt. Moses Harris and Troop M of the First Cavalry. One of his first duties was stationing troops at all the popular locations in the park. These included Norris Geyser Basin, Lower Geyser Basin, Upper Geyser Basin, the Grand Cañon, Riverside on the Madison River, and Soda Butte. Baronett was the only assistant to be kept on, this time as a scout. Harris noted in a report, "Baronett has been employed as a scout and guide under authority received from the War Department, and, owing to his long experience and perfect familiarity with the mountain trails, his services are invaluable. It is to be regretted that it has been found inexpedient to authorize the employment of more than one of these experienced scouts."[195] While praising Baronett, Harris lamented that he could not engage more men of this caliber.

---

195. "Report of Capt. Moses Harris, First Cavalry, Acting Superintendent, Yellowstone National Park, Office of Superintendent," Mammoth Hot Springs, WY, October 4, 1886.

WORKING IN WONDERLAND

Jack was employed from September through November 1886, January through April 1887, and September 1887. He was paid at a rate of $75 per month.[196] However, after September 1887, he was forced to retire due to an old foot injury. Early in 1885, Jack whacked his foot with the axe while cutting wood. The wound never healed properly, and it caused him problems for many years.[197] In the spring of 1887, *Forest and Stream* reported, "We continue to hear favorable accounts from the Yellowstone Park of the game which has wintered there. Jack Baronett, the scout, was sent last month by Captain Harris over to Specimen Ridge to look for bison. He found a herd there, of which he counted eighty, all of the herd not being in sight."[198] But buffalo numbers were decidedly declining. Gen. Sheridan reported in 1882 that as many as two thousand of the noble beasts had been killed the previous winter in and around the park.[199]

Buffalo populations were estimated by the various superintendents over the years, with six hundred reported in 1880, dropping to two hundred by 1885, and between 1896 and 1901, a mere twenty-five to fifty animals remained.[200] Captain George Anderson, who took over as Yellowstone's acting superintendent in 1891, made protecting the park's wildlife his crusade. He posted scouts at various points around the park during the winter to be on the lookout for poachers, particularly in Soda Butte Valley and Hayden and Pelican Valleys. Early in 1894, scouts noticed suspicious sled tracks in Pelican Valley. A man named Ed Howell from Cooke City was seen passing the Soda Butte station at night, raising suspicions. On March 12, 1894, Anderson received a telephone call from Lake Hotel that Howell had been caught red-handed with five freshly killed bison, the trophy heads of which he was in the process of severing. His captors reported that Howell was promptly apprehended, and they were en route to the Mammoth guardhouse.

It just so happened that Emerson Hough, a correspondent for *Forest and Stream* magazine, was a guest of Captain Anderson when news

---

196. Jack Baronett, Vertical Files, Biography, US Army Civilian Employment Records, National Archives, RG 92, Files 1886-635 and 1887-634, YNP Archives.
197. "Personal Points," *Livingston Enterprise*, February 7, 1885, p. 3.
198. Elwood Hofer, "Winter in the Wonderland," *Forest and Stream* (April 28, 1887): p. 246.
199. Haines, *The Yellowstone Story*, vol. 2, p. 59.
200. Haines, *The Yellowstone Story*, vol. 2, p. 483.

of Howell's bison slaughter and capture arrived at park headquarters. Hough was in Mammoth, merely by coincidence, preparing to launch a *Forest and Stream*–sponsored Yellowstone Park Game Expedition, guided by Billy Hofer and documented by F. J. Haynes, to survey the park's dwindling bison populations. Hough immediately wired an account of this appalling incident to editor George Bird Grinnell. Incensed by the senseless killing of park buffalo, Grinnell traveled to Washington, DC, where he and a few influential friends lobbied Congress to enact a bill to protect Yellowstone wildlife. On March 26, a mere two weeks after Howell's arrest, Rep. Lacey of Iowa introduced a bill to Congress to make the killing of park wildlife a crime punishable by law. Bolstered by public outrage, courtesy of Hough's *Forest and Stream* articles, Congress passed the Lacey Act on May 7, 1894.

In early January 1887, the Grand Winter Expedition was formed by *Century Magazine* in conjunction with *New York World*, a sensationalist

Self-portrait of Thomas Elwood Hofer eating in his cabin near Gardiner. He was frequently dubbed Billy or Uncle Billy. (Brigham Young University, MSS 9008 Item 7)

Lt. Schwatka

> Lt. Frederick Schwatka was born in Galena, Illinois, on September 29, 1849, graduated from the US military academy in 1871, and was appointed a second lieutenant in the Third Cavalry. He studied law and medicine, was admitted to the bar in 1875, and received a medical degree in 1876. He took a leave of absence from the military in 1878 and spent most of the next six years exploring the Arctic and the wilds of Alaska. Schwatka made a 3,251-mile journey by sled during his travels. He resigned from the military in 1884 and, in 1886, led another exploration expedition to Alaska under the auspices of the *New York Times*.

magazine, to explore the wilds of Wonderland during the winter. The *World* was published by Joseph Pulitzer, a pioneer in yellow journalism, and he hoped to gather fame and the sale of newspapers with this exploration. It was to be led by Lt. Frederick Schwatka, who was made famous by an 1883 expedition to the Yukon and an 1878–1880 expedition to the Canadian Arctic to look for written records by members of Capt. John Franklin's lost expedition. Yellowstone was certainly forbidding in the winter, but travel through the park was not wholly unusual. There were winter keepers at all the hotels who traveled about, and soldiers patrolled the backcountry.

Having spent time in the northern environs, Schwatka should have been quite familiar with winter travel. But the expedition ended up being an embarrassment for him and the *World*. The trip was manned by photographer F. Jay Haynes; Henry Bosse, a sketch artist; two expert snowshoers; and Schwatka's seventy-five-year-old father-in-law, J. W. Brackett. Charles A. Stoddard, David Stratton, Charles H. Taylor, and James A. Blakely were engaged as equipment handlers, accompanied by scouts and guides Jack Baronett and Ed Wilson.[201] Elwood "Billy" Hofer had spent many years in Yellowstone, was familiar with safe winter travel,

---

201. William L. Lang, "'At the Greatest Personal Peril to the Photographer': The Schwatka-Haynes Winter Expedition in Yellowstone, 1887," *Montana: The Magazine of Western History* (Winter 1983), p. 20.

and was an excellent skier. He met part of the group in February and sarcastically noted in his newspaper article that they "followed a first-class wagon road thirty feet wide, cut through the forest and planted with telephone poles every two hundred feet." Hofer also reported enough baggage was packed on wagons or sleds to equip twenty men and required three days just to reach Norris Hotel. Ironically, Schwatka was about the last man to straggle in. A few miles past the hotel, Schwatka suffered lung hemorrhaging. Baronett, whose foot was bothering him, volunteered to escort him back to Norris Hotel to recuperate and eventually return to Mammoth.[202]

Haynes, Wilson, Stoddard, and Stratton continued on to Old Faithful and Firehole. After exploring and photographing the spectacular winter geyser basin landscapes at Norris and Old Faithful, they returned to Norris Hotel. Haynes, Wilson, and his two companions skied over to view and photograph the Grand Canyon. Apparently thinking it quicker to go over Mt. Washburn to John Yancey's hostelry, the men quickly got lost in a blinding snowstorm. Struggling for three days with few supplies, no tents, and little food, the bedraggled survivors finally reached the safety of Pleasant Valley. Staying with "Uncle John" Yancey overnight and being amply fed, they returned to Mammoth, where the other trekkers had gathered.[203]

The expedition did, of course, receive a lot of newspaper headlines, but different from the type that Mr. Pulitzer desired. F. Jay Haynes essentially became the hero of the trip, while Schwatka was the zero. Many Western papers chastised the "great Yukon explorer" for his inability to cope with Wyoming's mountains. The *Billings Gazette* commented, "Schwatka is no tender foot, though he has been beaten in this last trip by Haynes, who has pluck and perseverance enough for several men of his size."[204] A headline from Salt Lake City declared, "Schwatka a Dude—The Famous Arctic Explorer Knocked Out by a Snowstorm."[205] Some time spent gaining familiarity with these mountains and becoming

---

202. "Elwood Hofer, The Yellowstone," *Philadelphia Times*, April 14, 1887, p. 1.
203. "Elwood Hofer, The Yellowstone," p. 1.
204. *Billings Gazette*, February 7, 1887, p. 2.
205. "Schwatka a Dude," *Salt Lake Herald*, February 13, p. 9.

F. J. Haynes

Frank Jay Haynes was the "official park photographer" in Yellowstone Park and obtained leases for four acres at Old Faithful and Mammoth Hot Springs, where he opened his first photo shop in 1884. His son Jack was also born that year and in later years would take over the family business. Frank eventually operated Haynes Photo Shops at all major locations in the park. He joined up with George Wakefield to form the Wakefield & Haynes Stage Co. in December 1885, but the concern was short-lived, and Haynes sold out in June 1886. Haynes and W. W. Humphrey started the Monida-Yellowstone Stage Co. in 1898 and operated from the Union Pacific rail line at Monida, Montana, into the park. When the Union Pacific completed its tracks to the boundary of the park, the company began operating out of West Yellowstone, Montana, in 1908. After the settlement of a lawsuit with Humphrey, Haynes changed the name of the enterprise to Yellowstone & Western Stage Company in 1913. Following the changeover to motorized transportation in the park, F. J. terminated his stage company after the 1916 season. In that same year, F. J. retired and turned over his successful photography business and photo shops to son Jack. Frank passed away on March 10, 1921, at age sixty-eight.

---

acclimatized to the higher elevations, as well as better planning, would have assisted Schwatka greatly.

A mystery occurred October 30, 1896, when Joseph F. Mullery, a Mammoth Hot Springs hotel clerk, wandered off into the woods, never to be seen alive again. He was known to be "slightly demented" and got lost quite quickly. His coworkers knew he was missing but, oddly, never attempted to locate him, much to their discredit. The army soldiers stationed at Mammoth then conducted a fruitless search for him. Jack Baronett got wind of the predicament and volunteered his services. "General Baronett deployed his troops making each cavalry man keep about 50 yards distant from his nearest companion ... and within 1–1/2 miles of the garrison they found Mullery's remains close to the Golden Gate canyon." His body was found lying down with a log for a pillow and his coat hanging on a nearby tree. Speculation was that Mullery believed himself to be in his own bed and went to sleep. Doctors declared he died from exposure, not starvation. The *Livingston Post* asserted that his coworkers' lack of action "will condemn them in the eyes of everyone who has the first instincts of humanity." Once more, Mr. Baronett succeeded where others failed.

Baronett was again called into action as a temporary deputy in July 1897 to assist in the search for an escaped prisoner being held for murder. One night, William Holmes (or Homes) played cards and drank at William Barber's cabin in Absarokee, Montana. As is typical during bouts of drinking, an argument broke out. Holmes was kicked out of the house, but the two men later met at a local bar and continued the argument. Fearing for his life, Barber attempted to locate the judge and marshal, but to no effect, and he was gunned down in cold blood by Holmes. Holmes fled on horse but was captured by a posse and placed in the local jail to await trial.[206] Holmes broke out of jail on September 3 and headed for the hills to escape.

Meanwhile, Baronett was apparently working on one of his prospects in the vicinity of Red Lodge and Absarokee when he was contacted by Marshal St. Clair. No doubt aware of Baronett's reputation as a noted frontiersman, the marshal gained his services as a tracker. Baronett, St. Clair, and a man named Frank McCumber started off on his trail. In early October, it was reported that "St. Clair and Baronet arrived at a horse camp eight miles from Fort Yellowstone 30 minutes after their man had left. He was afoot, and they could not follow the trail on horseback. They returned to Mammoth Hot Springs to notify McCumber, who had stopped at Cooke City to enlist the aid of the military in the capture. It was believed the culprit was headed toward Jackson's Hole."[207] Some two months later, St. Clair was notified that his man had been located in Washington state, and he traveled there to retrieve the murderer.[208]

An obscure sort of informal society developed in the border towns of northern Yellowstone Park. Some of the men in Gardiner, Bear Gulch,

---

206. "May Be a Hanging," *Bozeman Weekly Gazette*, July 9, 1897.
207. "Jail Breaker Holmes, Convicted of Murder, Two Days Ahead," *Anaconda Standard*, October 6, 1897, p. 2.
208. "Local Brevities," *Red Lodge Picket*, December 4, 1897, p. 3.

Emigrant, and Cooke City did not "appreciate" the rules and regulations that were being enacted in Yellowstone. Many of these pioneers had been prospecting, hunting, and fishing since before the park was established and somewhat considered the park their personal domain. Hunting was a profitable business, as men in the mining communities surrounding the park paid good money for game meat. Buffalo, prized for their head mounts and meat, were also killed, bringing the herd numbers down to unsustainable levels by the mid-1880s. Hiram Chittenden noted that Cooke City was of interest "only on account of its notorious hostility to the Yellowstone National Park."[209] Chittenden's opinion was likely shared by the park superintendents as well.

Jack Baronett, George Huston, Adam "Horn" Miller, Yankee Jim, J. W. Redington, and others became informal members of this sardonic group. Several monikers were attached to this "society"—A.O. Society, A.O. Tribe, A.O. Scouts, Yellowstone A.O.'s, or simply the A.O.'s. The meaning of the name is questionable, and while there was a saloon in Cooke City called the A.O. Saloon, which name came first is debatable, and it was likely a local hangout for the men when in town. Among the earliest written references to the A.O.'s was a letter from John W. Redington, who was a lead scout for the army during the Nez Perce rebellion in 1877, to Horn Miller. As a sort of postscript, Redington explained, "Formerly of the 'A. Out Scouts' in 1877."[210] Two letters after the *A* are crossed out and unreadable. Some have speculated that the *A* related to a specific posterior body feature. Reportedly, Horn Miller once approached President Arthur and declared himself leader of the Yellowstone A.O.'s. Arthur had no idea what he meant, but when Baronett explained the meaning, the president was said to have had a "conniption fit."[211]

Baronett's accomplishments in Yellowstone were many and varied, from guiding paupers to helping a president to performing as a deputy

---

209. Hiram M. Chittenden, *The Yellowstone National Park*, 3rd ed. (Cincinnati, OH: Robert Clarke Company, 1900), p. 264.

210. Redington to Miller, March 16, 1887, accessed May 18, 2022, https://www.colorado-west.com/cooke/hornletter2.jpg.

211. "Montana Matters," *Helena Independent*, September 14, 1883, p. 7; "Horn Miller in Town," *Livingston Post*, April 16, 1903, p. 1.

A.O. Saloon, Cooke City, hangout for Baronett and the A.O. Scouts. (Photo ca. 1890s, Buffalo Bill Center of the West, online digital file P5-1868)

marshal, army scout, assistant superintendent, tracker, bridge builder, and storyteller. As an article in 1882 describes him,

> *He has lived so many years where the slightest noises often mean peril that he has an air of constant watchfulness. His voice is low and his utterances slow and cautious, like one who instinctively guards against betraying his presence to a listening enemy.*
>
> *He is a man of more than medium size, but his steps are as noiseless as those of a cat, and, although he is considerably over 50 years of age, he is as agile and as a keen-sighted boy, and does not look more than 37 years old.*[212]

Baronett's legacy in Yellowstone exhibits his remarkable versatility, resilience, and spirit, leaving a lasting mark on the history of this extraordinary national park.

---

212. "The Scout," *Butte Miner*, February 21, 1882, p. 1.

CHAPTER SEVEN
Prospecting in Paradise

But can't you hear the Wild?—it's calling you. Let us probe the silent places, let us seek what luck betide us; Let us journey to a lonely land I know. There's a whisper on the night-wind, there's a star agleam to guide us, And the Wild is calling, calling . . . let us go.[213]

—Robert W. Service

Baronett was generally tending his bridge or searching for gold when not guiding or pursuing other duties in Yellowstone. In 1879, Baronett prospected in Crevice Gulch, a tributary of Bear Creek known as Bear Gulch to prospectors; by the turn of the century, it was dubbed Jardine, Montana. Joe Brown, John Zimmerer, Dan Royer, and another man had discovered placer gold at the mouth of Bear Gulch in 1866 and pulled out $8,000. The following year, Lou Anderson, A. H. Hubble, George W. Reese, Caldwell, and another man found the shiny yellow metal at the mouth of Crevice Gulch.

A Helena paper announced in July 1879 that "Messrs. Dewings, Baronette, Stone and others have recently struck rich gold-bearing ore in Crevice gulch. Parties who have examined specimens of the ore pronounce them equal to any found in Bear Gulch." Jack displayed a choice specimen to a newspaperman, who proclaimed, "The specimen is about four inches thick and nearly a foot square, and shows free gold in great profusion on nearly every surface. It is from a ledge owned by Baronett,

---

213. Robert W. Service, *The Spell of the Yukon and Other Verses* (New York: Barse & Hopkins Publishers, 1907), p. 39.

Dr. Monroe, and others. Jack says he refused $100 for the specimen."[214] Any chunk of ore, usually quartz, that sports visible stringers of gold is rich indeed. Much of the gold mined in the last one hundred years comes from ore, where gold is not even visible to the naked eye. Of course, it requires vast quantities to make it a paying proposition.

Brief Early History of Bear Creek

Excerpt: *Cultural Resource Inventory and Evaluation Project*, Homestake Mining Co., Jardine, MT, September 30, 1994

While the discovery of gold in Bear Creek has been credited to several individuals, there is no doubt that "Uncle Joe" Brown was to become a prominent figure in the first three decades of Bear Gulch mining history. In May 1866, Brown is credited with taking $1,800 worth of gold from placer deposits near the mouth of Bear Creek, sluicing surface gravels, and also seeking placer gold in ancient stream channels on Bear Creek. . . . From 1866 to 1884, Joe Brown and his partner, Mr. Vilas, worked placer ground on a modest scale. In 1870, Joe and James Graham located gold-quartz veins on Mineral Hill [above the current town of Jardine]. They constructed an arrastra, mined some ore, and milled it on a small scale. Between 1866 and 1869, Campbell, Cohen, and Long constructed a ditch from the head of Bear Creek to supply water for placer mining. Between 1875 and 1877, Joe Brown and his partners constructed another series of water ditches for placer operations. In later years, these ditches provided water for hydraulic operations and an electric power plant on Bear Creek.

Although sporadic work on placer grounds and lodes continued in the 1870s, no claims were surveyed or patented until the 1880s [1882]. The first recorded claims were the Graham Lode, filed by James Graham and Joe Brown on April 18, 1882. In 1884, Joe Brown and his partners sold their placer claims to Major George O. Eaton and Thomas Sturgis, who started the Bear Gulch Placer Company.

---

214. "Gallatin County," *The New North-West*, July 25, 1879, p. 3; "Crevice Gulch and Clark's Fork," *Helena Independent*, May 3, 1879, p. 3. Bear Creek flows into the Yellowstone near the mouth of the Gardner River.

Also in 1879, Baronett prospected the New World Mining District and located a number of claims. The district had been formed on July 19, 1872, in the Clark's Fork area northeast of Yellowstone Park. A miners' meeting was held that day in order to combine the New World and Blackmore mining districts (named after William Blackmore) into the New World Mining District. Although detailed information on the Blackmore District is lacking, it was formed by at least 1875. George Huston was elected deputy recorder with C. B. Werks (?) as recorder.[215] Various rules and regulations regarding mining claims were voted on and approved.

The following year, Eastern banker and financier Jay Cooke Jr. visited the area and became interested in investing in several larger claims. He went so far as to give a $5,000 bond to Huston as a purchase option on his mine properties, including the Great Republic, New World, and Greely claims.[216] The miners in the area were elated and envisioned money rolling in from the son of the Northern Pacific railroad magnate. In excited anticipation, the gold diggers decided to create a formal town site. The miners figured if they named their town after Cooke, it would help with the town's interest.

A meeting was held on June 11, 1880, to elect town officials and arrange to survey town lots. Miners who desired stock in the new town included Huston, Baronett, Jimmy Dewings, Col. P. W. Norris, Adam Miller, X. Beidler, J. W. Ponsford, James Gourley, Bart Henderson, Z. H. Daniels, J. H. "Pike" Moore, J. V. Bogert, W. W. Alderson, F. D. Pease, George Ash, Mathias "Cy" Mounts, and H. B. Potter. The list was a veritable "Who's Who" of the Upper Yellowstone and Bozeman areas. The community, known as Miner's Camp, was also called Clark Fork City and Galena City (and sometimes erroneously referred to as Shoo-Fly). It was eventually renamed Cooke City. Lots could only be legally sold and registered once the US government established a treaty with the Crow nation to release the strip of land bordering the north

---
215. F. V. Hayden christened Mt. Blackmore to honor the recently deceased Mary Blackmore. The mountain can be seen from her gravesite. Hayden also named a new mineral Blackmorite in honor of William Blackmore. It is not clear when the Blackmore District was established.

216. Robert V. Goss, *Pack Trains and Pay Dirt in Yellowstone* (Gardiner, MT: Self-published, 2007), pp. 48–50.

Crow Cession of Lands in 1882 Relevant to Bear Creek and Clark's Fork Region

Excerpt: Act of April 11, 1882—Congressional Act to Allot Land to Crow Indians on Reservation (initiated June 12, 1880)

Whereas certain individual Indians and heads of families representing a majority of all the adult male members of the Crow tribe of Indians occupying or interested in the Crow Reservation in the Territory of Montana have agreed upon, executed, and submitted to the Secretary of the Interior an agreement for the sale to the United States of a portion of their said reservation, and for their settlement upon lands in severalty, and for other purposes: Therefore . . .

Beginning in the mid-channel of the Yellowstone River at a point opposite the mouth of Boulder Creek; thence up the mid-channel of said river to the point where it crosses the southern boundary of Montana Territory, being the forty-fifth degree of north latitude; thence east along said parallel of latitude to a point where said parallel crosses Clarke's Fork; thence north to a point six miles south of the first standard parallel, being on the township-line between townships six and seven south; thence west on said township-line to the one hundred and tenth meridian of longitude; thence north along said meridian to a point either west or east of the source of the eastern branch of Boulder Creek; thence down said eastern branch to Boulder Creek; thence down Boulder Creek to the place of beginning. (Act of April 11, 1882. 22 Stat., 42, chap. 74, https://indianlaw.mt.gov/_docs/fed_state/acts_of_congress/crow/22_stat_42.pdf.)

boundary of Yellowstone.[217] But certainly lots were informally claimed and built on in anticipation of that time.

Another miners' meeting was held on April 10, 1882, the day before the official opening of the miners' desired lands. A record book was created that dictated specific stipulations for the New World Mining District. Adam Miller was elected president, and Orlando Dewing was chosen as recorder. Meetings would be held annually, and new officers

---

217. "Sandwiches," *Bozeman Avant Courier*, June 24, 1880, p. 3; "New Town at Clark's Fork Mines," *Bozeman Courier*, March 27, 1884, p. 3.

would be selected at that time. The first order of business was a detailed description of the district's boundaries. Other provisions noted, "A claim shall be fifteen hundred feet in length and three hundred feet on each side from the center of the lode ledge or deposit." It was also stated that marked four-inch stakes were to be affixed on a mound or monument at all corners of the claim. Claimants of land for a mill site would be allowed five acres for that purpose.[218]

Huston bought at least nine city lots at that time. Whether Baronett did is unknown, though he owned shares in several mines in the district. Regrettably, Jay Cooke Jr. eventually bailed out of the project and abandoned his plans in Cooke City; however, Huston did make a cool $5,000 on the forfeited deal. The miners kept on a-diggin' anyway, and two years later Col. George O. Eaton bought into the same properties that Cooke had turned down, so Huston ended up with a sizable amount of money from his claims.[219]

Records indicate that on June 20, 1879, Baronett and H. Harris filed for a claim near the Huston Lode in the New World District that became the White Foot Lode.[220] The following February, S. D. Henderson sold his rights and claims of the following mines to Baronett for $1,000: one-third interest in Peacock Lode, one-sixth interest in Alta California Lode, one-half interest in the Fraction Lode, and one-half interest in the West Point Lode.[221] In 1882, a ledger indicated that Baronett claimed 500 feet of the Yellow Jacket Mine, while four others each owned 250 feet of that claim. He also owned one-sixth of the Mexican Lode and a share of a 160-acre placer mining claim on Clark's Fork.[222] How much Baronett actively worked these claims is unknown, as miners often hired crews to sweat and toil for them. Like the stock market, claims were

---

218. New World Mining District, *Ledger Book 1*, 1882, #2350, Special Collections, Montana State University, Bozeman, MT. Also, New World Mining District, *Record Book A, 1879–1880*, Donna and Larry Teeter Private Collection.

219. Goss, *Pack Trains*, pp. 48–50.

220. New World Mining District, *Record Book A*, p. 6. This was one of a series of record books that tracked claims for the two individual mining districts before 1879 and for the New World district between 1880 and 1882, when the area was ceded to the State of Montana from the Crow Indian Reservation.

221. *Record Book A*, p. 105.

222. New World Mining District, *Ledger Book 1*, Sections F003, F005, F006.

frequently bought and sold depending on local economic conditions and potential buyers. It was also common for claims to be purchased sight unseen by investors in the Eastern United States and Europe.

Jack continued to prospect and mine in the area, as he had time between other ventures and even lived in Cooke City with his wife, Marion, for a spell in the mid-1880s. One would assume he built or rented a cabin in town. Eventually, he acquired a one-third share in the Little Daisy Mine. It was located on Henderson Mountain just east of the Homestake Mine and shared the same rich lode. One newspaper reported, "Wire gold in galena; wire gold in quartz; wire silver all through . . . a vein ranging from 50 to 109 feet wide and extending 700 feet up the face of the mountain. . . . All the old miners who have visited it pronounce it the richest they ever saw."[223] George Huston reported that the tunnel was blessed with "wire gold, wire silver, black sulfurets of silver . . . and native silver, the richest in the world."[224] There was no doubt a touch of exaggeration in the articles, as papers were wont to do with new gold strikes, but, nonetheless, it was rich.

Col. Eaton

Col. George Oscar Eaton was a native of Maine and served in the Civil War as a volunteer. He attended West Point, graduated in 1873 as a second lieutenant, and attended the School of Mines at Columbia College in New York. Eaton served in the cavalry in the Western states and was a member of Gen. Sheridan's staff. After he retired from the cavalry, he headed to Montana in 1881 and invested heavily in the mines at Cooke City. Eaton was president of the Republic Mining Co., which owned mines around Cooke City, such as the Great Republic, Greeley, Huston, and the New World. He was also president of the company that operated the hydraulic placer mines in the Bear Gulch (Jardine) area and built the first quartz mill in the area.

---

223. "Richest in America," *Bozeman Weekly Chronicle,* July 30, 1884, p. 3.
224. "Good News from Cooke," *Bozeman Avant Courier,* July 31, 1884, p. 3.

PROSPECTING IN PARADISE

In 1882, Col. George Eaton bought out Joe Brown's Legal Tender Mine in Bear Gulch and invested in other mine properties in that area. The following year, Eaton purchased Baronett's remaining half interest of the War Eagle Mine in the Clark's Fork district for $9,000[225]—a tidy sum indeed (over $280,000 in 2024 dollars)! In the fall of 1883, William H. Armstrong of Washington, DC, purchased Baronett's shares in the Little Daisy Mine and other properties in the area. Apparently, Baronett had trouble obtaining his share of the purchase price and resorted to a lawsuit. The decision was against Armstrong and three other men, declaring that Baronett was "entitled to the possession, and entitled to have and receive the one-third of the money, the purchase price for a certain quartz lode, to-wit: The 'Little Daisy' quartz lode, situated in the New World Mining District."[226] Information regarding the result of the suit has yet to be located. Although Jack was always ready to spin a good yarn, he was generally reticent about his personal life and activities.

Late in 1883, Baronett and Archie McKinley were busy working the Yellow Jacket #2 claim, while Jack and George Eaton had a crew mining the War Eagle lead. The smelter at Cooke began production shortly, and "silver bricks from the first smelter in Gallatin county will begin to arrive in Bozeman." The *Montana Record-Herald* was assured the flow of silver would muzzle the nay-sayers and critics of the mines at Cooke.[227]

Another of Baronett's haunts for gold was the Boulder River, which has its head in the Absaroka Mountains and flows south into the Yellowstone River near Big Timber, Montana. In 1883, he filed a claim in the Mill Creek district with partners James Connell and J. Davies. The men proclaimed it a valuable find and planned to sink a 50-foot shaft to verify its worth. Baronett and David Noble located several leads in the area the following year. In 1889, Jack spent two months prospecting the Boulder District and enthusiastically predicted great potential for the area; he located numerous claims during this time.[228]

---

225. "Montana Melange," *The Madisonian*, February 24, 1883, p. 2.
226. "Summons," *Bozeman Weekly Chronicle*, March 12, 1884, p. 4.
227. "From Clark's Fork," *Montana Record-Herald*, October 4, 1883, p. 3.
228. "Town Talk," *Billings Herald*, August 2, 1884, p. 3; "Local Matters," *Livingston Post*, July 18, 1889, p. 3.

The Republic Smelter in 1883. It was located on the mountain south of Cooke City, across the valley from the Homestake mines. (Open Parks Network, YELL_14_028 #2353, Yellowstone National Park #33247)

"Black gold" was another resource in which Baronett invested his time and effort. Better known as coal, it was present in at least three locations in southern Park County, Montana: Mount Everts in Yellowstone near Gardiner; Little Trail Creek, not far from Bear Creek above Gardiner; and the communities of Horr and Aldridge, north of Gardiner. The *Livingston Daily Enterprise* noted on January 12, 1884, that Baronett and Zed Daniels had a coal mine near Gardiner[229]; although the specific area was not mentioned, it was likely Mount Everts, as it is known that Jack was working the area. Major Pease and Baronett purchased a coal mine near Bear Creek less than a month later. Another newspaper observed, "It showed several fine veins of coal, some of them being six feet in thickness."[230] Later that month, it was reported that Baronett, Brown (Joe?), and James McCartney put a man at work on the Mount Everts bituminous coal outcropping.[231] That coal was shipped up the hill

---

229. "Local Layout," *The Daily Enterprise*, January 12, 1884, p. 3.
230. "Montana Matters," *Helena Independent*, February 1, 1884, p. 7.
231. "Jumping the National Park," *Helena Independent*, February 27, 1884, p. 7.

for use at the National Hotel in Mammoth Hot Springs. Coal was also a valuable product for the Northern Pacific Railway locomotives that began traveling from Livingston to Gardiner in 1883.

Baronett was employed at Fort Ellis for much of 1889, "where he has been in charge of the government property at Fort Ellis the past year. He expects to return to the Park the coming season and again operate his toll bridge on the Cooke road."[232] He was also known to do blacksmithing at the fort, perhaps to while away the winters. The following year, he was prospecting in the Sunlight Basin and Clark's Fork region with Horn Miller; Col. Pratt, a mine owner at Crevasse; and Cooke miner Jake Malin. They found some excellent prospects, "rich deposits of copper, silver and galena ores, and spent nearly two months there prospecting and locating claims. The prospects are fine and will develop into mines one day, but the district was too difficult to access for these people at the time."[233] Jack later wrote a letter to Wilbur E. Sanders, son of Montana senator Wilbur Fisk Sanders, describing the rich ores they had found. Jack was unsure whether the location was inside Yellowstone Park, but he asked Fisk to speak with his father and request that he prevent new land from being added to the park in that area. Jack also requested secrecy so as not to start a stampede.[234] The areas remained in the public domain, but whether Fisk had anything to do with it is doubtful.

The Telluride quartz district, located 50 miles southwest of Red Lodge, was originally discovered by Horn Miller in 1877. However, he was chased out by the Bannock and forced to walk out to civilization. Thirteen years later, Miller, accompanied by Baronett, F. A. Pratt, and Jake Malin, returned to the area in the fall of 1890. The men made six claims in the district. The following season, many more claims were made by numerous other parties, which were said to be quite rich. "The main lead is 80 feet across, and nine thousand linear feet are located upon it." The vein included ore of lead, silver, and copper pyrites.[235]

---

232. "Personal Points," *Livingston Enterprise*, May 31, 1890, p. 3.
233. "A Bit of Early History," *Gardiner Wonderland*, June 5, 1902, p. 3.
234. Baronett to Sanders, December 8, 1890, Wilber Fisk Sanders Papers, 1856–1905, MC53, Box 2, Folder 3, Montana Historical Society, Helena, MT.
235. "Along the Belt," *Picket Journal*, December 5, 1891, p. 3.

YELLOWSTONE JACK

During March 1893, an acquaintance of Baronett had been spending time in the area trapping and poisoning wolves and coyotes. It may have been Joe Kountz, who shared a bar business in Bozeman with Ponsford. Kountz also herded sheep, a well-known target for wolves and coyotes. The price of wolf pelts was in the $3–$4 range, and something less for coyotes, providing dual motives for his actions.

On returning home one day, Kountz began experiencing spasms. His wife quickly contacted Baronett, "who readily saw that the man had been poisoned, and having had experience in such cases in former years, proceeded to administer the usual antidotes at hand." It was surmised that he had eaten snow to allay his thirst and residues of the strychnine from his gloves had mixed with the snow. Thanks to Jack's knowledge and quick actions, Kountz recovered, but only after multiple painful spasms.[236]

Earlier that year, Jack had located a source for sapphires. Although well known in the west central portions of Montana, it is said they can also be found in the Beartooth Mountains, where he was working. Jack had a "handsome ring" made with a setting of sapphires and was showing it to friends. He claimed a value of $100 but, of course, would not reveal the precise location of its source, as he intended to return and prospect for additional gems.[237]

Most of the summers of 1892–1895 were spent in Sunlight Basin, which became known as the Telluride District. Jack was working with Jake Malin, and William and Earl Wittich of Livingston, while Horn Miller also mined in the area. One day, Jack stopped by the office of the *Red Lodge Picket* and "showed us some 'eye openers' in the way of copper carbonate and gray copper from their copper group on Sulphur creek."[238] Other samples showed "$110 in gold and silver; other ore carrying $1,342 in silver and $42 in copper, and gray copper ore, averaging 2 per cent."[239] Jack and Earl Wittich owned ten claims in the Sunlight Basin and Stinking Water District (now Bighorn River) and planned to spend

---

236. "Accidently Strychnined," *Bozeman Courier*, March 13, 1890, p. 3.
237. "Local Layout," *Livingston Enterprise*, January 7, 1893, p. 5.
238. "Mining Matters," *Red Lodge Picket*, November 12, 1892, p. 3. Sulfur Creek is in Wyoming and feeds into the Bighorn River (formerly Stinking Water River) near Cody.
239. "News from Telluride District," *Red Lodge Picket*, April 16, 1892, p. 3.

the summer of 1895 working those claims, one of which assayed at 366 ounces of silver per ton, $30 gold and a considerable amount of lead.[240] The *Picket Journal* alleged that Baronett "owned interests in many of the riches camps of the globe, making small fortunes in each."[241] There were likely some embellishments about his fortunes, but he certainly possessed claims in countless districts in the West. In 1895, Baronett, George Taft, George Turner, and J. M. Gray produced samples from Telluride that assayed quite well. A newspaper declared them "a splendid assay"[242] and about as rich as any miner would desire.

For many years, it was known that gold existed in the sands and bars of the Yellowstone River in areas surrounding Livingston. Gold from the New World mines, Bear and Crevice gulches, and the Emigrant mines washed into the river and was ground into dust from the intense friction. However, no one had been able to profitably capture the fine gold flakes. But in 1896, Newton Baily (or Bailey), a longtime seasoned Montana miner, discovered a simple process for capturing the precious mineral. "His apparatus for recovering or saving the gold is of simple construction, yet so thorough is the work that practically all the gold is saved, scarcely a color being found in the tailings."[243] He began working the islands and sand bars in the Livingston area and earned a decent living. By early 1897, a small rush was on, and men toiled away to coax out the king of metals from the sand bars in the Yellowstone River from Livingston downriver to the Billings, Montana, area.[244] Jack Baronett, never one to miss an opportunity, joined in the boom in April 1897 and, with a few men, proceeded downriver to the mouth of Duck Creek near the current town of Laurel and reportedly struck "good diggings."[245] Other parties on the river reported averaging $7–$8 a day. It doesn't sound like much today, but it would now be worth a couple hundred dollars.

---

240. "Local Matters," *Livingston Post*, May 31, 1894, p. 3.
241. "Mining Matters," *Red Lodge Picket*, November 12, 1892, p. 3.
242. "A Splendid Assay," *New Idea* (Red Lodge), July 18, 1895, p. 1.
243. "Gold in the River," *Anaconda Standard*, May 18, 1896, p. 9.
244. "Gold in the River."
245. "Local News," *Livingston Post*, April 22, 1897, p. 3.

CHAPTER EIGHT
Gold Rush to the Black Hills

As well might the eastern miners walk with shot guns into a gulch lair of Hogback Grizzlies, as to arouse Barronette, the Buchannons and other comrades from the upper Yellowstone.[246]

—J. S. Farrar

As a prospector, Baronett and his peers were perpetually on alert for word of new gold strikes. Going back a few years to 1874, General Custer's Expedition to the Black Hills in Dakota Territory discovered gold deposits. The land was owned by the Sioux, and the US Army attempted to prevent white men from secretly entering the Hills to prospect. However, their efforts failed, and by 1876 a full-fledged gold rush was on. Naturally, Baronett jumped at the opportunity and joined the throngs of hopeful miners.

In 1868, the United States brokered a treaty at Fort Laramie, Wyoming, between the US government and the Sioux nation. Once again, the Sioux territory grew smaller, but the Black Hills, considered a sacred homeland and the western half of the Dakotas, was promised to them. But it was not long before the white men again broke their promises. Interior Secretary Columbus Delano was among the first to speak out. In an 1872 memo regarding the Black Hills, he claimed, "I am inclined to think that the occupation of this region of the country is not necessary to the happiness and prosperity of the Indians, and as it is supposed to be rich in minerals and lumber it is deemed important to have it freed

---

246. J. S. Farrar to P. W. Norris, February 26, 1877, P. W. Norris Collection, Henry E. Huntington Library, San Marino, CA.

as early as possible from Indian occupancy." To follow up on this idea, Delano authorized an expedition to the Black Hills in 1874 to determine the value of its natural resources. Lt. Col. George Custer led the group under orders from General Alfred H. Terry.[247]

This event profoundly changed the northern plains and Rocky Mountains for Native Americans and white men alike. The Custer Expedition brought praise from prospectors, miners, businessmen, and settlers. However, it inspired wrath and retribution from the Sioux for the violation and eventual loss of their beloved homelands in the Black Hills. The purpose of the expedition was ostensibly to explore a little-known section of that country, scout out locations for a fort, and secretly prospect for gold, although gold was not a primary goal. Between 1,000 and 1,200 men were in the expedition, along with teamsters, horses, cattle, newspapermen, photographers, scientists, and civilian prospectors.

The group's geologists and prospectors did discover gold in the southern Hills and various other locations. In one of his reports, Custer noted, "I referred in former dispatches to the discovery of gold. Subsequent examinations at numerous points confirm and strengthen the existence of gold in the Black Hills. Almost every panful of earth produced gold in small yet paying quantities on some of the water-courses. Our brief halts and rapid marching prevented anything but a very hasty examination of the country in this respect."[248] The *New York Herald* disclosed, "The explorations for gold were not very extensive, but were enough so to satisfy all that gold abounds in unlimited quantities. . . . Gold was discovered at various points, also plumbago [graphite ore], iron, lead and silver, galena and gypsum in unlimited quantities. The country is as rich as any in the United States." The country was also rich in lumber, water, and other resources.

Between May and October 1875, yet another government expedition to the Black Hills was conducted, led by Lt. Col. Richard Dodge. Mining professor Walter Jenney was in charge of the geological explorations,

---

247. Cynthia-Lou Coleman, *Environmental Clashes on Native American Land: Framing Environmental and Scientific Disputes* (Switzerland: Springer Nature, 2020), pp. 111–12.

248. Rev. Peter Rosen, *Pa-ha-sa-pah, Or, The Black Hills of South Dakota* (St. Louis, MO: Nixon-Jones Printing Co., 1895), p. 304.

accompanied by eight companies of troops from Fort Laramie. With his staff of prospectors and miners, Jenney could officially corroborate the 1874 reports of gold. Realizing the value of the previously neglected Black Hills, financial interest in the area perked up.

Despite attempts to keep the news silent, exaggerated rumors of the gold discoveries spread quickly. The US Army was mandated to keep white men out of the Hills and succeeded on many occasions, but they could not continuously patrol such a large, mountainous region. Miners surreptitiously traveled there to try their luck with varying success. It was a journey fraught with dangers—deadly attacks from the Sioux and threats by the army of arrest and confiscation of equipment and possible imprisonment. However, the risks were justified to the many men searching for their dreams of wealth.

Negotiations soon began between government officials, the army, and the Sioux to purchase the Black Hills. The Sioux opposed any transgressions on their sacred lands by the white men and were steadfast in their opposition to the sale. In November 1875, President Grant ordered all the Sioux back to their reservations by the end of January, well aware that with the relentlessly harsh winters of the Northern Plains, the Sioux would be unable or unwilling to obey the order.[249] Now deemed delinquent, this subterfuge allowed the government to justify war with the recalcitrant Sioux and permitted President Grant to invalidate the 1868 Treaty with the Sioux, also known as the 1868 Treaty of Ft. Laramie. No longer was the army required to control white miners and their quest for the Black Hills. The race was on for prospectors, miners, and tradesmen mining the miners. The decision to open the Black Hills ultimately led to the Battle of the Little Bighorn in 1876 and other atrocities in the following years.

After Gen. Custer's defeat in June 1876 at Little Bighorn, Congress responded by attaching a "sell or starve" rider to the Indian Appropriations Act of August 15, 1876. The government, which had been unable to negotiate the purchase of the Black Hills, created this clause that essentially "cut off all rations for the Sioux until they terminated hostilities

---

249. David Lavender, *Fort Laramie and the Changing Frontier: Fort Laramie National Historic Site, Wyoming* (Washington, DC: US Department of the Interior, 1983), pp. 120–22.

"Sell or Starve" and the Act of 1877

After the defeat at the Battle of the Little Bighorn in June 1876, Congress responded by attaching what the Sioux call the "sell or starve" rider (19 Stat. 192) to the Indian Appropriations Act of 1876 (19 Stat. 176, enacted August 15, 1876), which cut off all rations for the Sioux until they ended hostilities and ceded the Black Hills to the United States. The Agreement of 1877, also known as the Act of February 28, 1877 (19 Stat. 254), is the most controversial treaty regarding the Black Hills land claims. The treaty officially took away Sioux land and permanently established American Indian reservations. Article 1 of the act modifies the boundaries of reservations stated in the 1868 Fort Laramie Treaty, while Article 2 allows the US government to establish roads for settlers to travel on when crossing the territory.

In addition, Article 7 states that only full-blooded tribal members residing on the reservation could abide by the agreements and benefits from this act, as well as past treaties. The controversies around this act state that the government purchased the land from the reservation, but there is no valid transaction record. This act also violated Article 12 of the 1868 Fort Laramie Treaty and consequently became a central point of contestation for land rights over the Black Hills.

and ceded the Black Hills to the United States."[250] The Agreement of 1877, also known as the Act of February 28, 1877, officially took away the Sioux homeland and permanently established American Indian reservations elsewhere, significantly reducing conflicts in the Black Hills and Cheyenne stage roads to the area.

The 1874 Custer Expedition's initial gold discoveries were made in the southern portion of the Black Hills in what became Custer City. However, the finds were relatively minor, and prospectors worked their way north, searching for more profitable ore. Significant deposits of gold were discovered in Deadwood Gulch in November 1875, and a stam-

---

250. *United States v. Sioux Nation of Indians* (Ct. Cl. 1979), 601 F.2d 1157, 1161; 19 Stat. 176 (chapter 289).

pede soon followed. There was no stopping the hordes. So many men from Montana joined the rush that, for a time, the Hills were known as "Montana, Junior." Fortune hunters from the Yellowstone area included Baronett, Bart Henderson, E. S. Topping, Frank Grounds, Billy Hofer, John Werks, Harry Horr, Ed Mendenhall, and George W. Reese.[251]

"The largest aggregation of stampeders to enter the Black Hills in a single body during the big gold rush of '76, was composed of more than two hundred men." Sometimes referred to as the Montana boys, the well-equipped and provisioned group included Jack Baronett, "miners, farmers, merchants and tradesmen of all kinds to be found in and around Helena, Deer Lodge, and other points in Montana territory." They were all experienced Westerners and armed with the most effective firearms obtainable. The men were "prepared to meet, and no doubt were expecting to meet, strong opposition from the hostile Sioux Indians. This notable outfit started out the first week of April, 1876." It was a safe but rugged journey until they reached Devil's Tower. A band of Sioux attacked while the men were setting up camp, killing one of the men. At the next camp, they were again assailed but encountered no fatalities. The Sioux finally backed off, and on May 10, 1876, the group reached what later became Spearfish, South Dakota.[252]

These miners settled into an area they called Montana City, located about two miles below Deadwood Gulch on Whitewood Creek. They were at that site by July 4 and held a celebration for the holiday. It seemed all the miners and businesspeople showed up to participate, having great bonfires, speeches, singing, shooting guns, and perhaps fireworks or actual black powder. Copious amounts of food and spirits no doubt abounded. The Montana boys definitely made their presence known. "In the absence of anvils and cannons, to fulminate the necessary thunder, a strong detachment of sturdy, buckskin clad mountaineers—Jack Baronett ... took a conspicuous position outside the main crowd with needle-guns, and ever and anon, as occasion required, poured volley after volley into

---

251. Robert V. Goss, *From Sail to Trail: Chronicling Yellowstone's E. S. Topping* (Gardiner, MT: Self-published, 2008), pp. 47–48.
252. John S. McClintock, *Pioneer Days in the Black Hills—Accurate History and Facts Related by One of the Early Day Pioneers* (Norman: University of Oklahoma Press, 2000), pp. 55–56.

Bustling downtown Deadwood, Dakota Territory, during the height of the gold rush in 1876. (Goss Digital Collection, public domain)

the massive mountain walls opposite. . . . The scene was grotesque, it is true, but the boys were doing their 'level best' and their salutes were as much enjoyed by themselves and appreciated by the other participants as if a heavy battery of artillery had been at their command."[253] The news of Custer's appalling defeat a week prior apparently had not reached the Hills, or the celebration might have been more subdued.

Horatio N. McGuire, a journalist of some note in the East who intended to write a promotional booklet about the Black Hills, described his interesting arrival in Deadwood Gulch. He asked Jack Baronett, "one of the pioneers of the Black Hills," how far it was to Deadwood:

"Only a mile and a half; that girl on the horse is going there now."

"Girl! What girl? I don't see anybody on a horse but that daredevil boy yonder."

"Why, that's a girl on that bucking cayuse; that's 'Calamity Jane.'"

---

253. "Centennial," *Black Hills Weekly Pioneer*, July 8, 1876, p. 4.

GOLD RUSH TO THE BLACK HILLS

> *And "Calamity Jane" she was, as I ascertained in getting some items in regard to her most remarkable career of ruin, disgrace and recklessness. There was nothing in her attire to distinguish her sex, as she sat astride the fiery horse she was managing with a cruel Spanish bit in its mouth, save her small neat-fitting gaiters, and sweeping raven locks. She wore coat and pantaloons of buckskin, gayly beaded and fringed, fur-trimmed vest of tanned antelope skin, and a broad-brimmed Spanish hat completed her costume . . . [and] at each leap of the fractious animal giving as good an imitation of a Sioux war-whoop as a feminine voice is capable of.*[254]

What a sight to behold, especially for an Eastern greenhorn.

Sometime in July 1876, Miss Calamity Jane did indeed come to Deadwood, as the *Black Hills Pioneer* announced on July 15: "Calamity Jane has arrived." Her presence was not her first foray into the Back Hills. Dressed as a bull-whacker, she joined the Jenney Expedition that set out for the Black Hills from Fort Laramie in the summer of 1875. More than 450 soldiers and the required wagons, supplies, mules, drivers, and so forth accompanied the expedition. Geologists, miners, mapmakers, botanists, and newspaper correspondents also tagged along. Jenney spied Calamity somewhere along the journey and ordered her to leave. She did, but merely to the back of the promenade, where she joined the mule drivers.[255] An Oregon newspaper provided a brief description of Calamity after her arrival in 1876: "At Deadwood City, in the Black Hills, there is a sweet girl known as 'Calamity Jane.' . . . Her profanity is said to be highly original and ornate; she chews tobacco elaborately, and is generally recognized as the incomparable and unrivaled Belle of Deadwood."[256] She certainly sounded like a woman hard to resist.

During the early gold rush, prospectors primarily focused on extracting placer gold from gravel bars and creek beds. Experienced miners, such as Baronett, knew how to locate rich deposits where streams had slowed

---

254. Horatio N. Maguire, *The Black Hills and American Wonderland* (Chicago: Donnelley Lloyd & Co., 1877), p. 304.
255. Linda Jucovy, *Searching for Calamity: The Life and Times of Calamity Jane* (Philadelphia, PA: Stampede Books, 2012), pp. 51–53.
256. "Calamity Jane," *Weekly Oregon Statesman*, September 15, 1876, p. 2.

down and deposited their load of gold. Some of these gravel bars and creek beds were situated well above any live water. This process required hard labor to either transport the gravel to water for processing or bring water to the deposits via flumes or canals. Baronett had been working claims on Rapid and Castle Creeks since July 5. These creeks were located south of Deadwood, about midway to Hill City and Castle Creek. The diggings were known to be among the richest in the Hills. He was quite successful and, while visiting Cheyenne, Wyoming, proudly displayed some of his gleanings to the newspaper editor. The newsman revealed in an article, "He brought with him a sack of the most beautiful gold that we have ever had an opportunity to feast our editorial eyes upon. There was no flour gold, but all in nuggets of the most fanciful shapes, and averaging in size from a grain of pearl sago to that of a Lima bean. The color is a rich orange, and assays higher than any other gold in the Black Hills."[257] Although the official US price of gold was around $20/ounce, miners might get only between $15 and $18/ounce, depending on the quality and pureness of the precious metal.

Baronett became an incorporator or trustee of the Estrella Del Norte Mining Co. in 1876. The company's property was on Rapid Creek, consisting of nineteen gulch claims, a water right, and 160 acres of bar diggings. The company's properties were valued at $1,192,500. Other associates included Jack's partner, judge W. L. Kuykendall, and newspaperman, lawyer, and judge Horatio N. Maguire. A reporter for the *Custer Chronicle* reported some uncertainty about the company's financial condition, "but I do know that if they will back up their wide-awake superintendent, Bart Henderson, with the necessary funds, he will make it a success."[258] Henderson worked for the company at least until 1885, when he left for the Coeur d'Alene mines and eventually journeyed to British Columbia, where he died in 1889. It is unknown how long Baronett was with the organization or when he sold his shares, but he may have cashed them in when he left the Hills for Montana in 1877.[259]

---

257. "Castle Creek," *Cheyenne Daily Leader*, November 30, 1876, p. 5. See also Letter to *Cheyenne Daily Leader* newspaper, November 30, 1876, WPA Subject 31—Black Hills Mining. Wyoming State Archives, Cheyenne, WY.
258. "Estrella Del Norte," *Daily Deadwood Pioneer-Times*, June 15, 1882, p. 4.
259. "The News," *Bozeman Avant Courier*, April 5, 1877, p. 2.

Map excerpt of the northern portion of the Black Hills, showing the towns of Deadwood, Lead, and Montana City. Also depicted are the gold-bearing streams and outcrops. (Rand, McNalley & Co., 1877, public domain)

YELLOWSTONE JACK

Brief History of Deadwood, South Dakota

Deadwood is located just northeast of Lead and about 40 miles northwest of Rapid City. The town lies in a canyon formed by Whitewood Creek in the northern Black Hills at an elevation of 4,530 feet. Built at the base of the steep wooded inclines of Deadwood Gulch and extending up the hillsides, it was named for the dead trees found in the canyon. The city was founded during the 1876 gold rush when about 25,000 miners swarmed the surrounding hills. Its turbulent reputation as a lawless outpost of frontier violence was magnified by the Deadwood Dick series of dime novels. Wild Bill Hickok, soldier, scout, and marshal, was killed in a Deadwood saloon on August 2, 1876, by Jack McCall and buried in Mount Moriah Cemetery. A railroad was built to connect Deadwood and Lead City and chartered in 1888. The line was later used to haul equipment for carving nearby Mount Rushmore. Gambling was central to Deadwood's history, but it was prohibited in 1905; gaming in Deadwood was again legalized through a state referendum in 1989.

In those early days, the Black Hills was a perilous country to prospect, mine, freight, or survive. Until early 1877, one of the primary dangers was from the Sioux, who still claimed ownership of their sacred Pahá Sapá. Later, their threats had greatly lessened, but violence committed by white bandits, road agents, and their ilk became the primary hazards. These "organized bands of outlaws or road agents, who, from their rendezvous in inaccessible mountain caves or canyons, swooped down on parties of placer-miners, murdered the men, and secured their gold; or ambushed a freight 'train' of supplies, killing the drivers, and taking what provisions they wanted. Or they would hold up the overland stage-coach, rob the express and mail sacks, frequently shoot the passengers, and be miles away before the news reached the settlements."[260] General George Crook sent in a young scout and detective by the name of Frederic M. Hans, aka "Lone Star," to help clean up the situation. In January 1877, Hans stumbled upon the lair of a gang of these banditti in a remote canyon and

---

260. T. R. Porter, "Lone Star: The Adventures of a Famous Scout," *The Wild World Magazine* 14 (October 1904 to March 1905), p. 245.

Fred Hans

In his day, Frederic Malon Hans (1861–1923) was a well-known railroad detective, frontier scout, American Indian hunter, and deadly marksman. Lone Star (or, as the Indians called him, "Chach-Pe-Wan-Ge-La") was one of the few of the famous "cross-arm" two-gun men. Hans started to roam the plains when he was sixteen years old. Perhaps no scout who ever lived was more familiar with the habits and methods of the American Indians than Lone Star. He derived his sobriquet from the Indians because, for the most part, he preferred to work alone.

According to the *Deadwood Daily Pioneer Times*, April 23, 1921:

> Lone Star's name is Fred M. Hans. He is a two-gun man—a real two-gun man. He has never been on the "silver sheet," but he still has the two ivory-handled blue 6-guns he used against outlaws and unruly Indians in the days when a fumble or the loss of a faction of a second in shooting meant death. Lone Star's gun-play is so lightning—like that should a bunch of five or six ordinary crooks interfere with him he probably would kill the entire bunch before any one of them could fire a shot even if they had their guns in their hands.

Letter: HEADQUARTERS, ARMY OF THE UNITED STATES
Washington, DC, December 16, 1886

> To Whom It May Concern:
> I have known Mr. Fred M. Hans ("Lone Star") for almost ten years. He was a scout and guide on the plains, serving with the troops operating against hostile Indians from 1876 to 1881. From personal knowledge and from reports of officers with whom he operated I take pleasure in recommending him for the gallant service he has rendered the army. For faithfulness, daring, endurance, and good judgment he is the superior of any scout and guide I have ever known.
> (Signed) P. H. Sheridan, Lieutenant-General

(Frederic Malon Hans, *The Great Sioux Nation: A Complete History of Indian Life and Warfare in America*, 1907)

feigned being a robber as well. He camped with them for several days and made an excuse to go to Custer City on business.

Meanwhile, the outlaws attacked two freighters, killed their horses, and stole their goods.[261] This act finally spurred miners and freighters into action, and a party of eighteen or twenty stalwart, well-armed men formed a posse to catch the murderers. Among these men was Jack Baronett, a fearless gun hand. When Hans arrived in Custer City, he discovered the US marshal was absent, so he teamed up with freighter Dick McCormick and the posse. They rode to the hideout and secretly surrounded the cave, hidden from sight. Hans bravely rode up toward the cave shouting greetings but was met by gunfire from the nine gunmen, who had figured out his duplicity. They killed his horse, which he used as protection while he and the posse sent in a hail of bullets. The posse killed all nine of the desperados and suffered no injuries in the gun battle. The posse gathered the stolen properties, cash, and gold and triumphantly returned to Custer City.[262] No doubt among their first stops was the local watering hole to celebrate.

The early part of 1877 brought significant changes for Jack when he was forced to defend himself in a violent altercation. He had been mining on Rapid Creek with Judge William L. Kuykendall, who had arrived in the Hills in 1875. In later years, Kuykendall wrote a book about his life in the Western frontier and included his version of Jack's shootout in early February 1877. Jack and other miners had discovered that mines recorder William L. Timblin was recording claims on Rapid Creek under the names of his friends in Iowa, who had never set foot in the Hills. Being highly unorthodox and illegal according to accepted mining laws, Jack and the other miners called for a miners' meeting to complain and resolve the issue. Kuykendall held court in the local saloon. After much deliberation and a few potent potables, the group decided Timblin's mining claims were falsely submitted and would be

---

261. Porter, "Lone Star," p. 247.
262. Frederic Malon Hans, "Diary of Fred M. Hans, 1877—Black Hills Road Agent," in *Scouting for the U.S. Army, 1876–1879: The Diary of Fred M. Hans*, ed. Michael L. Tate, Grace Lakota Hans Pawol, South Dakota Historical Collections (1981), pp. 27–34; unidentified newspaper clipping in Fred M. Hans Papers in possession of Grace Lakota Hans Pawol, Omaha, Nebraska.

void and closed. Those claims were again reopened for proper recording. Timblin was highly miffed about the affair and vowed vengeance on Baronett, whom he saw as the culprit.[263]

A few days later, Timblin, likely emboldened by firewater and gripping a pistol at his side, rode up to Baronett's cabin. A few tense words were exchanged, and then suddenly Timblin raised his weapon and fired a shot that narrowly missed Baronett. Jack was accustomed to being under fire, so he knelt and calmly pulled out his revolver and shot Timblin square on. Falling off his horse, Timblin tried to get off another round, but Baronett walked up and put his gun to Timblin's head as a warning. Some of the onlookers carried Timblin into the cabin, where he later admitted being at fault before he died. Luckily, Baronett was surrounded by his many friends, who prevented Timblin's friends from seeking any hotheaded revenge.

A preliminary trial judged Baronett innocent due to self-defense.[264] Of course, like any violent altercation, there were various versions of the event—the number of shots fired by either party, the location, whether Timblin was on a horse (or if both were), and so forth. Since Kuykendall was Baronett's partner and a judge, this version appears to be the simplest and is generally supported by other accounts. It was later said by an unknown wit about the Montana boys, "As well might the eastern miners walk with shot guns into a gulch lair of Hogback Grizzlies, as to arouse Barronette, the Buchannons and other comrades from the upper Yellowstone." Jack was not prone to violence, and this seems to be a singular event, but woe betide those who tried to cross him.

Timblin had a $5,000 life insurance policy with the Connecticut Mutual Life Insurance company, and his grieving wife, Sarah, was trying to collect on the policy, but the company refused to pay up. The contract, in part, stipulated that Timblin was permitted "to reside and travel in any civilized abode north of the 32d parallel, but became void if he overstepped those limits, or died in violation of law." The company argued that a territory "where two men can empty their pistols at each

---

263. William L. Kuykendall, *Frontier Days: A Striking Narrative of Striking Events on the Western Frontier* (J. M. and H. L. Kuykendall Publishers, 1917), pp. 207–9.
264. Kuykendall, *Frontier Days*, pp. 207–9.

Kuykendall's Description of the Shooting

A few days after the trial, "a man rode with the Recorder to Barnett's [Baronett's] cabin, and, on approaching, noticed Barnett standing in the door and saw the Recorder get his pistol out and hold it down by his side. When near the cabin, he called Barnett out and after a few words the Recorder shot at Barnett, who in a flash drew his revolver and shot the former off his horse. The Recorder tried to shoot again after he fell, but was prevented through Barnett placing his revolver against his head with the command to drop his pistol. He was carried into the cabin, where he soon expired. . . . The Recorder in this case was a new man in a mining country, without knowledge of its ways, while Barnett was an old hand in the business, a great hunter, a deadly shot and well versed in every phase of strenuous western life."

other, and the armed citizens stand by to see that a third man does not interfere with the sport" could not be considered a civilized abode. They also deemed the shooting to be a duel.[265] The shooting was not a duel according to generally accepted standards of the West at that time, as a man fired on was usually allowed to return deadly fire with a self-defense excuse. Moreover, most accounts agreed that was true, as even Timblin reportedly fessed up to firing first.

The insurance company issued a report published by an insurance journal in 1879. It is quite amusing, certainly not one that would be acceptable in modern days. The article begins, "The verdict of a coroner's jury after a re-encounter between two men in which one was killed, was, that the deceased came to his death by being too slow on the trigger. If a coroner's jury had been empanelled in the case of Mr. W. H. Timblin, whose widow is now suing the Connecticut Mutual Life insurance company on a life policy, the verdict would have been a similar one, no doubt, with, perhaps, the addition that it served him right." The piece ends with the statement, "The rest of us can scarcely be expected to pay losses on

---

265. "Review of the Month," *Insurance Journal: A Monthly Review of Fire and Life Insurance* 7 (1879): p. 84.

a man whose expectation of life is bounded by his accuracy of aim and quickness with the trigger."[266] Who says insurance people don't have a sense of humor? In May 1879, a court decided against the insurance company and awarded Sarah Timblin $5,485 including interest.[267]

After the initial excitement of the shooting died down, Jack continued his mining activities on his claims, though he was ever watchful for potential trouble from Timblin's friends who sought vengeance. A newspaper claimed in February 1877 that Baronett hit a silver-bearing crevice seven-feet wide on the Gen. Custer lode that he was working.[268] Three months later, he probably sold his claim and left the Hills when he received word that the army wanted him for scouting duty. In any case, it was in his best interest to leave the Hills, as some of Timblin's cohorts still carried a grudge against Baronett. He left town and traveled 200 miles to the Tongue River Cantonment in southeast Montana.

---

266. "Review of the Month."
267. "The Deadwood Case," *Pittsburgh Daily Post*, April 18, p. 4; May 31, 1879, p. 6.
268. "Iron Creek," *Cheyenne Daily Leader*, February 22, 1877, p. 4.

CHAPTER NINE

Nez Perce Burn Jack's Bridge

Gallant Charley Reynolds
Kind and cheerful was thy bearing.
Firm and martial was thy tread;
First among the brave and daring
Art thou numbered with the dead.[269]
—P. W. NORRIS

After the shootout in the Black Hills, Baronett traveled in the spring of 1877 to the Tongue River Cantonment in Montana Territory, which was renamed Fort Keogh the following year. Gen. Nelson Miles commanded the camp and hired Jack as a guide for the last half of May and as a scout in June.[270] The army ordered Capt. Michael Sheridan, brother of Gen. Philip Sheridan, to the Custer battle site to mark and inter the remains of Gen. Custer's men who had perished in the previous year's horrific battle. On the first of July, Baronett, along with Crow scouts G. Herndon White and Curley (who were scouts with Custer's command); Half Yellow Face, who was with Maj. Reno; and several other Crow scouts led Troop I of the 7th Cavalry from the mouth of the Bighorn River to the battle site.[271] Curley, not participating in the violent massacre, is said to have watched

---

269. John S. Gay, "Charley Reynolds," *Montana: The Magazine of Western History* 14, no. 3 (Summer 1963), p. 49.
270. Jack Baronett, Vertical Files, Biography, US Army Civilian Employment Records, National Archives RG 92, File 1886-635. Yellowstone National Park Archives.
271. "Burying the Brave," *Dodge City Times*, July 21, 1877, p. 5.

it from a distance and afterward rode to divulge the defeat of Custer's detachment, becoming the first to deliver this grim news.

Sheridan forbade any photographers to accompany the expedition to prevent newspaper exploitation or disrespect of the battlefield and remains. On arrival, the men were aghast at the battered, broken, and deteriorated remains of Custer and his men, scattered helter-skelter across the site. It was a grisly scene, and Sheridan and his men tried to identify the men as much as possible under the savage conditions. The remains of George Custer, his brother Tom, Capt. Keogh, and some other officers were packed in grass in ten crude coffins. The rest were lightly covered with earth, and name stakes were placed for those they identified. Then "the train and cortege slowly and silently wended its way from the lofty cactus desert to the deep valleys of cottonwood and willow that fringed the rivers of this Indian battle land."[272] The coffins would be shipped to West Point, where Custer was to be buried, with the remaining officers sent to other cemeteries in the East.

At the same time, Philetus W. Norris was en route to Yellowstone Park to assume his superintendence. In April, Norris received word of his appointment, and he contacted James McCartney at Mammoth Hot Springs to become temporary superintendent until his arrival.[273] The previous superintendent, Nathaniel Langford, was a man with perhaps good intentions but little follow-up. He rarely spent time in the park, and wildlife was being decimated, natural features defaced, and artifacts looted. Norris would be the first superintendent to live in the park full-time.

Norris wanted to survey the Custer battlefield in an attempt to locate the remains of his friend Charley Reynolds. Norris was also a freelance reporter for the *New York Herald* and planned on writing a report on the aftermath of the battle. He attempted to overtake the military command but was too late and met them near the mouth of the Bighorn River on their return. Norris encountered Baronett, with whom he was well acquainted, and asked him to guide him back to the Custer battle site

---

272. "Burying the Brave."
273. Aubrey L. Haines, *The Yellowstone Story*, vol. 1 (Denver: University Press of Colorado, 1996), pp. 216–17.

NEZ PERCE BURN JACK'S BRIDGE

John H. Fouch, in the company of Baronett and P. W. Norris, took the first photographs of the Little Bighorn battle site in 1877. The photo had gone undiscovered for 113 years until Dr. James Brust acquired it in 1990. ("The Mystery of Custer's Horse, Vic, at the Little Bighorn," Notes from the Frontier, accessed November 16, 2024, www.notesfromthefrontier.com/post/the-mystery-of-custer-s-horse-vic-at-the-little-bighorn)

so he could find the remains of "Lonesome Charley."[274] Although Norris had met Charley only once in 1875 in Yellowstone, he became enamored of the scout and his deeds, and they quickly developed a close friendship. In 1875, Reynolds had scouted for Col. William Ludlow's exploration of Yellowstone under the auspices of the Army Corps of Engineers. That night of the aforementioned big storm, Norris holed up at Baronett's place with Ludlow and Reynolds.[275]

---

274. James S. Brust, Brian C. Pohanka, and Sandy Barnard, *Where Custer Fell: Photographs of the Little Bighorn Battlefield Then and Now* (Norman: University of Oklahoma, 2007), pp. 19–20.
275. Gay, "Charley Reynolds," pp. 40–51.

Baronett took Norris to the battle site, guided by a map that trader and Arikara interpreter Fred F. Gerard had sketched. Gerard was with Reno's command, survived the battle, and personally saw Reynolds fall. Although Sheridan had enacted a press ban on the expedition, Norris surreptitiously managed to bring photographer John H. Fouch along; he took the first photographs of the Custer battlefield.[276] The men located what they thought were Charley's remains. Norris commented, "All that we could find were a few small bones which were but partly covered over with earth . . . a few tufts of his auburn hair, which clung to the earth after wolf or ghoul had removed the skull . . . the hair, small bones and pieces of clothing were gathered up into a handkerchief for burial elsewhere."[277] What happened to those remains is a mystery—perhaps they were buried in the Norris Cemetery in Michigan or even with Norris's own burial.

Yellowstone's new superintendent, Philetus W. Norris, along with Jack Baronett and the tourist trade, faced significant challenges in 1877. The Nez Perce had existed peacefully in portions of Oregon, Idaho, and

John H. Fouch

Born in Ohio in 1849, by age nineteen Fouch lived in Minnesota by Lake Minnetonka, where he owned a photo studio. After the death of his first wife, Jane Tennis, Fouch moved to the Montana Territory at the Tongue River Cantonment (Fort Keogh), where he owned a studio in 1877. He photographed Chief Joseph after he surrendered at Fort Keogh and was also the first to photograph the Custer battlefield and Custer's Crow scouts. In 1878, he visited Yellowstone and took sixteen photographs that were included in the "Stereoscopic Views of the Yellowstone Country." In 1879, he moved back to his home in Minnesota, where he reproduced the photos in the "Artistic Views of the Yellowstone Country and Yellowstone National Park, Series of 1876, 1877, and 1878." Most of the Yellowstone photos came from the summer of 1878. Fouch died August 7, 1933, in Glendale, California.

---

276. Brust, *Where Custer Fell*. The photos were not located until 1990.
277. P. W. Norris, "The Field of Death," *Indiana Democrat* (PA), August 26, 1877.

Washington but were now being rounded up to live on a reservation in Idaho in late summer. Miners and settlers were flooding into the country, creating violent incidents with the Nez Perce. Rather than attempt to keep the white men out, the government reduced the Nez Perce lands by 90 percent to accommodate the newcomers. The 1863 Treaty of Ruby Valley created a small reservation where the tribe would be required to live and farm. However, the treaty was signed by only a portion of the leaders. The other nontreaty Nez Perce felt they did not have to abide by the white man's paper. They preferred their migratory hunting and gathering lifestyle and continued to roam the larger area. But now they were being forced onto the reservation. Resisting relocation and determined to stay free, they decided to fight and flee. Violence broke out during protests, and a large group escaped and hit the trail through eastern Idaho to the Big Hole Valley and over to the western entrance of Yellowstone.

Gen. Oliver O. Howard, a Civil War veteran who became commander of the Department of the Columbia in 1874, was involved in the negotiations with the Nez Perce, and it was his duty to round up and bring back the resistors. He and his cavalry troops were hot on their trail, but, despite engaging in numerous bloody battles, the tribe managed to remain a few steps ahead of their enemy.[278]

Reaching Yellowstone around the middle of August, the Nez Perce proceeded up the Madison and Firehole Rivers to the Fountain Flats area. The Radersburg party from near Helena was enjoying their jaunt through Wonderland, along with eight or nine groups of tourists scattered about the park. Suddenly the Nez Perce appeared, and their trip turned from heaven to hell. They were forcefully taken captive and driven over the Mary Mountain trail toward Hayden Valley. Along the route George Cowan was shot and left for dead, and Al Oldham was shot through the jaw but managed to escape. Meeting a second party

---

278. This is a complicated story that has been discussed in detail in many sources, so just some of the relevant basics will be presented. See Jerome A. Greene, *Nez Perce Summer, 1877* (Helena: Montana Historical Society Press, 2000); Robert V. Goss, *Pack Trains and Pay Dirt in Yellowstone* (Gardiner, MT: Self-published, 2007); Bruce Hampton, *Children of Grace: The Nez Perce War of 1877* (New York: H. Holt, 1993); Orrin H. Bonney and Lorraine G. Bonney, *Battle Drums and Geysers: The Life and Journals of Lt. Gustavus Cheyney Doane, Soldier and Explorer of the Yellowstone and Snake River Regions* (Chicago: Sage Books, 1970).

Howard's March From Henry's Lake to Lower Geyser Basin.	THE HOSTILES' ATTACK AT MAMMOTH HOT SPRINGS.
Oldham Found on the Trail Shot Through Both Jaws.	Richard Dietrich Killed.
Dietrich Shot Through the Heart.	Slaughtering Cattle and Burning Bridges.
Burning of Baronett's Bridge and Henderson's Ranch.	BOZEMAN, September 2. [SPECIAL DISPATCHES TO THE HERALD.] Prof. Dietrich was killed at the Mammoth Springs. Doane's advance guard found the body still warm.
Rumors About Impending Troubles With the Crows.	The Nez Perces are still at East Fork killing Beatty's cattle. They have burned Baronett's bridge and Henderson's ranch.
BOZEMAN, M. T. September 2d, 1877. To the Editor of the Herald:	P. KOCH. BOZEMAN, September 2.—

Newspaper headlines about the Nez Perce and their violent rampage through Yellowstone, August 1877. (*Helena Weekly Herald*, September 6, 1877, p. 2)

of tourists from Helena near the Grand Canyon, the Nez Perce killed Charles Kenck and wounded two men on Otter Creek while the others fled into the woods.[279] Unaware of the fracas, George Huston and Texas Jack Omohundro were separately guiding tourists around the park and unknowingly managed to avoid encountering the Nez Perce,[280] which was probably advantageous for them, for both Huston and Omohundro were experienced frontiersmen and certainly well armed.

In the meantime, Baronett was stationed with Lt. Hugh Scott at Judith Gap in Central Montana on the lookout for Nez Perce. He had been hired by 1st Lt. Gustavus C. Doane, commander of the Crow scouts. In a letter to the Yellowstone Command on the Bighorn River, Doane noted, "I have also brought along Mr. Jack Baronett a man well known in the mts who has been Marshall for the Yellowstone Park and

---
279. Goss, *Pack Trains*, pp. 26–30.
280. Goss, *Pack Trains*.

Lt. Gustavus C. Doane, ca. 1875. Doane was transferred to Fort Ellis in 1869 and given command of Company F, Second Cavalry. (Goss Digital Collection, public domain)

has rendered good service [and] was of use on many occasions to the Party of the Secretary of war in 1875. I know the man to be one of tried valor and honesty and a thorough mountaineer—I would respectfully request and urge that he be put on your rolls as a first-class Scout and be attached to my party from May 16, 77. I have promised him this if it could be had. He knows both the people and the country well."[281] Since Doane, Baronett, and the scouts found no sign of the Nez Perce in the area northeast of Bozeman, they returned to Fort Ellis to resupply.

Lt. Doane then proceeded up the Yellowstone Valley on August 31 with Baronett and other soldiers. Nearing Cinnabar Mountain, they saw smoke rising in the distance. Baronett, Private William White, and scout/interpreter Jirah Allen were sent ahead to discover the cause. On

---

281. Lt. Doane to Yellowstone Command, June 13, 1877, Collection 2211—Doane Papers, 1860–1939, Series 2: Military papers, 1864–1893, Box 2, Folder 8. Montana State University Special Collections, Bozeman, MT.

returning, they reported that James and Bart Henderson's ranch was burning.[282] 2nd Lt. Hugh Scott volunteered to investigate, accompanied only by Baronett, but Doane dictated that they take ten other men with them. Some of the Nez Perce had gone down from Mammoth to Cinnabar Basin and set the Henderson Ranch on fire and were stealing horses. Sterling Henderson, Joe Brown, John Werks, George Reese, and William Davis were staying at the ranch, and several of them were fishing on the nearby Yellowstone River. The others, seeing Nez Perce approaching down the hill from Mammoth, gathered arms and ammu-

Lt. Doane

Gustavus Cheney Doane was born May 29, 1840, in Galesburg, Illinois. He traveled with his parents by ox train to Oregon in 1846. He graduated from college in California and enlisted in the US Army in 1862; he was commissioned first lieutenant in 1864. He retired from the military after the war but rejoined the army in 1868 and was appointed second lieutenant in the US Regulars and stationed at Fort Ellis in 1869. Early in 1870, he was a participant in the massacre of a Piegan village on the Marias River in which 173 Piegans were killed, only 33 of whom were men. He accompanied the Washburn Expedition of 1870 with a small contingent of soldiers. The following year he guided the Hayden Expedition into the park. Doane was with the first command to reach the devastated Custer battle site in 1876 and assisted with rudimentary burial duties. Late that year, he and a small crew attempted to float the Snake River from its source to the mouth at the Columbia River. The boat capsized early in the trip and the attempt was given up. He volunteered for Arctic duty late in 1877. In 1878, he married the daughter of the founder of Hunter Hot Springs in Springdale, Montana. He became a captain in 1884 and died in Bozeman on May 5, 1892.

---

282. A. B. Henderson built this ranch around 1872. It was the last vestige of civilization and facilities for tourists and other parties passing up the Yellowstone River to Mammoth Hot Springs. He lived there with his wife and eight children, of whom Sterling was the older. James Henderson was A. B.'s brother.

NEZ PERCE BURN JACK'S BRIDGE

nition and hurried down to the river to the shelter of some rocks.[283] Thus commenced a two-hour firefight in which, miraculously, no one seemed to be injured. When the Nez Perce observed Scott and Baronett rapidly proceeding up the valley, they gathered all of Henderson's horses and expeditiously rode for the hot springs. The men at the ranch told the scouts that the attackers had headed back up to Mammoth.

Lt. Scott, Baronett, and the rest followed and, on reaching McCartney's cabin, "found a white man lying dead at the door, not yet cold. [Richard Dietrich of the Cowan party] had been standing in the doorway, looking out, when one of the Indians we were chasing rounded the point and shot him. He plunged forward on his face, and was shot again."[284] The men chased the Nez Perce as far as Lava Creek but returned to Henderson's Ranch at Baronett's insistence to join forces with Doane. Jack was concerned their small squad might encounter a more significant force of the Nez Perce or be ambushed from the top of a nearby ridge at dusk. Doane then ordered Lt. Scott "to proceed to join, by the shortest possible route and with as little delay as possible, the regiment at Clark's Fork."[285] Doane reached Baronett's Bridge several days after Gen. Howard had crossed and continued to Clark's Fork.

Gen. Howard's troops pursued the fleeing Nez Perce through the northeastern portion of the park. One group from the tribe crossed Baronett's Bridge and set it afire to slow the cavalry advance. The ends of the stringers burned through, but the ends of the timbers dropped into the river, dousing the flames. Howard approached the bridge soon after, on September 6, 1877, and found it impassable due to the fire. According to the *Bozeman Weekly Chronicle*, "the bridge hung over the chasm by the skin of its teeth. A trooper volunteered for the occasion and carefully crawled over, had he not, he and the bridge would have crashed down into the roaring torrent. But he made it by a scratch and with his

---

283. Lt. Doane, Letter to Yellowstone Command, June 13, 1877. The Henderson Ranch, established around 1872–1873, was located about two miles downriver from Gardiner, on the edge of the Cinnabar town site.
284. Hugh Lenox Scott, *Some Memories of a Soldier* (New York: The Century Co., 1928), pp. 60–64.
285. Col. Sturgis to 1st Lt. Doane, September 2, 1877, Collection 2211-Bo2-F11, Doane Papers. Montana State University Special Collections, Bozeman, MT.

Naming Names

> John Shively, a gold miner from the Black Hills prospecting in Yellowstone, had been captured by the Nez Perce. He speculated that Little Bear, a Shoshone chief, had led the party that burned the bridge. Nez Perce chiefs White Hawk and Many Wounds, during a visit to Yellowstone in 1935, claimed their fathers Wottolen and White Hawk were among the party that burned the ranch and bridge. (Peter Nabakov and Lawrence Loendorf, *American Indians and Yellowstone National Park*, Yellowstone Center for Resources, YCR-CR-02-01, 2002, p. 222.)

picket-rope and a log he soon secured the bridge so that stouter soldiers could cross."[286] Baronett's cabin, now deserted, stood close by, and the soldiers "requisitioned" some of the timbers and boards to make repairs so that the entire command could cross.[287]

According to Gen. Howard, the bridge damage stopped their chase for roughly three hours. He later described their efforts:

> *Our bridge has just been finished; the beams, shortened by the fire, were tied to some heavy timber that was fortunately on hand. Mr. Baronet's house ... stood a few hundred yards away, on Joseph's side of the river ... and much of its lumber was brought to the river, for re-planking. The bridge ... had but one intermediary support, and that fearfully near to demolition. As the first animals were started across the patched-up structure it trembled, and swung laterally very perceptibly ... our improvised bridgemen, standing as they did, on the shore, crouching and peeping under to watch the shaky pier and the ropes, and ever calling out, till they were hoarse, "Why don't you go on there? She is all right; the men mustn't step together," in the short space of half an hour the work was done; led horses, loaded pack-mules, and marching men had crossed the flood. I think we must have realized*

---

286. "Baronett's Bridge," *Bozeman Weekly Chronicle*, September 30, 1885, p. 3.
287. "Baronett's Bridge."

something of the feeling of the Israelites when they had reached the other shore of the Red Sea and looked back.[288]

Ultimately, the Nez Perce made their way through the park to the Clark's Fork area and headed north, hoping to gain safety in Canada. General Howard and his troops were worn out after weeks in the saddle, so they faded back, hoping the Nez Perce would think they had escaped. The fugitives managed to reach the Bear Paw Mountains near the border, where they stopped to rest the women and children. Unbeknownst to them, Col. Nelson Miles was approaching from Fort Keogh; he caught up with them the next day and attacked the camp. After several days of fighting, Chief Joseph surrendered on October 5 and gave his famous "I will fight no more forever" speech. While some were able to slip through the army lines and cross into Canada, over four hundred Nez Perce surrendered, including men, women, and children. Chief Joseph and his people were not allowed to return to Oregon despite the promises

Gen. O. O. Howard

Gen. Oliver Otis Howard (November 8, 1830–October 26, 1909) was a career US Army officer and a Union general in the Civil War. As a brigade commander in the Army of the Potomac, Howard lost his right arm while leading his men against Confederate forces at the Battle of Fair Oaks/Seven Pines in June 1862, an action that later earned him the Medal of Honor. He was the army general who helped pursue the Nez Perce during the 1877 wars. His troops blazed a trail over Mary Mountain during the pursuit. That route was used for tourist travel until 1892, when the road over Craig Pass from Old Faithful to West Thumb was completed. Howard died in Burlington, Vermont, on October 26, 1909, and is buried at Lakeview Cemetery in Burlington. At his death, Howard was the last surviving Union Army general to have held the permanent rank of a general in the regular US Army.

---

288. Oliver O. Howard, *Nez Perce Joseph: An Account* (New York: Lee and Shepard Publishers, 1881), pp. 246–48.

and protests of Howard and Miles. They were sent to Kansas and the Oklahoma Indian Territory until 1885, when the Nez Perce were finally allowed to return to Washington. Still, Joseph was refused permission to live in his homeland in the Wallowa River Valley in Oregon.

George Huston, Adam "Horn" Miller, S. G. Fisher, and J. W. Redington were among the scouts who kept on the trail to the Bear Paw Mountains. Redington later declared, "S. G. Fisher was one of the best, and so was George Huston [and] Horn Miller was one of the best old souls that ever lived." *Harper's Weekly* published an article in November about the affair, probably written by 2nd Lt. C. E. S. Woods, an aide to Gen. Howard. The piece deemed the guide, George A. Huston, "a man of sterling integrity and indomitable pluck. He is the most famous and reliable 'Yellowstone Guide,' the hero of many a thrilling bear or Indian fight, told so modestly that you do not suspect him of being principle actor."[289] It was quite a tribute for the grizzled old mountain man.

The atmosphere was relatively peaceful in Yellowstone in 1878. The Nez Perce had caused death and destruction the previous year. But there was now a new sense of fear in the air due to a Bannock uprising, and the citizens were alarmed that the circumstances of 1877 would be repeated. The Bannock, located on the nearby Fort Hall Reservation in southeast Idaho, were facing starvation and in an uproar. White ranchers had destroyed their food sources in the Camas Valley while their cattle and horses grazed, and pigs uprooted the camas root, a staple of the Bannock diet. To compound the problem, the government was failing to provide adequate rations as promised. War broke out in the Camas Valley in May; eventually, around forty soldiers and civilians were killed.[290]

In late August, a group of roughly one hundred Bannock traveled the Nez Perce route through the park in an attempt to gain safety with Sitting Bull in Canada.[291] Reaching Henry's Lake, they encountered a camp of the

---

289. C. E. S. Wood, "The Surrender of Joseph," *Harper's Weekly* 1, November 17, 1877, p. 906, cited in Goss, *Pack Trains*, 38.

290. Dick d'Easum, "Bannock War at Camas Prairie," Idaho State Historical Society, no. 474, 1969, accessed September 4, 2024, https://history.idaho.gov/wp-content/uploads/0474_Bannock-War-at-Camas-Prairie.pdf.

291. Allie Patterson, "Nez Perce and Bannock Flight Through Yellowstone National Park," accessed June 20, 2022, www.intermountainhistories.org.

NEZ PERCE BURN JACK'S BRIDGE

Hayden Expedition, where they attacked and ran off the stock and gathered up most of the food provisions. Harry Yount and topographer A. D. Wilson escaped into the woods and made it to safety in Yellowstone on foot. A troop of soldiers from Fort Ellis engaged the Bannock two days later and captured fifty-six head of stock, but the Bannock escaped into the park.[292]

Following the route used by the Nez Perce in 1877, the Bannock made their way up the Clark's Fork. General Nelson Miles, leading troops of the Fifth Infantry, with Crow warriors and scouts, discovered the Bannock camp on an unnamed tributary of the Clark's Fork River. On September 4, 1878, Captain Andrew Bennett and eighteen or so of his men attacked the numerically superior camp, which was caught unawares. For a good while, "H—l was a-poppin'" during the battle with the recalcitrant Bannock. After eleven warriors were killed and others wounded, the rest were eventually convinced to surrender. The wounded were cared for, and the group was trudged off to Fort Keogh.[293] Miles's letter was published in the *Helena Weekly Herald*, reading, "Dear Sir: We were successful yesterday at daylight in capturing a small camp of Bannocks on Clarke's Fork. As near as I can ascertain there were eleven Bannocks killed, thirty-one captured, and about two hundred horses, mules and ponies. Those who escaped I think will be picked up in the hills and mountains by the Crows." Also killed was Captain Bennett, a Crow warrior and an interpreter, while another soldier was wounded.[294]

Meanwhile, Gen. Miles, P. W. Norris, Fred A. Hunt, and other soldiers were on a pleasure excursion to Yellowstone. Unaware of what was transpiring, they traveled up the Yellowstone River, past the Bottler Ranch, to Mammoth Hot Springs, where they camped. They later continued on to Baronett's Bridge. After crossing what remained of the bridge, Fred Hunt poignantly observed, "All that was left of his [Baronett's] shack were some blackened and crumbling walls and a black kitten and the remains of his bridge. The complete desolation of the place was emphasized by that skinny little black kitten. The outfit passed very

---

292. Haines, *The Yellowstone Story*, vol. 1, pp. 238–39; Richard A. Bartlett, *Yellowstone: A Wilderness Besieged* (Tucson: University of Arizona Press, 1989), pp. 27–28.
293. Fred A. Hunt, "A Purposeful Picnic, III," *The Pacific Monthly* 19 (May 1908), pp. 523–30.
294. "The Battle of Clark's Fork," *Helena Weekly Herald*, September 19, 1878, p. 4.

gingerly over the remains of the bridge, and while the tardy passage was being made a couple of soldiers fished with grasshoppers and caught over one hundred pounds of brook trout in the two hours."[295] The group continued on with their "picnic" through Wonderland.

While all of this was occurring, Jack Baronett was guiding a party of sixteen with Lt. Douglas, T. B. Sackett, Judge Patton, and Englishman Walter C. Chamberlain and his brother. Unbeknownst to the group, the Bannock passed through the park's northern section while they were at Mud Volcano. Worried about Baronett and his party, Superintendent Norris sent a scout to locate them and later reported, "My scout Hibbard, found the Lt. Douglas and Barronette party of sixteen persons at the Mud Volcano, all safe and well."[296] In a letter to Gen. James Brisbin, published the following February, Chamberlain exclaimed that "Jack Baronett, our guide, was a first-rate man, and from first to last gave us the most entire satisfaction. He is the best 'rustler' I ever came across—always active and doing something, and at the same time most careful and thorough in all he does."[297] It is no wonder that Norris was concerned for the safety of the party, as the Chamberlains were brothers to the famed radical British parliamentarian Joseph Chamberlain, who fathered Prime Minister Neville Chamberlain.

---

295. Hunt, "A Purposeful Picnic." Hunt was awarded the Congressional Medal of Honor for "Gallantry in Action" with Col. Nelson A. Miles's attack on Crazy Horse's camp in the Wolf Mountains on January 8, 1877. He later became a prolific writer of Western US history for numerous magazines.
296. "Hurrah for Norris," *Bozeman Avant Courier*, September 12, 1878, p. 2.
297. "English Tourists," *Helena Weekly Herald*, February 27, 1897, p. 1.

CHAPTER TEN

Jack's Bridge: The Exodus

In my opinion the only thing that keeps the bridge up is the grace of God.[298]

—S. H. Crookes

P. W. Norris assisted Jack Baronett and John Ponsford in rebuilding the bridge in the fall of 1878 after it had been set afire by the Nez Perce in 1877. Due to Norris's experience as a millwright, they managed to convert the bridge from a single-stringer pack train bridge to a structure with two queen-post trusses capable of handling wagon traffic.[299] A newspaper reported in June 1878 that the bridge had been rebuilt enough so traffic to the mines would have no trouble crossing the river. Since General Howard had used some of the lumber from Baronett's cabin to temporarily repair the bridge in 1877, Baronett and his friends rebuilt the cabin to have comfortable lodging before the long cold winter.

In concert with the bridge repairs, a group of thirty or so miners from Cooke City banded together that spring to effect repairs and improvements on the road between the bridge and Cooke. They estimated the project would take four to six weeks to complete, just in time for the warming weather and melting snow to allow them to return to their mining operations.[300] The miners themselves needed to repair and improve

---

298. Crookes to Goode, September 10, 1900, Army Files, Letter Box 8, Item 15, Doc. 3700, YNP Archives.
299. Aubrey L. Haines, *The Yellowstone Story*, vol. 1 (Denver: University of Colorado Press, 1996), p. 243.
300. "Town Talk," *Helena Weekly Herald*, April 27, 1882, p. 7.

YELLOWSTONE JACK

Baronett's Bridge ca. 1882, three years after the Nez Perce burned sections of the original structure. Late in 1878, Superintendent Norris helped Baronett and Ponsford rebuild the bridge with two queen-post trusses that allowed wagon travel. (Frank J. Haynes Stereoview #1264, "Barronett's Bridge, Yellowstone River," Montana Historical Society)

the road, as it was not a tourist route, and Norris was disinclined to spend his limited budget and manpower on that route. He was more concerned with improving roads within the park interior for visitors.

The *Bozeman Times* reported on June 6, 1878, that Baronett, Horn Miller, Pike Moore, and George Roland had recently "left the Yellowstone Bridge for the Clark's Fork Mines."[301] The men had also spent the previous winter at the bridge. There was plenty of wildlife and fish to feed on while keeping an eye on the bridge and travelers throughout the long winter.

In his *Calumet of the Coteau*, Norris noted the bridge was "the first, and for ten years the only, bridge ever crossed any portion of the mighty Yellowstone River." In a poetic frame of mind, Norris rhapsodized:

> *The ruins of the famous Baronet cabin, upon the high, huge granite*
> *boulder-strewn basaltic point above the confluence*
> *of the two forks of the Yellowstone River.*
> *Above the ceaseless dash and roar, Where mountain torrents greet.*[302]

---

301. *Bozeman Times*, June 6, 1878, p. 2.
302. P. W. Norris, *Calumet of the Coteau* (Philadelphia: J. B. Lippincott, 1883), pp. 205–6.

John W. Ponsford

James "John" W. Ponsford was born March 21, 1847, and at age twenty-two was a private with the Second Cavalry stationed at Fort Ellis. He took part in the 1870 massacre of an American Indian village on the Marias River in Montana that took the lives of primarily women and children. He was at Fort Ellis when he retired after 1870. By mid-1870, Ponsford owned several billiard halls/saloons in Bozeman. Ponsford also prospected in the Clark's Fork area with Baronett and others. He was among those miners who desired stock in the new town of Cooke City on its creation in 1880. Ponsford also operated coal mines near Bozeman in the 1880s. By 1883, he was a deputy sheriff in Bozeman and pulled the spring that hanged a man named Clark, who had been convicted of murder. It was the first legal hanging in Bozeman. In 1893–1894, Ponsford served as chief of police in Bozeman. Famed Montana lawman and dispenser of vigilante justice John X. Beidler dictated his biography to Ponsford in the late 1880s, who was a pallbearer at Beidler's funeral in 1890. Ponsford died September 16, 1912, and is buried in Sunset Hills, Bozeman.

Indeed, it was not until around 1881 that another bridge crossed the Yellowstone River north of the park boundary.

In 1880, Superintendent Norris and his crew were undertaking road repairs and building new routes for the tourist trade. He intended to improve the road to enable wagon traffic from Mammoth to Baronett's Bridge and Tower Fall. He enlisted Baronett's assistance, and together the two men struggled to find a passable route that was not too steep or rugged. Norris noted that "on the 3rd and 4th of July the two men adopted a route which I had previously explored with only a moderate amount of grade and bridging and passing between the vertical basaltic walls of a very modern lava overflow, and an impassable fissure vent fully 1,000 feet deep to Elk Creek, and through a geode basin through the famous 'Devil's Cut' or Dry Canyon [as he preferred to call it] to the stream skirting Pleasant Valley." The men then scaled a sharp hill to "escape an impassable canyon in reaching Pleasant Valley, and to traverse a boggy canyon to avoid a craggy cliff in leaving it, near the forks of the Yellowstone and by steep grading and climbing reached the cliffs overlooking Tower Falls." Baronett was paying Norris back for his knowledgeable assistance in rebuilding the bridge while improving his prospects, allowing larger and heavier traffic to use his bridge.[303]

William W. Wylie (who later established the Wylie Camping Company in Yellowstone) traveled through Yellowstone in the early 1880s and commented in his 1882 travel book, "This Bridge has been built and used chiefly by those interested in the Clark's Fork Mines, which are eastward from this Bridge thirty-five miles. Tourists who visit Specimen Mountain, Soda Butte Springs, and Hoodoo Basin, cross the Yellowstone upon this Bridge. As there does not [appear] one tourist in 500 visit these points."[304] It would be twenty-five years before visitors regularly traveled along the impressive route from the bridge to Cooke City and beyond.

Sensing the changing tides of official assessments, Baronett and Ponsford sent letters to the Interior Department regarding the bridge. Ponsford wrote in 1880 offering to sell the bridge to the Interior Department and sought an inspection and report by an Interior official but received no reply.[305] Baronett followed up in 1881 and proposed to either sell or be granted a permit or license to maintain the bridge. He argued that the bridge was a necessity and required maintenance, and at "great cost he constructed a bridge on the Yellowstone to enable the miners to come and go to the Clark's Fork Mines ... that it was absolutely necessary for that purpose, that without it mining could not have been carried on only a very short time each year."[306] Baronett had spent an additional $2,000 putting in new stringers and iron floor braces only a year earlier. Park officials acknowledged that the bridge performed an essential service and required regular maintenance. However, they also realized there were inadequate funds in the budget to purchase the bridge or build a replacement. It was an uncomfortable limbo for all parties involved.

---

303. P. W. Norris, "Fifth Annual Report of the Superintendent of Yellowstone National Park" (Washington, DC: Government Printing Office, 1881), pp. 9–10.

304. William W. Wylie, *Yellowstone National Park, Or, The Great American Wonderland* (Kansas City, MO: Ramsey, Millett & Hudson, 1882), p. 70.

305. "Lamar River Bridge," *Yellowstone Roads and Bridges*, HAER No. WY-12 (1968), p. 3.

306. "Lamar River Bridge," p. 5.

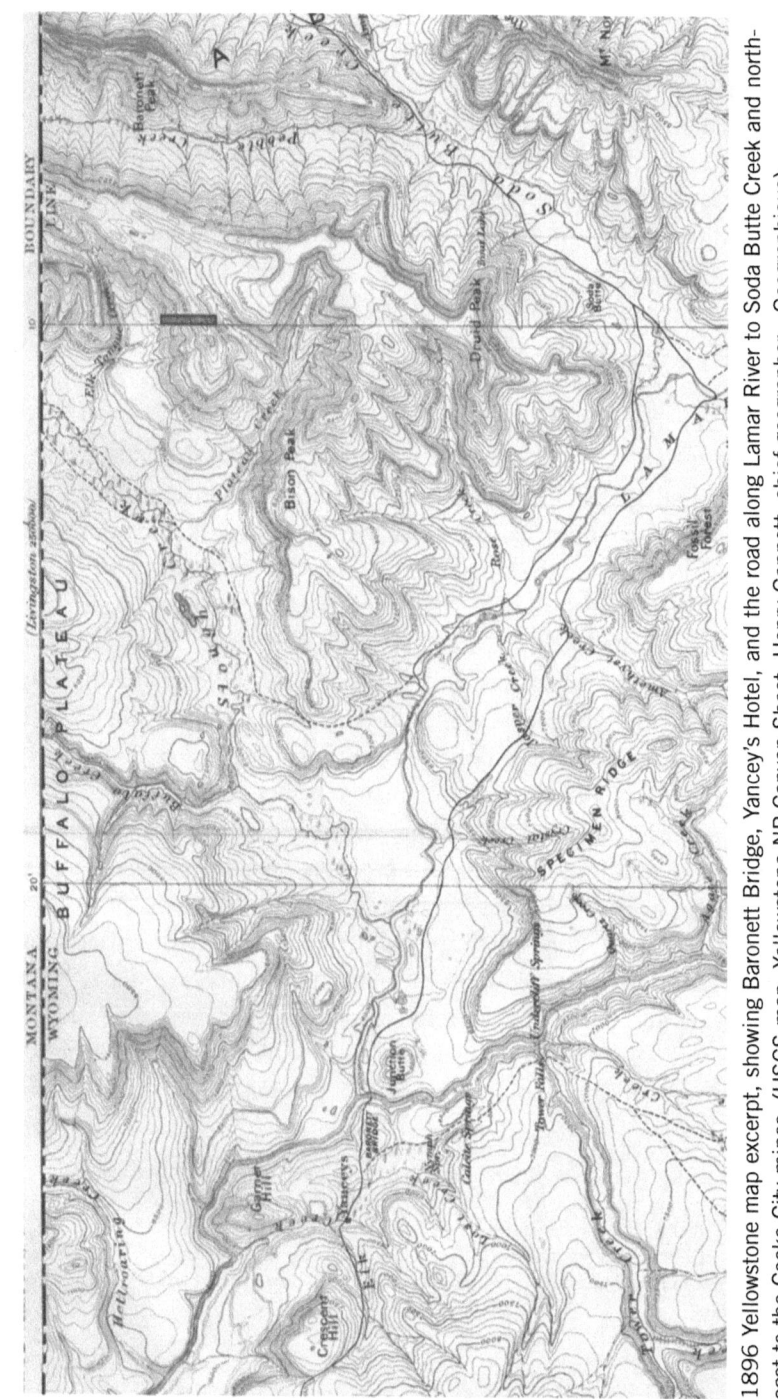

1896 Yellowstone map excerpt, showing Baronett Bridge, Yancey's Hotel, and the road along Lamar River to Soda Butte Creek and northeast to the Cooke City mines. (USGS map, Yellowstone NP Canyon Sheet, Henry Gannett, chief geographer—Geographicus)

Ponsford and James L. Sanborn reportedly purchased an interest in the bridge in 1882, although it may have been more of a partnership or lease, as the terms are unclear. Although Ponsford helped build the bridge in 1871, along with other miners, he may not have had any financial interest in the enterprise. And, no doubt, any monies Sanford and Ponsford gave Baronett certainly did not cover the accumulated costs Baronett had invested in the bridge over the years. It is a confusing situation, and there appear to be no records of the transactions. It was likely a gentleman's handshake agreement. When Baronett was compensated by Congress in 1899, there was no mention of Sanford (who had died in 1890) or Ponsford receiving any monies.

Nonetheless, one stipulation of the agreement was that Ponsford and Sanborn "shall make the approaches to the bridge in a good passable condition for a six-mule team to cross over. The work is to be done early this spring, in time for the travel to the Clark's Fork country. Price paid, $2,500."[307] In April 1882, Jack Allen, who later became the proprietor of the Cosmopolitan Hotel in Cooke City, left Bozeman with a four-horse team and wagon traveling to Cooke City. He crossed over the improved bridge and is believed to be the first to cross with a freight wagon.[308]

It was a risky venture at best for both Ponsford and Sanborn, as the army and various governmental bureaucrats believed (and rightly so) that having a privately owned bridge in a national park was improper, especially one that was charging tolls for its use. Norris preferred to have a new bridge built by the government, but he seemed unable to find a more suitable location; besides, funding was not available. Consequently, Baronett's Bridge continued in use for another twenty-five years.[309]

Ponsford and Sanborn attempted to expand their operation and proposed "keeping a stopping point for travellers subject to any restrictions the Honorable Secretary may impose." They requested ten acres of land

---

307. "Territorial News," *Butte Miner*, April 5, 1882, p. 8. There are few, if any, references to Ponsford actually tending the bridge. J. L. Sanborn was Ponsford's partner in numerous enterprises but was killed in 1890 when his horse threw him against a building.

308. Robert Flather, "Bridges," MSC007_04.01, YNP Archives. According to Flather, Baronett sold his interest to Ponsford around 1884, who then took on Sanborn as his partner and again began collecting tolls.

309. "Lamar River Bridge," pp. 3–5.

JACK'S BRIDGE: THE EXODUS

near the junction of the roads to Clark's Fork and Mount Washburn.[310] Interior denied their proposal, as John Yancey already maintained a mail station and cabin near that same location and was granted a ten-year lease in 1884 to build a hotel on ten acres that would provide lodging, dining, and, more important, drinking facilities.

Baronett and Ponsford again requested they be granted a lease for their bridge in November 1884. They explained, "We built the bridge in 1870 and respectfully refer to President Arthur who knows us and the bridge." In another letter dated November 22 to Yellowstone Superintendent Carpenter, the two men inquired whether they should apply for a lease. They claimed that when President Arthur was touring the park, he replied regarding a lease that "we should not be bothered & that we deserved credit for putting the bridge there."[311] They thought invoking the name of the president might aid their case.[312]

The secretary of the interior finally recommended buying the bridge in 1887, noting the acting superintendent of Yellowstone, Capt. Moses Harris, suggested $2,000 for the purchase, based on an appraisal at a later date. Harris also noted in his 1887 report, "I have attempted no interference with the business as conducted by these parties, as it would seem that the long period in which they have been permitted to carry on their business unmolested has given them a certain right of possession which should be settled by investigation and a judgment." He also believed the "pleasure ground of the people" was being obstructed by the toll bridge and free passage should be enacted.[313]

Despite general agreement on the purchase of the bridge and elimination of tolls, it was not until 1891 that a bill was introduced in Congress to buy the bridge, but there was no action. Bills were introduced every year after that, but nothing happened except for back-and-forth

---

310. Ponsford and Sanborn to Secretary of Interior, February 5, 1884, RG 48, No. 62, Roll 2, Letters Rec'd Interior 1883-84, YNP Archives.

311. Ponsford and Sanborn to Carpenter, November 22, 1884, RG 48, No. 62, Roll 2, Letters Rec'd Interior 1883–84, YNP Archives.

312. Baronett and Ponsford to Secretary of Interior, November 22, 1884, RG 48, No. 62, Roll 2, Letters Rec'd Interior 1883-84, YNP Archives.

313. Capt. Moses Harris, "Superintendent's Annual Report, 1887" (Washington, DC: Government Printing Office, 1887), pp. 6–7.

dickering among various bureaucrats. Meanwhile, in 1890, Yellowstone acting superintendent Capt. Frazier Boutelle sent a letter to notify Baronett that he could no longer reside in his cabin per Department of Interior regulations. In this letter, Boutelle reproached Baronett for not previously paying attention to what he was told and demanded, "You must not again attempt a residence in the park without the authority of the Secretary of the Interior."[314] Baronett's home and refuge in the park was being taken away from him, and he would soon lose his bridge.

At this time there was no mention of Ponsford relative to the bridge. By the early 1890s, Ponsford and Joseph Kountz had become partners in a brewery/liquor store and billiard hall in Bozeman. Meanwhile, Ponsford and Kountz were occupied with prospecting, mining, and managing a cattle ranch. So it is likely that Ponsford was not concerned with the bridge negotiations.[315]

Capt. George Anderson, acting superintendent of Yellowstone, submitted a report to the Interior in 1893 recommending that Baronett's claim be extinguished and that he be compensated $5,000 for his losses.[316] Baronett officially lost possession of his bridge in 1894, but no payment was sanctioned then.[317] By that time, Baronett had acquired the services of Attorney Edward M. Dawson in Washington, DC, to represent his case. Letters were exchanged between the lawyer and various government officials. However, the cogs of Congress turned slowly and accomplished nothing for another five years.

Baronett wrote a letter to Capt. Anderson in November 1894 requesting his assistance. He enclosed a letter from his lawyer and asked Anderson to forward it to Washington with his blessing. Jack noted, "It would do me the greatest favor that could be conferred upon me. I am getting at the age I need the money."[318] Jack again wrote Anderson

---

314. Boutelle to Baronett, November 10, 1890, Bound Vol. 215, Vol. 111, Letters Sent, 1890, p. 186, YNP Archives.
315. Various Bozeman newspapers from 1890 to 1899.
316. Anderson to Dept. of Interior, October 27, 1893, Army Files, February 1895, YNP Archives.
317. Aubrey L. Haines, "The Bridge That Jack Built," *Yellowstone Nature Notes* 21, no. 1 (January–February 1947): pp. 3–4.
318. Baronett to Capt. Anderson, November 23, 1894, Army Files, LB2, Item 4, Doc. 788, YNP Archives. See also Documents #789–792, 1152, and 2321–2324.

JACK'S BRIDGE: THE EXODUS

in February 1895, complaining he did not collect any tolls the previous summer, as he was not able to attend to the bridge, and reasoned that if a man was put on as tender, he would spend all the tolls, and Jack would not have realized any monies anyway. He also claimed the "United States Government has used my bridge since 1877 without paying a dollar with the exceptions of Gen'l Sheridan, when he crossed he paid for doing so."[319] Jack was then around sixty-five years old, the phase of life when hard work began to hinder everyday activities, making his prospecting and mining even more difficult and less fruitful. People back then were on their own to provide for old age, as there was no government relief to fall back on—merely a local poorhouse.

Capt. Anderson reported in 1895 that he had directed his men to repair the bridge enough to provide safe passage for wagons and tourists. He also arranged to make temporary repairs on the road to Cooke "to accommodate the tourist travels that comes in from the east side."[320] The repairs were greatly needed, but in a mere five years, the bridge had seriously deteriorated even more.

At long last, the secretary of the Treasury authorized payment in 1899, "To C. J. Baronett, of Gardiner, Montana, for the bridge known as 'Baronett's Bridge,' over the Yellowstone River, and the approaches thereto, five thousand dollars."[321] Baronett claimed it cost him more than that in attorney fees and travel to obtain his money. How much he actually made on the bridge tolls will never be known. It certainly could not have made him rich at two or four bits a head, especially since he was often absent and left his bridge in charge of others.

S. H. Crookes, a civil engineer from Livingston, inspected the bridge in 1900. He was dismayed to report that it "is in very dangerous condition—the planking is entirely gone at south end of bridge and batter braces at north end have rotted away so much that the bolts have slipped 3" through the timbers. In my opinion the only thing that keeps the bridge up is the grace of God." The letter was forwarded to Capt. Chit-

---

319. Baronett to Capt. Anderson, February 19, 1895, Doc. #2324, Army Files, YNP Archives.
320. "Cooke Letter," *Livingston Enterprise*, June 8, 1895, p. 1.
321. Baronett Bridge, *The Statutes at Large of the United States*, vol. 30, chap. 314 (Washington, DC: Government Printing Office, 1899), p. 918.

tenden of the Army Corps of Engineers, who made temporary repairs and noted that the bridge required reconstruction. However, funds were not available, and the deteriorating bridge could be used only for light traffic until a new bridge was constructed.[322] The bridge continued in use for a few more years, despite its fragile condition.

In anticipation of a new steel bridge, in 1902 a temporary wooden bridge was erected upstream near the current Tower Bridge site. But, due to a strike, the mills failed to produce the necessary steel. The temporary bridge served for another year until the new steel bridge could be completed in 1903. Fabricated with a steel deck truss, a light metal lattice railing, and a 130-foot span, the new bridge was based on a design by the American Bridge Company.[323] Interestingly enough, the steel bridge was named the New Baronett Bridge to honor Jack Baronett's legacy.[324] Hiram Chittenden noted in his 1915 tome that the name was indeed transferred to the new bridge.[325] Even as late as 1920, a government report still referred to it as the Baronett Bridge,[326] and it has not appeared to have received any other formal name. The bridge was strictly functional, with no outstanding architectural attributes to warrant a moniker other than the Yellowstone River Bridge. Tourists used the bridge infrequently until at least after 1915, when private automobiles were allowed into Yellowstone and it became necessary to significantly improve the road to Cooke City.

The fate of Baronett's cabin is not well known. The fourteen-square-foot log building was among the earliest residences in the park. The cabin "served as a gathering place for mountaineers and as an occasional overnight stopping-place for travelers," in addition to a residence for the toll-takers during Baronett's absences. Though likely built around the

---

322. Crookes to Goode, September 10, 1900, Army Files, Letter Box 8, Item 15, Doc 3700, YNP Archives.

323. "Lamar River Bridge," p. 6.

324. Kenneth H. Baldwin, *Enchanted Enclosure: The Army Engineers and Yellowstone National Park* (Washington, DC: Office of the Chief of Engineers, US Army, 1976), pp. 107–9.

325. Hiram M. Chittenden, *The Yellowstone National Park* (Cincinnati, OH: Stewart & Kidd Co., 1915), p. 320.

326. Baronett Bridge, *Reports of the Department of the Interior, Fiscal Year Ended June 30, 1920* (Washington, DC: Government Printing Office, 1920), p. 210. The 1903 bridge was replaced in 1961 and is due for replacement in 2026.

JACK'S BRIDGE: THE EXODUS

The New Baronett Bridge located near Tower Junction, upstream from the original. Completed in 1903, it was very utilitarian. A more modern bridge replaced it in 1961. (YNP Archives photo #29454)

same time as the bridge, the first known historical reference to it was by Paul LeHardy of the Jones Expedition in 1873.[327] A report issued many years after the bridge was demolished claimed the cabin was still in use in the 1920s, although by whom is unknown, perhaps backcountry rangers, researchers, road maintenance crews, and the like. The site was again recorded in 1985, and the roof and upper walls were gone. Ann Johnson, a park archaeologist, reported in 1989 finding "a wagon road, and remnants of several outbuildings, tin cans, and glass bottles. The remaining walls of the cabin had burned in the fires of 1988, leaving a trench where the bottom row of logs had been."[328]

During a trip exploring the area in the early 2000s, I could see traces and outlines of some of the buildings, along with assorted historic trash,

---

327. Aubrey L. Haines, "Baronett's Cabin," Haines Papers, Series 4, Box 33, Place Names Data, pp. 31–60. Montana State University Special Collections, Bozeman, MT.

328. Mary Ann Franke, *Yellowstone in the Afterglow: Lessons from the Fires* (Yellowstone National Park, WY: Yellowstone Center for Resources, 2000), p. 39.

Remains of the Baronett Bridge stone embankment on the east side of the Yellowstone River in 2006. View from upriver. (Goss photo)

nails, broken glass, and other debris. Stone walls from the old bridge were still partially in place, along with conspicuous traces of the old road to Yancey's Hotel site. There were also ruins of an old log cabin below the site, along the Yellowstone River, perhaps used by Horn Miller, George Huston, Ponsford, or other miners seeking shelter. Vestiges of the road to Soda Butte that passed north of Junction Butte were still evident and easy to follow. According to former Yellowstone ranger and researcher Robert Flather, after passing north of Junction Butte, the road then crossed "Crystal, Specimen, Jasper and Amethyst Creeks [on the south side of Lamar River], crossed the flats to the Lamar ford above the mouth of Chalcedony Creek, crossed Soda Butte 2 miles from this ford and did stay north of Soda Butte until the pull-out east of Ice Box Canyon. Here, it crossed Soda Butte and stayed to its south until the Cooke City area." From the 1880s through 1915, the road's primary purpose was to provide access to the soldier station and ranch at Soda Butte and for the miners at

JACK'S BRIDGE: THE EXODUS

Cooke. Because it was not a standard tourist route, road maintenance was marginal and ill kept, sometimes improved by miners, sometimes by the army, and occasionally not at all. A report in 1886 described it as the worst road in the park and "well nigh impassable a large portion of the year."[329]

When the New Baronett Bridge was built in 1903, the road followed the old route north of Junction Butte. It was several years before the road was reconstructed south of Junction Butte, where the highway currently runs. Numerous minor realignments were made over the years, and seasonal flooding regularly washed out other bridges and road sections. Sometime after automobiles were allowed in Yellowstone in 1915, improvement of the road system became necessary.[330] Today, the road is a well-maintained but less traveled route through Lamar Valley used primarily by wolf and buffalo watchers, hikers, campers, and Cooke City residents. The byway continues through the northeast entrance to Cooke City, with seasonal access to Cody, Wyoming, or over the breathtaking Beartooth Highway to Red Lodge, Montana.

In August 1935, Nez Perce chiefs White Hawk and Many Wounds traveled the Nez Perce trail with historian and author L. V. McWhorter in an attempt to retrace the Nez Perce route taken in 1877. Along with Yellowstone Park naturalist William E. Kearns, they traversed Yellowstone looking for trail remnants, campsites, and other evidence. White Hawk was around fourteen years old in 1877 and was a horse-tender for the group. Many Wounds, the great-grandson of Chief Red Bear, who had met with Lewis and Clark during their travels across the West, was a young man on a reservation in Idaho in 1877. However, his father, Wottolen, or Hair Combed Up Over the Eyes, was a prominent leader of the Nez Perce. Both White Hawk (ta'mapcá'yoxayxáyx, aka John Miller) and Wottolen were among the party that burned the Henderson Ranch and set fire to Baronett's Bridge.[331] After the battle in the Bear Paw Mountains, they were among the group that escaped to Canada.

---

329. "Lamar River Bridge," p. 4.
330. Robert Flather, "Cooke City Miner's Road," Catalog No. 210545, Box 3, Files 03.02, 03.03, 04.01, YNP Archives.
331. Peter Nabakov and Lawrence Loendorf, *American Indians and Yellowstone National Park* (Yellowstone National Park, WY: Yellowstone Center for Resources, YCR-CR-02-01, 2002), p. 222. See also "Turtle Island Storyteller Rosa Yearout," *Wisdom Blogger*, accessed October 12, 2022, https://wisdomoftheelders.org/turtle-island-storyteller-rosa-yearout/.

In 1935, Nez Perce chiefs White Hawk and Many Wounds retraced the 1877 Trail in Yellowstone, near the site of Baronett's Bridge. (Washington State University, Special Collections #pc_085_b02_f10_001)

While in Yellowstone, White Hawk and Many Wounds ('ilexni'eewteesin' or Sam Lott) visited the bridge site on August 13 and were very interested in the area. They "spent considerable time searching for some slight token as evidence of [their] visit."[332] William Kearns took several photographs of the men during their trip, with one photo showing the two chiefs standing at the edge of Baronett Rapids, just above the bridge site.[333] Frank Jay Haynes published a stereoview between 1881 and 1884, titled "1265—Barronett's Rapids." It remains the only known commercial view of these rapids.

Yellowstone Park historian Mary Shivers Culpin prepared a Multiple Property Documentation Form in 1995 nominating the bridge site for the National Register of Historic Places, which is mentioned in her

---

332. W. E. Kearns, "A Nez Perce Chief Re-Visits Yellowstone," *Yellowstone Nature Notes* 7, nos. 7–8 (June–July 1935): p. 41.

333. Open Parks Network.org, Yellowstone Photo Album 29, page 28, #10306-1, https://openparksnetwork.org/single-item-view/?oid=OPN_NS:671CB4C1E05F982216D36016D16EC0FA.

JACK'S BRIDGE: THE EXODUS

History of the Construction of the Road System in Yellowstone National Park, 1872–1966.[334] The document states, "A nomination for another associated resource, the Baronett Bridge site has been prepared by the Wyoming State Historic Preservation Office. This site will be included in the Multiple Property nomination form for this project." It would have been eligible under Criterion D at the state level in that

> *The Baronett Bridge Site is significant at the State Level for its position as the first bridge to cross the Yellowstone River. The bridge, which predated the creation of the Park by one year, gave access to the Cooke City mines from the Yellowstone Valley. As one of the first of two private parties doing business in the Park at the time of its establishment, the site is also important for Concessions History which will be developed later. The site's cultural deposits can contribute to our understanding of the late nineteenth century transportation frontier and the settlement and development.*

According to the Wyoming State Historic Preservation Office in August 2022, the nomination was never formally submitted or approved; it is not clear why there was no action.[335]

---

334. Mary Shivers Culpin, *The History of the Construction of the Road System in Yellowstone National Park, 1872–1966.* Historic Resource Study, vol. 1. Selections from the Division of Cultural Resources, no. 5. National Park Service, 1994.

335. Culpin, Multiple Property Documentation Form, 1995. Email conversation with Wyoming State Historic Preservation Office on June 15–16, 2023.

CHAPTER ELEVEN
Alaska Beckons and Jack Fades from the Frontier

> *There's gold, and it's haunting and haunting;*
> *It's luring me on as of old;*
> *Yet it isn't the gold that I'm wanting*
> *So much as just finding the gold.*[336]
> —Robert W. Service

Prospectors first discovered gold in British Columbia, Canada, in 1856. Officials kept the news quiet until 1858. When word leaked out, some thirty thousand hopeful miners descended on the area, most from the California mines. Much of the activity was centered on the junction of the Fraser and Thompson Rivers. Miners faded in and out over the years, and new prospects were discovered at other locales. Even as late as 1889, the mines produced over $3 million in gold.[337] In June 1887, Jack Baronett headed for Juneau, Alaska Territory, and British Columbia in search of riches. His activities there are unknown, although a tourist group that included ex-Montana governor Samuel Hauser; US senators George Vest, Donald Cameron, and Charles Farwell; and others noted one of the Montanans they met in Juneau was "Capt. Jack Baronnette, formerly

---

336. Robert W. Service, "The Spell of the Yukon," *The Spell of the Yukon and Other Verses* (New York: Barse & Hopkins, 1907), p. 18.
337. Angus Macleod Gunn, "Gold and the Early Settlement of British Columbia, 1858–1885," master's thesis, University of British Columbia, 1965, pp. 25–35.

guide and special agent of the government in the National Park who is now located at Juneau."338 Returning to Montana in November, he set about his usual activities, mining, prospecting, and tending to his bridge, where he often spent the frigid winters.

A decade later, Baronett again sailed for Alaska to join the sensational new gold rush on the Klondike, Yukon Territory, Canada. Fabulous gold deposits were discovered in August 1896, and men became wealthy almost overnight. Two ships full of miners and their wealth of gold from Alaska arrived on the West Coast in July 1897. The *Portland*, with $1 million in gold, docked in Seattle on July 16, and the *Excelsior*, with $500,000 in gold, arrived July 14 in San Francisco.339 The *Tacoma News Tribune* pro-

The "Ton of Gold" ship, the *Portland*, docked in Portland, Oregon, on July 17, 1897. Aboard were sixty-eight miners and reportedly a ton of gold bullion. (Seattle Museum of History and Industry)

---

338. "Personal Points," *Livingston Enterprise*, August 13, 1887, p. 3.
339. "Like News of the Old West," *San Francisco Examiner*, July 17, 1897; "Gold from the Yukon River," *San Francisco Call*, July 15, 1897, p. 8. Half a million dollars would be worth around $15 million today.

ALASKA BECKONS AND JACK FADES FROM THE FRONTIER

claimed on the front page, "THE GOLD FEVER—Steamship Portland Arrives from Alaska Confirming Tales of Fabulous Wealth Recently Discovered at the Klondike. Has a Solid Ton of Gold Nuggets. Many People Dropping Everything to Return North by the Next Steamer."[340] The allure of golden riches was irresistible and had profound impacts on people's lives. People quit everything—ships lost crew, merchants' employees fled, and many businessmen closed their shops and rushed to what they all believed were sure-fire fortunes. Word quickly spread throughout the states, territories, and the world—the rush was on in 1897.

Even in Livingston and Park County, Montana, men dropped what they were doing to join the multitudes. A century later, historian Dick Dysart of Livingston compiled a list of local persons leaving for Alaska in 1897–1898. He gathered over one hundred names from old newspapers and documents, many of them well known in local history, including George Colpitts (crafter of the Old Faithful Inn clock), Bart Henderson, Ed and John Bailey (Bailey Lake), Mr. and Mrs. Henry Hefferlin (Livingston Hefferlin Stores), Ed Howell, Joe Keeney, Alex Lyall (storekeeper at Mammoth), Frank Phiscator, Amos Shaw (boat captain on Yellowstone Lake), Frank Tolhurst (taxidermist), and Adolph Wetzstein (liquor dealer). Phiscator, formerly of the Yellowstone and Gardiner area, may have been the most successful. He had a rich claim on the Klondike and brought home almost $100,000 in gold. In addition, he owned a claim he later sold for $1 million. Many of these men formed the Montana Exploring Company, buying shares for the purchase of a boat and transportation costs to Alaska. Amos Shaw, a former pilot on Yellowstone Lake and one of the founders of the Shaw & Powell Camping Co. in Yellowstone, was captain of the *Alton*. Once in the Yukon, some men gravitated to other professions: Joe Keeney became a marshal in Dyea, Alaska; others became merchants, mining the miners; a few performed as musicians; and at least one man became a faro dealer. Many a man whose luck or skills failed at mining or business returned to the States broke,[341] a familiar story during the numerous gold rushes in the Old West.

---

340. "The Gold Fever," *Tacoma News Tribune*, July 17, 1897, p. 1.
341. Dick Dysart, "Park County People Who Went to Alaska," September 24, 2001, Yellowstone Gateway Museum, Livingston, MT.

Frank Phiscator

Frank Phiscator, a millionaire Alaska miner, ended his life on December 31, 1905, in his apartments at the Grand Hotel in San Francisco. Despondent over female troubles, he slit his throat with a razor. Phiscator was one of the pioneers of the Klondike gold rush and was at Forty Mile at the time of the great discoveries. He built the first house in Dawson, possessed rich claims on Bonanza Creek, brought home $96,000 in gold, and sold a claim for $1.3 million in 1897. Phiscator came originally from Baroda, Michigan, but was a resident of Park County for many years, making his home in the Gardiner area for the greater part of the time. He was at Cinnabar, the old terminus of the Northern Pacific Railway, for a spell. He engaged in various occupations: mail carrier on the Cooke City and Mammoth route, wood cutter, seller of "coated specimens," and other odd jobs.

Joining that surge of humanity at almost seventy years of age must have been grueling for Baronett. The journey stymied men half his age, but Baronett was not one to give up, and he was still a strong and stalwart man. Such adversities would not impede him, especially with gold waiting in "them thar hills." Phiscator, on his return from Alaska a rich man in 1897, declared, "There is only one kind of man that can get to the creeks—one trained in the hardships of the wilderness, hardened by years of hard fights with actual frontier life and one versed in all the accomplishments which are acquired in a country where the best man is he who gets his pistol out first. . . . The man who gets through it comes out only by accident, the rule being that his bones are left in the ice and snow." It may have been a bit of excess hyperbole, but it could be and was, for many, a ruthless journey. But Jack definitely measured up to that description.

Typically, prospectors and miners would travel to Seattle and board a ship north to the ports of Dyea and Skagway in southeastern Alaska. From there, the usual route was over the steep passes of the Chilkoot or White Pass to the Yukon River and sailing down to the Klondike River. It was a long, arduous journey through the wilds of Canada. The Mount-

ALASKA BECKONS AND JACK FADES FROM THE FRONTIER

Gold cargo from Alaska at Seattle dock on July 17, 1899. The gold bullion was weighed, packaged, and crated by the Canadian Bank of Commerce in Skagway, Alaska. (Photo #1988.33.234, Seattle Museum of History & Industry)

ies compelled all miners to carry roughly 2,000 pounds of supplies and food, enough to last for a year. That required hauling on their backs as much as they could carry up the steep pass and then returning time and time again for more goods. Once over the pass, one needed to acquire or build a boat to float across lakes and traverse down the treacherous river. The early arrivals fared well, but later prospectors found the best lands already claimed. These stouthearted men faced bitter cold, snowstorms, and rugged terrain.

One article claimed that Jack Baronett prospected in Alaska in 1899 and traveled back to his home country before returning to Alaska; then he traveled down to California and back again to Alaska.[342] While relatively few men returned triumphantly from the Klondike wealthy, others at least made a respectable gain for their efforts. But many more returned penniless and broken in body and spirit. Was Jack one of the latter? It would appear so, though due only to bad luck and not lack of expertise or ability.

---

342. *Gardiner Wonderland*, May 7, 1903, p. 2.

YELLOWSTONE JACK

Regrettably, there is no confirmed information concerning Jack's travels and whereabouts in Alaska. A few newspapers mentioned his departures and arrivals from the States. Baronett may have been well known in Montana, Wyoming, and the Dakotas, but in Alaska he was merely an anonymous miner trying to fill his poke or strike it rich. There are undoubtedly many enriching stories about his time in Alaska; if only they could be located, it would enhance our perception of the man.

For decades, Jack had been lured by the siren call of Khrysos, the god of gold and wealth, for the treasure that "neither moth nor rust devoureth it; but the mind of man is devoured by this supreme possession."[343] But this "supreme possession" ultimately led to his financial downfall; nonetheless, his spirit carried on, and he was loath to give up. Baronett had something of the Midas Touch when locating gold claims. He found good-paying lodes at Emigrant, Bear Gulch, Cooke City, Boulder River, Clark's Fork, and others. The problem is, Jack was among the breed of prospectors for whom the search and the "Eureka! moment" was the crowning event. Working away at a claim day after day with the unrelenting mundane toil, dirt, and sweat was not in their blood. They would mine enough of the golden glitter to fill their pockets and move on to bigger and better finds, which seemed to be their modus operandi. That Jack returned from Alaska destitute is puzzling.

Jack returned to the States in late March 1901 aboard the sidewheel steamboat *North Pacific*. It was built in 1871 and had undergone a complete overhaul before Jack's ride. It provided daily service between Victoria, BC, and Seattle.[344] He returned with little money, but, for unknown reasons, accounts of the opposite flooded the newspapers. A flurry of papers across the country reported in 1901 that Jack's unnamed brother was killed during the Second Boer War. Supposedly Jack was the only heir to a fortune left by his brother, a quarter-million dollars by some accounts. To add intrigue, many newspapers reported Jack missing. However, it is more likely he was just out and about prospecting in the

---

343. Khrysos is a Greek spirit of gold and riches. Her name means gold. Her father is the Greek god Zeus, lord of Olympus and the sky. Quote from Greek poet Pindar, Fragment 222 (trans. Sandys), Greek lyric fifth century BCE.

344. *The Province*, March 13, 1901, p. 7; *Victoria Daily Times*, March 24, 1901, p. 7.

hills somewhere, as was his wont. One story declared that he had boarded a wheat ship bound for England to collect his inheritance. Another described him visiting with Orion Clemens, brother of Mark Twain, at the Rabbit Mine in Shasta County, Northern California.[345] Orion was in Nevada politics and moved to the Meadow Lake area in California for a time, but by the 1870s he had returned to the East. However, there was indeed a Rabbit Mine at which Baronett may have sojourned.

Much sensational and mostly creative publicity about Jack was published, and by the time he surfaced alive and well he had become a legend in his own time. Numerous fanciful newspaper accounts boasted of a check for $5,000 waiting in the hands of William J. Seymour in Tacoma for Baronett to pick up and travel to England to collect his inheritance. Headlines about his "inheritance" and being lost graced the pages of newspapers across the West—from Dawson, Canada, to Victoria, BC, as well as San Francisco, Los Angeles, Salt Lake City, Montana, and Washington. Examples of some of the headlines about Baronett declared, "Heir to Great Fortune," "Heir to a Title Lost in Tacoma," "No Trace of Missing Heir," "Wealth Waits for an Heir," "Fortune Awaits an Englishman Who Is Missing," and "Jack Baronett's Fortune." The *Tacoma Daily Ledger* claimed Baronett was in England with some mining friends and, with his inheritance, chartered a boat called the *Royal George*. The *George* was shipwrecked around Cape Horn, and the survivors struggled to reach Valparaiso, Chile, where they worked their way up to Seattle.[346] While perhaps true, there is no other documentation for that story. The *Livingston Post* cleared the air of rumors in 1903 when it announced, "The story which gained wide circulation to the effect that a fortune had been left the old timer was fairy tale. Jack hasn't any money except that which he has made, and is no pampered heir of a vast estate, thank you."[347]

Even though he may not have been blessed with a large inheritance, surely, with his vast mining experience and talent, he would have unearthed or acquired profitable claims in Alaska. Yet Jack came back from the Alaska goldfields busted—why? It makes sense only if his

---

345. "No Trace Here of Missing Heir," *The Searchlight* (Redding, CA), April 17, 1901, p. 6.
346. "Heir to a Title Lost in Tacoma," *Tacoma Daily Ledger*, April 13, 1901, p. 5.
347. "Local News," *Livingston Post*, May 7, 1903, p. 5.

CAPT. BARONETTE.

KNOWN TO EVERY OLD TIMER, HAS FALLEN HEIR TO A LARGE FORTUNE

LEFT HIM BY HIS BROTHER

Who Fell in the Boer War — However, Jack Is Not to Be Found at Present, But Will Be Hunted Up by Friends

Captain "Jack" Baronette, known to every old timer west of the Mississippi, and who lived in the vicinity of the Yellowstone National Park for years, has at last fallen heir to a large fortune from his brother, who was killed during a fight between the English and Boers.

"Capt. Baronette, Known to Every Old Timer, Has Fallen Heir to a Large Fortune." (*Livingston Enterprise*, April 20, 1901, p. 1)

treasure was lost; perhaps his ship capsized, sending his gleaming gold back to a river bottom or along the treacherous coast. Research shows that between 1878 and 1915 alone, at least eighty-seven ships were wrecked along Alaska's rugged coast,[348] and this does not include all those ships sunk on the open seas, along other coasts, or in the many interior rivers and lakes filled with snags and ice floes.

His various biographies generally agree with the capsized ship story but differ significantly in the details. Aubrey Haines related in his biography of Baronett that "he left the Yellowstone country with his money, from

---

348. "Shipwreck Online Exhibit," Alaska State Library, accessed May 5, 2022, https://library.alaska.gov/hist/exhibits/shipwrecks.html.

ALASKA BECKONS AND JACK FADES FROM THE FRONTIER

the sale of his bridge, for an expedition to Nome, Alaska during the last great gold rush. But his schooner and his hopes were both crushed in the arctic ice."[349] Baronett did leave for Alaska in 1897 but was not paid for his bridge until 1899. Chittenden tells a similar story, claiming that the money from the sale of his bridge "was invested in an expedition to Nome, Alaska, during the last great 'gold rush,' but his schooner and his hopes were both crushed in the Arctic ice."[350] Thrapp's story is much the same as that of Chittenden. The capsized ship portion of the story rings true through almost all of the stories, and it makes sense and explains his being broke. William Hover of the Associated Charities of Tacoma, which was formed in 1892 to help families and children in Seattle and King County overcome life's challenges, declared he "gathered from his [Jack's] remarks that the expedition to the new northern gold fields during which the schooner was wrecked, was the project of an English syndicate which appointed Baronette commander and guide, he having been in Alaska previously."[351]

There are also many confusing reports concerning Jack's whereabouts from 1901 to 1903, a few of them by supposed old friends, but none can be substantiated. However, the following 1901 account by William Hover is the most believable.[352] Hover reported, "Baronette had been a frequent visitor at the offices of the Associated Charities during the months of January and February, that institution being in the habit of supplying work or assistance for the indigent." Hover also mentioned that Baronett "came in for work, but was very feeble and scarcely in a condition to satisfactorily perform such work as was obtained for him." Baronett told Hover of friends he knew in Wallace, Idaho, "for which place Mr. Hover had eventually, on February 27, obtained transportation, the old man going the next day."[353] How long Baronett stayed in Idaho or his whereabouts until the spring of 1903 has yet to be determined.

---

349. Aubrey L. Haines, "Biographical Appendix," *Yellowstone National Park: Its Exploration and Establishment*, vol. 2 (Washington, DC: US Department of the Interior, National Park Service, 1974), p. 442.

350. Hiram M. Chittenden, *The Yellowstone National Park, Historical and Descriptive* (Cincinnati, OH: Robert Clarke Co., 1895), pp. 291–92.

351. "Capt. Baronette," *Livingston Enterprise*, April 20, 1901, p. 1.

352. "For Thanksgiving," *Tacoma Daily Ledger*, November 19, 1901, p. 5. This ad verifies Hover and his position.

353. "Capt. Baronette," *Livingston Enterprise*, April 20, 1901, p. 1.

Battered by his travails, Baronett returned to Livingston, Montana, in late April 1903.[354] The *Bridger Free Press* reported on his whereabouts in recent years: "Since leaving here four years ago Mr. Baronette has had a varied experience. He has been in California; has attempted the voyage around Cape Horn and been wrecked; has been across the ocean to Great Britain several times; has been for a year in Chicago and has finally come back to Montana to reside."[355] Just one more story to add to Jack's trails and tales.

In May, he went down to Gardiner to visit his old haunts and swap yarns with his remaining comrades.[356] Sadly, by that time, many had already passed away, including his friends George Huston and Bart Henderson. The *Gardiner Wonderland* reported, "Jack Barnett [Baronett], one of the real old timers of the country, and whom most everybody thought dead and out of the game, returned last week. He left here six years ago and went to Alaska, drifting from there to the old country and back to Alaska and then to California."[357] Jack returned to Livingston, where he spent his remaining few years but, regrettably, in a manner he neither desired nor was accustomed to. The *Livingston Enterprise* on April 20, 1901, described Baronett during his golden years—minus, of course, any actual gold: "John H. Baronette, the elderly Englishman . . . career picturesque in the extreme, the last few years, however, as is so often the case of adventurous lives, having been one continuous struggle for existence. As pioneer, scout, miner, soldier, sailor, Baronette has spent some forty years in the great west . . . the strenuous life he has lived is beginning to leave its mark."[358]

On June 6, 1904, the Park County Board of Commissioners "ordered that J. C. Baronett be admitted to the county poor farm, he being sick and without means."[359] And, indeed, records for the poor farm, or poorhouse, indicate that Baronett was admitted the following day.[360] It was a lamen-

---

354. *Gardiner Wonderland*, May 7, 1903, p. 2.
355. "Scout's Varied Experience," *Bridger Free Press*, May 15, 1903, p. 2.
356. "Local News," *Livingston Post*, May 7, 1903, p. 5.
357. *Gardiner Wonderland*, May 7, 1903, p. 2.
358. "Capt. Baronette," *Livingston Enterprise*, April 20, p. 1.
359. "County Business," *Livingston Enterprise*, June 18, 1904, p. 1.
360. "Park County Poor Farm Records Index 1896–1924," accessed July 14, 2023, https://sites.rootsweb.com/~mtpcgs/media/Park%20County%20Poor%20Farm%20Records%20Index%201896-1924.pdf.

table and humbling fate for a pioneer of his caliber, who had achieved so much in his life, to be forced to live as one of the poor and downtrodden. He, of that breed of self-sufficient men and women, did not cotton to charity and handouts.

To comply with state law, the town of Livingston built a poorhouse in 1892. Caretakers, as well as physicians, were contracted for the care of indigent, poor, or infirm residents without alternate resources. It was not a desirable option for these folks, but often they had no choice. These contractors were selected based on the lowest bid to provide food, clothes, medical supplies, care, and other necessities. They were fain to spend any more money than compulsory, so living conditions could sometimes be appalling. Being a Civil War veteran, Baronett also relied on aid from the Grand Army of the Republic (GAR), established by the Union Army after the war, and the Women's Relief Core, an auxiliary of the GAR. Considering Jack's service with the Confederacy, receiving aid from these societies likely rankled both his sense of Western pioneer independence and his Southern sympathies.

John H. "Collins Jack" Baronett remained at the poor farm the last few years of his life and bid his final adieu on November 28, 1906, at the Park County Hospital in Livingston. The GAR conducted the funeral, and Baronett's body was interred in the town's Mountain View Cemetery. A tombstone later placed read, "John H. Baronett; 1834–1906. Sailor, Soldier, Prospector, and Builder of the First Bridge Over the Yellowstone River."[361] His birth date on the stone was in error, as it is believed he was born in 1829, which made him around seventy-seven years old at his death.

About a week after Baronett's death, an unknown friend wrote a fitting tribute to Jack:

The old-timers are like the free plains of the west, fast being gathered by a permanent owner. A few short years and what is now the '49–

---

361. "Death of an Old Timer," *Livingston Enterprise*, December 1, 1906. According to Aubrey Haines, the current tombstone was placed in September 1998. It is unknown whether previous markers had been erected. Jack Baronett, Hand-written Note Cards, Aubrey L. Haines Collection No. 2231, MtBC, us, Montana State University Special Collections, Bozeman, MT.

Baronett tombstone, Mountain View Cemetery, Livingston, Montana. (Goss photo, 2008)

65–76 boys will all be in their last camp. The children of today little think of the meaning of old timer. They cannot appreciate the gladness in the hand clasp when one of the earliest settlers runs across a friend of former days. Those long gray beards or the crippled step of the old man are as "apples of gold in pictures of silver" to the dimmed eyes of the boys of the plains or the early mining camps of the west. Time, O, time, stop in thy flight and give a thought to the passing of the pioneer.[362]

A fitting tribute to a man of action who, although well known and a legend in his own lifetime, gradually faded from the memories of ensuing generations.

As we now lay him away for his last sleep let us say kindly, Jack Baronette, in your dreams you are amongst those who will miss you.[363]

And also among those of us who had not the privilege of knowing him.

---

362. "A Friend's Tribute," *Livingston Enterprise*, December 8, 1906.
363. "A Friend's Tribute."

EPILOGUE

The Beautiful Wonder World
To see our Yellowstone, those will
go who never went before, and
those who went, will go
the more.
     —Jack Cheney

Bart Henderson opened the wilderness of Yellowstone with his road building; Jack Baronett's bridge enabled the prospectors and miners to more easily travel to and from Clark's Fork, while Adam "Horn" Miller and George Huston explored the northern portion of Yellowstone and the mining potential. All four men played a large part in the development of the mines and the establishment of Cooke City and its future as a tourist destination.

But as the days of the original Yellowstone pioneers and old-timers rapidly came to a close, Jack was among the last to succumb. Many of Jack Baronett's trail mates had already trekked over the Great Divide—including such stalwart men such as P. W. Norris in 1885, George Huston in 1886, Bart Henderson in 1889, Ed Wilson in 1891, Walter de Lacey in 1892, Gustavus Doane in 1892, Truman Everts in 1901, and John Yancey in 1903. Jack's passing in 1906 was followed by that of John Ponsford in 1912 and Horn Miller in 1917.

The era of the early pioneers ultimately gave way to a more polished group of concessionaires and government leaders. The new National Park Service had taken over the reins from the US Army and were making significant changes to the administration of Yellowstone. Automobiles

YELLOWSTONE JACK

now commandeered the roads that were once traversed by the old-time stagecoaches and noble steeds. A short poem penned by Cottage Hotel builder George L. Henderson, published in 1886, was a portent of the future and a fitting tribute to the old-timers:

> *Death may strangle Yankee Jim,*
> *Reduce Jack Barronette to dust,*
> *Blow out Horn Miller's will and vim,*
> *Give Henderson to rot and rust;*
> *But neither panic, time nor death,*
> *Can blot their mem'ries from the hills*
> *Where they expended thought and breath;*
> *Their deeds the early records fills.*[364]

Historian Frederick Jackson Turner has been credited with claiming that "the West, not the East, was where distinctively American characteristics emerged . . . [which] produced a new type of citizen—one with the power to 'tame the wild' and one upon whom the wild had conferred strength and individuality."[365] This description undoubtedly applies to all the men who played a significant role in the annals of Yellowstone's "Old West." The memories of Jack Baronett and his bold compatriots continue to live on and are woven into the historical fabric of Yellowstone National Park.

---

364. G. L. Henderson, "The National Park," *Sioux City Journal*, January 30, 1886, p. 2.
365. Frederick Jackson Turner, *The Frontier in American History* (New York: Henry Holt & Co., 1921); Allan Taylor, "The Old Frontiers," *The New Republic*, May 7, 2008.

ACKNOWLEDGMENTS

The Yellowstone region has hosted a legion of fur trappers, explorers, prospectors, businessmen and -women, and government and concessionaire employees for nearly two hundred years. These hundreds or thousands of personalities have influenced the park's history, most of whom are well known, but many are still little known or obscure. Having worked in Yellowstone National Park for thirty years and a gold mine for six years, I had a chance to study the myriad historical personalities involved. Many of these characters have been examined and written about by a variety of historians. Others are just names barely mentioned. It is this group that has spurred my historical interest.

Over the years, I have researched and written about some of these individuals who never received the attention they deserved. These include storekeepers/businesspeople such as sand artist Andy Wald, coated specimen craftsman Ole Anderson, storekeepers Henry Klamer and George Whittaker, and the Trischman sisters, store operators at Mammoth and Canyon. I have also written of prospectors, miners, and explorers George Huston and Z. R. "Red" Sowash.

Jack Baronett, who built the first bridge over the Yellowstone River in Montana and the park, falls into this last category. I have been amassing information, news clippings, and so on, for over twenty years on ole Jack. It was in early 2022 that I began composing drafts about his life. Several hundred drafts and countless edits later, I have finally produced a book about him!

Of course, there are many folks who were of great assistance in this project, and I would like to give them due credit. Yellowstone researchers, historians, and authors Bruce Gourley and Tamsen Hert were instrumental in the early stages of editing and organization. Yellowstone research librarians at the Yellowstone Heritage Center provided valuable materials regarding Bart Henderson's diary and other photos and documents. Conversations with former ranger Robert Flathers on the Cooke City road and bridge were invaluable.

Gary Barnhart and Jodi Allison Bunnell of Montana State University Archives and Special Collections supplied copies of articles by Aubrey Haines from the *Yellowstone Interpreter* and other important Haines papers. Karen Reinhart, former curator at the Yellowstone Gateway Museum in Livingston, Montana, furnished Baronett articles by local historian Doris Whithorn. Zoe Ann Stoltz, reference historian at the Montana Historical Society Research Center in Helena, contributed copies of letters by Wilbur Fisk Sanders. Donna and Larry Teeter provided valuable copies of 1879–1880 New World Mining District record books. Thanks also to the Fray Angelico Chavez History Library in Santa Fe, New Mexico, for furnishing copies of William Blackmore's Diary #6 (his 1872 Yellowstone trip).

Last, but certainly not least, I wish to express my thanks to historian, researcher, lecturer, and author Elizabeth A. Watry for her immense assistance in tediously editing and reediting my manuscript, while providing valuable aid for organization and structure, without which I would be adrift in a sea of confusion. Thanks also are due to my literary agent, Chris Cauble, with Riverbend Publishing, for believing this story is worthy of publication, along with those at Globe Pequot who provided their edits and suggestions. Thanks to you all!

APPENDIX

Jack's Stories—Truth or Fiction?

Notes from the Author. 165
Jack's Bear Stories 167
   "Westland Trails," by H. C. Reagan 167
   "A Bear That Used a Rifle". 169
   "An Awful Bear Story". 173
   "His Story of a Bear Fight" 175
Jack's Sea-Serpent Stories 177
   "The Serpent Far Astray—The Serpent Season". 177
   "Extremely Large Snake Discovered" 178
   "The Sea Serpent Outdone". 178
Jack's Old Scout's Stories 181
   "Thrice Captured". 181
   "Blood Indian War in Montana". 182
   "A Lodge of Indians Surprised". 183
Jack's Biography by Hiram Chittenden 185
Jack's Biography by Aubrey L. Haines 187

NOTES FROM THE AUTHOR

These stories harken back to the days of the early Mountain Men, who were well known for the imaginative and amusing stories they told to help pass the long, cold winter nights. Some of their stories were pure fantasy; others were a combination of truth and fanciful yarns. Jack Baronett continued this tradition with stories he spun around the campfire at night. Others were narrated to unsuspecting rubes searching for an interesting newspaper article. This tradition continued with the stagecoach drivers in Yellowstone, such as Geyser Bob, who related whoppers and tall tales to many of the unsuspecting tourists.

All of these stories are written verbatim from the original sources, except perhaps for some minor punctuation for clarity. There have been no judgments made as to truthfulness or falsehoods, as the stories may have elements of each, and some may be completely imagined by the authors. With the exception of the Chittenden and Haines biographies, they are presented for enjoyment, amusement, and an insight into the concepts of making legends in the nineteenth century. Some statements may not be politically correct in our current social atmosphere, but history is neither politically correct nor incorrect; it simply exists. It is the interpretations and the viewing of past events through modern eyes and precepts that make those differences. Enjoy them through the perceptions of those who lived in a different era.

JACK'S BEAR STORIES

"Westland Trails"
H. C. Reagan, "Westland Trails—Camp Fire Stories,"
Carbon County News (MT), October 14 and 21, 1926, p. 2

This man was a hunter and trapper with no fixed abode except when he built the bridge across the Yellowstone River at Junction Buttes for the miners at Clarks Forks now known as Cooke City. Assisting Baronette at that time was Bart Henderson[366] and Uncle Charlie Millard.[367]

Baronette and Uncle Charlie concluded to prospect over the mountains near Yancey's Ranch settled on by Uncle John Yancy. As all prospectors or hunters did, they took their rifles with them for game and emergency. Along with them went Dick, a small black terrier dog who formerly belonged to Mr. Leitchner of frog legs fame. The two men separated to meet again at the top of the mountain. Dick in this case went with Baronette. After a time Uncle Charlie heard the report of a rifle and not paying any attention to it, believing Jack had probably shot an elk. In a short time he heard a crashing in the bushes near him.

The dog Dick came out with his hair standing on ends. He barked and yapped at Uncle Charlie who asked him what was the matter. Dick

---

366. Abel Bartlett Henderson is believed to have prospected for gold in California and the Far West at least by the 1860s. He began prospecting in and around Yellowstone Park in 1867. He discovered gold in the Cooke City area in 1869–1870 with Adam "Horn" Miller, Ed Hibbard, and James Gourley; he also named Soda Butte and Soda Butte Creek during that trip. With help from James Gourley and Horn Miller, he began building a road in 1871 from Bottler's Ranch near Emigrant to Mammoth Hot Springs.

367. Charles Millard, described as "veteran Montana argonaut," was one of the territory's early gold miners. He prospected at Alder Gulch, Virginia City, Last Chance Gulch, and likely the greater Yellowstone country. He passed away in Livingston in 1920.

still groveled and looked behind him and hair still standing on his back straight up, about this time Uncle Charlie heard more crashing and crackling in the brush towards which Dick was barking. Uncle Charlie saw emerging from the bushes Baronette who was coming like a locomotive trying to make up lost time. Yelling to Uncle Charlie, a bear by hell, a bear, and just behind Baronette was a real sure enough silver tip bear who seemed to have some desire to reach Baronette who was just as anxious that he should not. Uncle Charlie said the situation been plain to him and that safety first was his idea. With an extreme effort Uncle Charlie got up speed and made a bee line for a clump of spruce trees whose limbs hung low. He said he looked back and saw that Baronette was still in the lead and coming for the same tree. The bear a close second. He said he never had been much of a climber but in this case he threw down his Sharps rifle and made double quick time up the tree.

How he did it he cannot tell but he got there before either Baronette or the bear. A yell came from Baronette to give him room in the tree. Up he came as from a catapult. Calling to Uncle Charlie to move higher in the tree so he could keep away from the dam bear, who was at the foot of the tree trying to reach him. Every time the bear would stand up Dick would get in his work on the bear by biting his on his hind quarters snipping him. The bear would try and strike Dick who was not there like the Irishman's flea. The bear continued to harass the men in the tree but could not reach them. Every time he made a fresh effort to get into the tree, Uncle Charlie says Baronette hollered to him to get up higher. After a time the silver tip gave it up as a bad job.

The bear retiring, the two men making sure he had gone far enough away dropped to the ground and got their guns and Dick. It was always a point of argument between Uncle Charlie and Baronette after this episode as to who could run the fastest, neither one claiming the championship under the circumstances. Dick received the credit of saving Uncle Charlie and Jack Baronette from that bear. Baronette Mountain is named after Jack Baronette.

"A Bear That Used a Rifle"
"A Bear That Used a Rifle," *Butte Inter Mountain*, August 17, 1901, p. 9

"Jack Baronett Was a Famous Romancer about Bears"
*Reeled Off a Strange Tale to a Party
of English Tourists—Told of a Bear
Who Handled a Winchester
Like an Export—Bruin Was
Not a Lucky Marksman
and Quit In Disgust.*

JACK Baronett, the old time hunter, scout and guide, who was among the pioneers of the Yellowstone National park, and who, according to newspaper reports of a few months ago, has fallen heir to a large fortune in England, and has shipped before the mast to claim It, was a character in his way that would be hard to match in any country under the sun. For many years he lived at Baronett's bridge over the Yellowstone, in the National park, and he put in his summers as best suited his fancy. He would hunt and fish a little and occasionally do a little scouting as a past-time. Should the right sort of a party seek his services as a guide he would consent to show the beauties of Wonder and as no one else could show them.

His favorite pastime was "loading" tender feet, and many is the good story he could tell of the adventures which befell him during his early days In the park. Bear stories were his specialty, and when his audience and his mood were both right, he would reel them off by the hundred yards and assert with the gravest phiz imaginable, that they were the truth, and nothing but the truth.

At one time, in the summer of 1881, he came to our camp near the Grotto geyser, in the upper basin for a little yarn spinning. He was camped near by, having come to that point to meet some young army officers who intended to make a tour of the park.[368] In our party were a couple of young Englishmen who were taking in the sights of the west.

---

368. These officers were likely Gen. Philip Sheridan and his staff, whom Baronett guided on a tour of Yellowstone.

They both had more money than brains and we were doing the best we could to show them the wonders of the park. They would not enthuse a bit over the wonderland display of hot water, the beautiful terraces, the many hued springs or the grand mountain scenery and they eagerly urged us to "cut out the 'ot water displays and show them something big to shoot at."

It did not take Jack long to size up his crowd and do it proper. In reply to the ever ready query as to where they would find some big game, he said that over on Specimen mountain[369] lived the biggest bear that ever went unkilled.

"I have hunted for him time and again," he said when pressed to tell more about the monster, and when his lips had been nicely wet by a taste from a black bottle produced by one of the Englishmen, "but only once have I ever secured a glimpse of him. That time was the week before last and, to tell you the truth, should I live for over 100 years, I do not want to see him again. He is bigger than any of your saddle horses and wiser than any tourist who has ever crossed the pond and I have good reason to believe that he bears a charmed life.

"Well! I started in to tell you how I came to see him. I was hunting for bear; not any particular bear but just any old member of the tribe of bruin who might present himself for a target. Presently I found the track of the big bear of the mountain. I knew it was 'Old Snooks' as we called him, and I determined that I would have his hide before night. I realized that I was up against a hard proposition, but I was not afraid and pressed on in hot pursuit after him.

"Presently I found him. As I entered little park in the timber not over 50 yards across, there he was, a big cinnamon-colored object looking to my excited eyes, as large as a circus tent. He was eagerly tearing away at a rotten log in search of worms. As quick as I saw him, for fear that I would lose my sand, I took a shot at him. Well! For the first time in my life, at that distance, I missed and missed him clean.

"The old fellow straightened up and looked as if his dignity was offended. He gazed all around as if in search of some one. Presently his

---

369. Located in Lamar Valley on the south side of the river, home to petrified trees.

little, piggish-looking eyes fell on me as I was industriously shinning up the nearest tree. With a growl he was after me, but by that time I was up among the branches out of harm's way.

"In order that I could climb more easily I did not take my gun with me and left It behind. In fact I did not miss it until I was up among the big branches and saw the Winchester lying upon the ground at the foot of the tree. Almost before I was settled on my perch 'Old Snooks' was tearing up the earth around the foot of the tree in a rage that was frightful to see. He would try to climb, but he was too big and fat and the tree was too small. Then, when he would slip down he would cuff the tree in a fury, tearing off great splinters of bark and hurling them across the clearing. His mouth frothed in anger and he appeared to be nearly beside himself with rage and disappointment at not being able to reach me. Occasionally he would go to the farthest end of the clearing and, taking a running shoot, he would jump at the lower branches. Once he came very near getting a foothold, tearing a heel off one of my boots which, fool-like, I had left dangling beneath my perch. After that I pulled my heels up under my body and roosted, turkey wise, during the remainder of his Interview.

"Presently 'Old Snooks' caught sight of my gun and a new idea seemed to strike him. He quieted down all of a sudden and began to handle the gun with the same curiosity that a child handles a new toy. He sat down on his hunkers and presently began working the lever. In some manner he threw out the cartridge shell (which I had left in the gun owing to my hurry to do some climbing) and threw a fresh one into the gun. Then, an Instant later, the gun went off, the bullet clipping a branch from the tree a few inches from my head.

"The knowledge that he could shoot the gun seemed to please the old fellow. He straightened up and, so help me goodness, he had a grin on his ugly face. He waddled under my tree until he was not over ten feet away, placed the gun to his shoulder as cleverly as any hunter could do, took careful aim at me and pulled the trigger. The gun snapped. He took it down from his shoulder, carefully nosed it over and it looked good to him. He threw in another shell, took aim at me and once more pulled the trigger. Again the gun snapped. Seven times he repeated this performance and every time the gun would snap. When he emptied all of the cartridges out of the gun magazine he approached still closer to me and motioned for me to throw him down my cartridge belt. I could not see it that way and told him so in very plain words. He was offended but proceeded to pick up the cartridges which he had pumped out of the gun and put them back into the magazine again. He was too clumsy to do this and after several vain attempts; he gave it up and threw the gun away in disgust.

"He sat under my tree for nearly two hours, evidently in a deep study. Finally, when I began to think that I could hold on no longer and that I would have to let go my hold and become his dinner, he got up and walked to where he had thrown the gun and picked It up again. He came directly under my tree and, reaching as high as he could, he handed me the gun butt end first, and then waddled off into the woods.

"Occasionally he would look back with a wise air, as if to leave the impression that I was harmless and that the gun was even more harmless. As soon as I got the old gun in my hands I examined It to see why 'Old Snooks' could not make it shoot. The reason was plain at a glance. A lot of hair had become wadded in between the hammer and the needle and the cartridges could not be exploded.

"Why didn't I follow him up and kill him, eh? Was I afraid?" snorted in answer to an insinuation made by one of the young Englishmen. "You young fellows can hunt 'Old Snooks' if you want to, but I advise you to have your lives well insured before you venture on the part of Specimen mountain in which he makes his home." And with a snarl of disgust, without even a good night, Jack tore himself off to his camp in a huff over being interrupted while telling his story.

JACK'S BEAR STORIES

"AN AWFUL BEAR STORY"
"An Awful Bear Story," *Dixon Evening Telegraph* (IL), October 30, 1886

Told in the Columns of a Contemporal
by Captain Quinton, U. S. A.

The papers speak of him now as Captain John Barronette. I suppose that Jack gets his title of Captain from the fact of being the boss story teller of Montana. When I was acquainted with him he was simply Jack, and was one of the curiosities of the park. He was then a hunter, guide, trapper, and a first-rate story teller.

But, while Jack could tell a good yarn, it was not always best for a listener to be too confiding, as nothing gave him more pleasure and delight than to help a fellow out who kept a diary, "one of them durn literary fellers." In 1873 I went through the Yellowstone Park under Jack's guidance, and during the trip of over hundreds of miles, and which lasted many weeks, Jack regaled me with many a tale of adventure by flood and field. One of these I remember, and tell you it as it was told to me.

"When I fust cum to this country," said Jack, "I was the greenest specimen of a pilgrim that you ever set eyes onter. I wus so green that the sap used ter regularly start outer me. I had killed a few deer, a mounting lion or two and was just a spilin' for a chance to go for a b'ar.

"Well, one day when I was out a-nosing round the mountains I spied a right smart grizzly a-histing in his dinner offen a thick clump of berry bushes. 'Thar is my chance,' said I to myself, 'and ef I don't git that arb'ar I'll sell my hide for saddle-bags.' So I began to approach him—kinder cautious like—aiming to git the wind so that it would blow from him onto me, as the nose of a b'ar is keener than a white man's eye. Well, I finally got around to a p'int where I had a full view of the b'ar—and as I come into full view I suddenly discovered that thar was two b'ars a fee-din, in that clump of bushes 'stead of one, and, what made it wuss still, the b'ars—both on 'em—discovered me jest as soon as I showed up and came rarring and a-charging straight for me. So I had to climb a tree that was—fortunightly for me—quite clus, and the way that I got into that tree was a caution to cats. I skun up thar quicker'n X. Beidler's[370] beaver did when the dogs were arter him. An' I took my Winchester up, too.

"Well, the b'ars charged right up to the roots of the tree and began a-scratchin' and a-diggin' like as they were mad. They had a kinder disappointed look about 'em, too, while they were a-growlin' and cavortin'. I sat thar and watched them for some time, and finally, knowin' that they would keep me thar until a day after eternity ef I did not make some move, I kinder climbed out on the limb of the tree, my gun pointing downward, and drawed a bead upon one of the b'ars. Well, jest as I was about to pull the trigger I heerd a kinder crackling, and you can land me in perdition ef that darned limb didn't give way—and down I came, my gun going one way, while I came down and landed right square on top of one of the b'ars. As I settled myself I reached for his ears with both hands, and let a yell outer me that was like to raise the dead, meanwhile kicking the b'ar in the ribs with both heels to make him git up and travel, and I think frum the way he lit out he thought a trip-hammer had gotten on to him. A quarter-hop wasn't a patchin' to the gait that b'ar struck. And he gave me the durndest, all-firdest ride that I ever had in my life for about two miles.

"I did not notice the country much, but as I kalkerlated that I was quite clear of the other b'ar I gave mine an extra kick in the ribs, raised another yell, and then slid off behind, kinder easily and quiet like, and ef suthin hesn't headed him off, I expect that arb'ar is a runnin yet. Lieutenant, say we take suthin, my throat's gittin' kinder dry."

---

370. John "X." Beidler was among those who participated in the "Bloody Kansas" rebellion but left for Texas following John Brown's death. He arrived in Virginia City, Montana, on June 10, 1863, just days after the gold discovery made by a group of miners. He joined the Vigilantes and became one of the group's most active members. In December 1863, along with twenty-four men, he swore a secret oath. Their mission was to hunt down, capture, and hang as many of the criminals as they could, Sheriff Plummer included. Later, in 1864, Beidler was appointed a deputy US marshal but continued his vigilante activities, which led many to accuse him of overstepping the bounds of established law and justice. John Beidler continued to serve as deputy US marshal until the late 1880s and also acted as a stagecoach guard. He is said to have guided a few times in Yellowstone. In 1888, his health began to fail, and, being destitute, he relied on the charity of friends. On January 22, 1890, he died at the Pacific Hotel in Helena from complications of pneumonia. The beaver reference is unknown, though he was a trapper for a time.

JACK'S BEAR STORIES

"His Story of a Bear Fight"
"A Visit to Wonderland," Letter No. 11, *Lacon Home Journal* (IL), October 11, 1882

His Story of a Bear Fight
As related by Spenser Ellsworth

"At Mammoth Hot Springs I joined a man named McGurk [Matthew McGuirk][371] in hunting grizzlies. We went up the mountain back of the Springs and got sight of two bears feeding. Singling out one, each of us fired and wounded his game but not seriously, and 'ere we had time to seek a place of safety both were charging like mad. We climbed trees, and waited for the bears to show themselves but as they failed to appear, we came down. My bear however was watching, and before I could shoot it was close upon me with jaws distended eyes glaring, and savagely growling. Somehow my gun went off prematurely and McGurk's was disabled. About seven feet above my head a dry limb projected which I seized and was drawing myself up when McGurk, hard pressed, and seeing no friendly tree caught me by the leg and sought thus to escape. The increased weight proved too much for the limb, which broke and both fell to the ground. The bear reached the tree just at the moment and we both fell astride the animal. Though expecting to feel his sharp claws in my flesh I could not resist laughing, but the bear was the worst scared of the three, and breaking away made off. My gun was soon ready again and a lucky shot broke his back. The other escaped."

---

371. Matthew McGuirk established McGuirk's Medicinal Springs in 1871 along the Gardner River near the 45th parallel. He created pools from the river rock for soaking and built a small cabin to live in. Superintendent Langford ordered him out of the park in 1874.

JACK'S SEA-SERPENT STORIES

"The Serpent Far Astray—The Serpent Season"
"The Serpent Far Astray—The Serpent Season," *Billings Gazette* (MT), August 2, 1886, p. 2

The Superintendent of the National Park congratulates himself upon a further and most surprising increase in the game of that wonderful region. The latest addition is a sea serpent, or something very like one, that was first seen by two tourists and a stage driver, out grazing near Yellowstone Lake. . . .[372] An account of these strange events was telegraphed to the Pioneer Press, and appeared in the issue of Friday last it omitted to mention the particular brand of wet groceries with which the snake hunters had fortified their courage before taking the field. It seems probable that if the National Park caravansaries continue to furnish that class of refreshments, the list of game reported by superintendent Weir last fall, will receive many new and strange additions in his next report. But it is to be hoped they will report something much larger before the

---

372. The name of the stage driver was not mentioned, but perhaps it was ole "Geyser Bob" Edgar, who loved telling whoppers. One of his favorites is also of a serpent: "The yarn that Geyser Bob liked to tell best was of the timid eastern lady tourist who expressed a deadly fear of snakes. Her continued expression of fear on this score made Geyser Bob nervous and he determined to give his questioner a real scare. As Bob drove his surrey past the terraces above Mammoth Hot Springs he suddenly halted the team. Nervously he handed the lines to the timid tourist. Bob walked silently up and down the road and without saying a word, returned to the rig. The curious woman had to ask what he was doing, and Bob replied: 'Last time I came up here a big snake jumped up and bit the wagon pole. His bite was so bad that the pole swelled up so much that it forced one of the horses over the cliff.' 'That lady never asked me another question,' said Bob when he told the story to the tourists. It was his way of informing people in his coach that he did not want to be a question box" (*Anaconda Standard*, August 27, 1913).

close of the season. It will not do for the World's Wonderland to be outdone by the monotonous prairies of Dakota, where the wheat growers have found a serpent over 100 feet long, disporting itself in the waters of Lake Kampeska.[373]

"Extremely Large Snake Discovered"
Cap't Quinton, U.S.A., from "An Awful Bear Story,"
Dixon Evening Telegraph (IL), October 30, 1886

I noticed recently a story in the papers going the rounds of the press, of an extremely large snake discovered among the other wonders of the National Park. The snake in form and shape is, barring the barnacles, of the fabled sea-serpent order, and is said to travel with his head threatening and with such fearful velocity—fifteen feet raised from the ground, while his even movement is accompanied with lone hissings and sizzlings like the frying of a dozen geysers concentrated in one. Jack Barronette is one of the discoverers of this Snake. The papers speak of him now as Captain John Barronette. I suppose that Jack gets his title of Captain from the fact of being the boss story teller of Montana. When I was acquainted with him he was simply Jack, and was one of the curiosities of the park. He was then a hunter, guide, trapper, and a first-rate story teller.

"The Sea Serpent Outdone"
"The Sea Serpent Outdone," *Eureka Daily Sentinel* (NV),
August 7, 1886

A Special from Cinnabar MT says: Last Monday a stage driver and two tourists, while near Yellowstone Lake, claimed to have seen an enormous reptile, which, while running through the grass, carried its head ten or 15 feet above the ground. They think it must have been at least 30 feet long. A party was organized at once to pursue the reptile yesterday. A number

---

373. Lake Kampeska is a natural lake located in the northeast portion of South Dakota. In July 1886, the *Rapid City Journal* reported the sighting of "a veritable sea serpent. Yes, indeed! nothing less than a great serpent, estimated at from ten to 100 feet in length, with fiery eyes and forked tongue, and its abiding place is Lake Kampeska, in Codington county." Many other papers reported vivid sightings of the serpent.

JACK'S SEA-SERPENT STORIES

of tourists, among them Colonel Wear, Superintendent of the Park, and his assistant, Captain Barronette, while near the cave of extinct geyser in the vicinity of the lake, heard a hissing sound coming from the cave and saw the head of a reptile thrust out some 15 feet, and immediately withdrew. Parties are watching for another sight of the monster. It is to be hoped that those persons at Yellowstone Lake who discovered the monster serpent not trample upon the worm. They ought to treasure him. The great mistake made by the ancients like Hercules and Meleager and Perseus was in killing the singular animals they encountered. Let the moderns profit by experience. Travelers will not believe the story in these days unless they can see the snake.

Note: All of the serpent stories seem to date from the year Baronett was hired by the US Army as a scout in Yellowstone. A coincidence? I think not. There seemed to be a rash of such stories from numerous localities across the country. Perhaps Jack was just doing his part to keep the ball rolling.

JACK'S OLD SCOUT'S STORIES

"Thrice Captured"
"An Old Scout's Story," *Butte Miner* (MT), February 2, 1882, p. 1[374]

"In 1857," said he [Baronett], "I went down to Fort Garland, did some trading with the Indians, and afterwards joined the regular army as a scout, under General Sydney Johnson. I afterward was with the regulars in Arizona. From there I drifted over to Mexico. The Mexicans got hold of me, and gave me the choice of joining them or being shot. They were fighting Maximilian. Why, I told them that was just what suited me—just what I came over for. When I say they were fighting Maximilian, I only tell part of their business. They were fighting anything that had money. They called themselves Mexicans, but most of them were Europeans, and all of them a bad lot. Before long I managed to get captured by another party of Mexicans, a little better than the first. They gave me the option of joining them or being shot, and I told them that just suited me; that what I came over there for was to join them. They were of Juarez's party.[375] From them I was captured—honestly captured that time, too, after a good solid fight—by some of Maximilian's troops.[376] Maximilian pardoned me and I joined his forces for a time, but a Mexican party got

---

374. Article originally from an interview with Jack Baronett by a reporter from the *New York Sun*. It was widely reprinted in other national newspapers.
375. Benito Juarez was a Mexican Liberal lawyer and statesman who served as the twenty-sixth president of Mexico from 1858 until his death in office in 1872. As a Zapotec man, he was the first indigenous president of Mexico and the first indigenous head of state in the postcolonial Americas.
376. As stated in the article, Baronett is believed to have served as a captain for Maximilian. The rest is likely an exaggeration. Maximilian I was an Austrian archduke who became emperor of the Second Mexican Empire from April 10, 1864, until his execution by the Mexican Republic on June 19, 1867.

hold of me again, and under the old custom I joined them once more. I hated to, for Maximilian was the noblest man that ever was in Mexico, and I hated to fight against him; but when a man has had the luck to be sentenced to be shot in cold blood a few times, the experience sort of takes out whatever nerve he has got for that sort of thing, and he is willing to make almost any sort of terms. Before long, however, I managed to get away from them, and left that country in disgust, going back up to Montana, where I was in the first Black foot and Blood Indian war."

"BLOOD INDIAN WAR IN MONTANA"
"An Old Scout's Story," *Butte Miner* (MT), February 2, 1882, p. 1

"Governor T. F. Meagher commissioned me to raise a company, and I did so at Helena, St. Louis Gulch and Last Chance Gulch. I had eighty-five splendid men, good fighters, well mounted and armed. All the mounting and equipping and fitting out of that company I did at my own cost, at an expense to me of $16,000—good dollars in gold.[377] That was in 1865. I don't know what the difference between gold and greenbacks was then in the East, but gold in Montana was five for one, and, in fact, people didn't want the paper anyway. Put a handful of greenbacks out on a bar for a drink and the barkeeper would take them all in, or else he'd shove them back and give you a drink. With me at that time were Charles Carson,[378] nephew of Kit Carson, and John Rann, now in the Whoop-up country, Charley Thomas,[379] and a lot more whose names I do not remember.

"At the close of the summer campaign the Black feet broke out again. Their first step was to kill their chief, Little Dog, a friend of the whites on the road between Fort Benton and Willow Round, on the Marias river. His son, who was a little distance behind, got up and demanded to know who had killed his father. The murderers stood around the corpse, silent and sullen. He made another demand, but they didn't answer him. He

---

377. That amount in gold would be worth about $350,000 these days—hardly an amount Baronett could afford.

378. Charles Carson was killed by Piegans by his ranch near the Dearborn River in Montana in 1866 and buried near the ford on the Dearborn. He was a nephew of Kit Carson, of frontier fame.

379. Charley Thomas did have a ranch up on the Teton River and lost horses and cattle to the Piegan.

calculated, however, that he could guess who did it, and went to work to get even. He only killed one, however, before they all turned in on him and killed him. They then dragged his mother out of the brush, where she had taken refuge, cut off her ears and turned her loose."[380]

"A LODGE OF INDIANS SURPRISED"
"An Old Scout's Story," *Butte Miner* (MT), February 2, 1882, p. 1

"I was ordered to go with a party of fifteen men I had gathered together to demand from the Black feet the murderers of Little Dog. I went according to orders, not that I had any idea of going with my fifteen men to make any demands from 1,000 to 1,200 lodges of Blackfeet, but I thought I'd get some Indians any way. We followed them until we got among their horses, and in full view of their lodges. There were more lodges than we could count, too many, we concluded, to make a fight with. But we knew where there was a small camp down on Pablo's island and made up our minds to go for them. We didn't know exactly how many of them there were, so Carson and I left the rest of the party behind about a mile when we landed on the island. We snaked around to get information, and got pretty close to the camp, when all of a sudden my mule, which had been raised among Indians, smelled them and made a break straight for the camp. I couldn't stop the brute, but by hard spurring sent him at a gallop right among the lodges. Carson stuck to me, and we went through there whooping and shooting. The Indians were stampeded at first and swore afterward that four or five hundred white men rode through the camp. I guess we made noise enough for that many. After that we hung about there and managed to raise some hair, but soon there got to be so many Indians after us that we thought we had better light out for Sun River, sixty miles below Fort Benton, and make a camp. On the road we were attacked by them at midnight, but after a fight of half or three-quarters of an hour, they pulled off, and we got down to Sun river, with them pursuing us and shooting from

---

380. The Piegan and Blackfoot were menacing and killing white trappers, traders, and ranchers in the country between Fort Benton and Helena. Chief Little Dog, who was friendly to the whites—perhaps too friendly—was attacked and killed by his brethren in 1865.

cover when they could get a chance. In the night we took four of them alive and hung them with our lariats, in full view of the others, daring them to come into the open and fight like men, instead of skulking in the bushes like squaws. They yelled back that before another moon our hearts would be on the ground. When we came to look it over and see how many there were of them, and that we had one wounded man on our hands, we thought maybe they might be right. So we pulled out from there again, and made for Helena, the Blackfeet following us and keeping up a running fight all the way to Dearborn river, where the last skirmish took place, and where Charley Carson was buried."[381]

---

381. There are a few elements of truth in this story. Charley Carson was killed by Piegans in 1866. In January 1870, the Marias Massacre (or Baker Massacre), led by Major Baker, was conducted on a tribe of the Piegan, probably mostly "friendlies," and some 170 were killed. But no evidence has yet been found that Baronett was involved in any of this activity.

JACK'S BIOGRAPHY BY HIRAM CHITTENDEN

JACK BARONETT
Hiram Chittenden, *Yellowstone National Park: Historical and Descriptive* (Cincinnati, OH: The Robert Clarke Company, 1895)

Note: Baronett is reported to have written to Chittenden in the 1890s, telling him of his life and some history about the park for Chittenden's new book. This biographical sketch is rather basic and to the point, and may be the most accurate, although the Black Hills event was in early 1877.[382]

Baronett's career was adventurous beyond the average man of his class. He was born in Glencoe, Scotland, in 1829. His father was in the British naval service, and he early began to follow the sea. In his multitudinous wanderings we find him on the coast of Mexico during the Mexican War; on the Chinese coast in 1850, where he deserted his ship and fled to San Francisco; in 1852, in Australia after gold; the next year in Africa, still on a gold hunt; then in Australia again and in San Francisco; next in the Arctic seas as second mate on a whaling vessel; back in California in 1855; courier for Albert Sidney Johnston in the Mormon War; later in Colorado and California searching for gold; scout in the Confederate service until 1863; then in Mexico with the French under Maximilian, who made him a captain; back in California in 1864, and in Montana in September of the same year, where he at once set out on a prospecting trip which took him entirely through the region of the Yellowstone Park; later in the service of Gen. Custer as scout in the Indian territory; then

---

382. The biography written by Dan Thrapp is under copyright, as is a short biography in Aubrey Haines's *Yellowstone Place Names*; these are not reprinted here. The Wikipedia entry is fairly accurate.

in Mexico and finally back in Montana in 1870; finder of the lost Everts; builder of his celebrated bridge in 1871; in the Black Hills in 1875, where he slew a local editor who had unjustly reflected upon him in his paper; scout in the Sioux, Nez Percé, and Bannock Wars, 1876–8; Indian trader for many years; engaged in innumerable prospecting ventures; and still, at the age of sixty-six, searching with his old time ardor for the elusive yellow metal (p. 291–92).

Baronett's Bridge crosses the river immediately opposite Junction Butte. It is the first and only bridge yet (1895) built across the Yellowstone within the limits of the Park. It was built by the well known mountaineer, J. H. Baronett, in the spring of 1871, for the convenience of Clark's Fork miners. It was partially destroyed by the Nez Perces in 1877, but was repaired by Howard's command, and still further repaired the following year by Baronett and Norris. In 1880, it was replaced by a more substantial structure. At present it enjoys the unique distinction of being a private toll bridge on a government reservation (p. 263).

JACK'S BIOGRAPHY BY AUBREY L. HAINES

JACK BARONETT
Aubrey L. Haines, *Yellowstone National Park: Its Exploration and Establishment* (Washington, DC: US Department of the Interior, National Park Service, 1974), appendix, 134–35

COLLINS JACK [JOHN H.] BARONETT
Born in 1827 in Glencoe, Scotland; still living as late as 1901. The rescuer of Truman C. Everts, who was lost from the 1870 Washburn party of Yellowstone explorers and wandered alone for 37 days in the wilderness.

Many of the details of the colorful career of Jack Baronett (better known as "Yellowstone Jack") come from the biographical sketch that Hiram M. Chittenden included in his 1895 edition of *The Yellowstone National Park* (p. 291–92). From it we know that he went to sea at an early age, but deserted his ship in China in 1850 in order to go to the gold fields of California. The lure of gold drew him to other strikes in Australia and Africa, and he made a voyage to the Arctic as the second mate on a whaling ship before returning to California in 1855. He served as a courier for Gen. Albert Sidney Johnston during the Mormon War and took part in the Colorado gold rush on the eve of the Civil War. Baronett's sympathies were with the South, so he joined the First Texas Cavalry. Abandoning the "lost cause" in 1863, he took service briefly with the French under Maximilian in Mexico.

Baronett came to Montana Territory in September 1864 and his movements afterwards are better known. He was a member of one of the prospecting parties that crossed the Yellowstone plateau that fall and was with the "Yellowstone Expedition" of 1866. He wintered at Fort C. F. Smith and was among those prospectors who made their way through the hostile Sioux to the Gallatin Valley to obtain relief for the nearly starved garrison of that northernmost outpost on the Bozeman road.

Service as a scout with General Custer's expedition to the Black Hills and another foray into the Yellowstone country in 1869 increased Baronett's familiarity with the region. Thus, when Truman C. Everts was lost from the Washburn party in 1870, Baronett was considered best qualified to search for him. As a result, the unfortunate explorer was found in time to save his life.

Immediately after the dramatic rescue of Everts, Baronett built a toll bridge over the Yellowstone River near its junction with the Lamar, and he operated it for many years as a vital link in the road to the mining region on the Clark Fork River. The care of his bridge was often left in other hands as Baronett guided hunting parties, scouted for the military, and continued his search for elusive mineral riches.

While in the Black Hills during the winter of 1876–1877, Baronett became involved in a dispute with W. H. Timblin over the recording of mining claims. Fired upon by Timblin, he returned the shots with mortal effect. This event led to the following comment: "As well might the eastern miners walk with shot guns into a gulch lair of Hogback Grizzlies, as to arouse Barronette, the Buchannons and other comrades from the upper Yellowstone."

Despite his service for the Confederacy, Baronett enjoyed the respect and confidence of his former enemies. He was the preferred guide of Gen. Philip H. Sheridan on several junkets through the park and also the only member of the original civilian police force to be retained when the Army took over management of the area in 1886. He thus became the first scout to serve the new administration (he had even been considered for the superintendence, upon the recommendation of the Governor of Montana Territory).

In 1884 Baronett married Miss Marion A. Scott, of Emigrant Gulch, at Bozeman, Mont., on March 14, 1884. His wife later held the position of postmistress at Mammoth Hot Springs in the park.

JACK'S BIOGRAPHY BY AUBREY L. HAINES

Baronett's 35-year association with the Yellowstone region has been justly recognized by coupling his name to an outstanding peak which flanks the road to the park's northeast entrance, but, otherwise, life did not treat him well. His toll bridge, in which he had invested $15,000, was taken from him in 1894, and he spent $6,000 in lawyer's fees to obtain from Congress a niggardly compensation of $5,000. That money was invested in an expedition to Nome, Alaska, during the last great "gold rush," but his schooner and his hopes were both crushed in the Arctic ice. Thereafter, the old man's health failed rapidly and he was soon too feeble to earn a living at the rough work available to him. The trail ends at Tacoma, Wash., in late January or early February of 1901, when he was given a ticket by a charitable organization to get him to a friend at Redding, Calif., and it ends with a touch of irony: Six weeks after Baronett's disappearance, he was sought as the only heir of a titled brother killed in the Boer War.

Sources used by Haines: Hiram M. Chittenden, *The Yellowstone National Park* (1895), pp. 291–92; "Capt. Baronette," *The Livingston Enterprise* (MT), April 20, 1901, p. 1; J. S. Farrar to P. W. Norris, February 26, 1877, P. W. Norris Papers, Henry E. Huntington Library, San Marino, CA.

BIBLIOGRAPHY

BOOKS

Baldwin, Kenneth H. *Enchanted Enclosure: The Army Engineers and Yellowstone National Park.* Washington, DC: Office of the Chief of Engineers, US Army, 1976.

Bartlett, Richard A. *Yellowstone: A Wilderness Besieged.* Tucson: University of Arizona Press, 1989.

Brust, James, Brian Pohanka, and Sandy Barnard. *Where Custer Fell: Photographs of the Little Bighorn Battlefield Then and Now.* Norman: University of Oklahoma, 2007.

Chittenden, Hiram M. *The Yellowstone National Park: Historical and Descriptive.* Cincinnati, OH: Robert Clarke Co., 1895; and 3rd ed., 1900.

———. *The Yellowstone National Park: Historical and Descriptive.* New and enl. ed., entirely rev. Cincinnati, OH: Stewart & Kidd Co., 1915.

Coleman, Cynthia-Lou. *Environmental Clashes on Native American Land: Framing Environmental and Scientific Disputes.* Switzerland: Springer International Publishing, 2020.

Cramton, Louis C. *Early History of Yellowstone National Park and Its Relation to National Park Policies.* Washington, DC: Government Printing Office, 1932.

Everts, Truman C. *Thirty-Seven Days of Peril.* San Francisco, CA: E&R Grabhorn & James McDonald, 1923.

Franke, Mary Ann. *Yellowstone in the Afterglow: Lessons from the Fires.* Yellowstone National Park, WY: Yellowstone Center for Resources, 2000.

Gerrish, Theodore. *Life in the World's Wonderland.* Biddeford, ME: Press of the *Biddeford Journal*, 1887.

Goss, Robert V. *The Chronology of Wonderland*, 5th ed. Gardiner, MT: Self-published, 2015.

———. *From Sail to Trail: Chronicling Yellowstone's E. S. Topping.* Gardiner, MT: Self-published, 2008.

———. *Pack Trains and Pay Dirt in Yellowstone.* Gardiner, MT: Self-published, 2007.

Gunn, Angus Macleod. "Gold and the Early Settlement of British Columbia, 1858–1885." Master's thesis, University of British Columbia, 1965.

Haines, Aubrey L. "Biographical Appendix." *Yellowstone National Park: Its Exploration and Establishment.* Washington, DC: US Department of the Interior, National Park Service, 1974.

———. "The Bridge That Jack Built." Yellowstone National Park, WY: Yellowstone Archives. *Yellowstone Nature Notes* 21, no. 1 (January–February 1947).

———. *Yellowstone National Park: Its Exploration and Establishment*. Washington, DC: US Department of the Interior, National Park Service, 1974.

———. *The Yellowstone Story: A History of Our First National Park*, vol. 1. The Yellowstone Association. Denver: University Press of Colorado, 1996.

———. *The Yellowstone Story: A History of Our First National Park*, vol. 2. The Yellowstone Association. Denver: University Press of Colorado, 1977.

———. *Yellowstone Place Names: Mirrors of History*. Denver: University Press of Colorado, 1996.

Hans, Frederic Malon. *The Great Sioux Nation: A Complete History of Indian Life and Warfare in America*. Chicago: M. A. Donohue, 1907.

Haupt, Herman. *The Yellowstone National Park*. New York and Philadelphia: J. M. Stoddard, 1883.

Howard, Oliver O. *Nez Perce Joseph: An Account*. New York: Lee and Shepard Publishers, 1881.

Jucovy, Linda. *Searching for Calamity: The Life and Times of Calamity Jane*. Philadelphia, PA: Stampede Books, 2012.

Kuykendall, William L. *Frontier Days: A True Narrative of Striking Events on the Western Frontier*. J. M. and H. L. Kuykendall, 1917.

Lavender, David. *Fort Laramie and the Changing Frontier: Fort Laramie National Historic Site, Wyoming*. Washington, DC: US Department of the Interior, 1983.

Leclercq, Jules, *Yellowstone: Land of Wonders, Promenade in North America's National Park*. Omaha: University of Nebraska Press, 2013. First published in France in 1886.

Maguire, Horatio N. *The Black Hills and American Wonderland*. Chicago: Donnelley Lloyd & Co., 1877.

McClintock, John S. *Pioneer Days in the Black Hills—Accurate History and Facts Related by One of the Early Day Pioneers*. Norman: University of Oklahoma Press, 2000.

Nabakov, Peter, and Lawrence Loendorf. *American Indians and Yellowstone National Park*. Yellowstone National Park, WY: Yellowstone Center for Resources, YCR-CR-02-01, 2002.

Norris, P. W. "Meanderings of a Mountaineer, or, The Journals and Musings of a Rambler over Prairie and Plain." Unpublished manuscript. P. W. Norris Collection, Henry E. Huntington Library, San Marino, CA, 1885.

———. *Calumet of the Coteau*. Philadelphia: J. B. Lippincott, 1883.

Pierrepont, Edward. *Fifth Avenue to Alaska*. New York: G.P. Putnam's Sons, 1884.

Richards, Mary Bradshaw. *Camping Out in the Yellowstone*. Salem, MA: Newcomb & Gauss, 1910.

Rosen, Rev. Peter. *Pa-ha-sa-pah, Or, The Black Hills of South Dakota*. St. Louis, MO: Nixon-Jones Printing Co., 1895.

Rydell, Kiki Leigh, and Mary Shivers Culpin. *Managing the Matchless Wonders: A History of Administrative Development in Yellowstone National Park, 1872–1965*. Yellowstone National Park, WY: National Park Service, Yellowstone Center for Resources, 2006.

BIBLIOGRAPHY

Scott, Hugh Lenox. *Hugh Lennox Scott Remembers Indian Country*. Norman: University of Oklahoma Press, 2016.

———. *Some Memories of a Soldier*. New York: The Century Co., 1928.

Service, Robert W. *The Spell of the Yukon and Other Verses*. New York: Barse & Hopkins Publishers, 1907.

Sheridan, Philip H., and William Tecumseh Sherman. *Reports of Inspection Made in the Summer of 1877 by Generals P. H. Sheridan and W. T. Sherman of Country North of the Union Pacific Railroad, and Report of Journey Made by General W. T. Sherman in the Northwest and Middle Parts of the United States in 1883*. Washington, DC: Government Printing Office, 1884.

Strong, General William E. *A Trip to the Yellowstone Park in July, August, and September 1875*. Washington, DC: US Government Printing Office, 1876; new impression, University of Oklahoma Press, 1968.

Thrapp, Dan L. *Encyclopedia of Frontier Biography: A–F*. Omaha: University of Nebraska Press, 1988.

Topping, E. S. *Chronicles of the Yellowstone*. Minneapolis, MN: Ross & Haines, 1968.

Turner, Frederick Jackson. *The Frontier in American History*. New York: Henry Holt & Co., 1921.

Varley, John D., and Wayne G. Brewster, eds. *Wolves for Yellowstone: A Report to the United States Congress*. Vol. IV: *Research and Analysis*. Yellowstone National Park, WY, 1992.

Wallace, Robert C. *A Few Memories of a Long Life*. Fairfield, WA: Ye Galleon Press, 1988.

Whithorn, Doris. "Jack Baronett—A Legend in His Lifetime." *Tales Twice Told on the Yellowstone*, vol. 2. Livingston, MT: Self-published, 1994.

Whittlesey, Lee H. *Yellowstone Place Names*, 2nd ed. Gardiner, MT: Wonderland Publishing, 2006.

Whittlesey, Lee H., and Elizabeth A. Watry. *Ho! for Wonderland*. Albuquerque: University of New Mexico Press, 2009.

Wiley, William H. *Yosemite, Alaska and the Yellowstone*. New York: John Wiley & Sons, 1893.

Wylie, William W. *Yellowstone National Park, Or, The Great American Wonderland*. Kansas City, MO: Ramsey, Millett & Hudson, 1882.

Journals and Magazines

De Lacy, Walter W. "A Trip Up the Snake River in 1863." *Contributions to the Historical Society of Montana* 1 (1876): pp. 113–43.

Engineering—An Illustrated Weekly Journal 44, July–December 1887 (London: October 14, 1887): pp. 362–63, 373, 415.

Everts, Truman. "Thirty-Seven Days of Peril." *Scribner's Monthly* 3, no. 1 (November 1871): pp. [1]–17.

Gay, John S. "Charley Reynolds." *Montana: The Magazine of Western History* 14, no. 3 (Summer 1963).

Goss, Robert V. "And Finding . . . a Hairless Cub, Called the Gulch Bear." *Montana Ghost Town Quarterly* 40 (Spring 2010).

Gray, John S. "Last Rites for Lonesome Charley Reynolds." *Montana: The Magazine of Western History* 13, no. 3 (Summer 1963).
Hans, Frederic Malon. "Diary of Fred M. Hans, 1877—Black Hills Road Agents." *Scouting for the U.S. Army, 1876–1879: The Diary of Fred M. Hans*, edited by Michael L. Tate and Grace Lakota Hans Pawol, South Dakota Historical Collections (1981): pp. 27–34. Unidentified newspaper clipping in Fred M. Hans Papers in possession of Grace Lakota Hans Pawol, Omaha, NE.
Hofer, Elwood. "Winter in the Wonderland." *Forest and Stream* (April 28, 1887): p. 246.
Hunt, Fred A. "A Purposeful Picnic, III." *The Pacific Monthly* 19 (May 1908): pp. 523–30.
Lang, William L. "'At the Greatest Personal Peril to the Photographer': The Schwatka-Haynes Winter Expedition in Yellowstone, 1887." *Montana: The Magazine of Western History* (Winter 1983).
Mitchell, Silas Weir. "Through the Yellowstone Park to Fort Custer." *Lippincott's Magazine* 25 and 26 (June and July 1880).
Porter, T. R. "Lone Star: The Adventures of a Famous Scout." *The Wild World Magazine* 14 (October 1904 to March 1905).
"Review of the Month." *Insurance Journal: A Monthly Review of Fire and Life Insurance* 7 (1879): p. 84.
Spouter, A. "Geysers in the Distance." *The Scholastic* 7, no. 29 (March 14, 1874): p. 225; vol. 7, no. 29 (March 21, 1874): p. 233; vol. 7, no. 30 (April 11, 1874): p. 258.
Taylor, Allen. "The Old Frontiers." *The New Republic*, May 7, 2008.
Walsh, Jim. "The Exploration and Mapping of Yellowstone National Park." *Meridian Journal*, no. 3 (1990).
Weaver, David B. "Early Days in Emigrant Gulch." *Contributions to the Historical Society of Montana* 7 (1910): pp. 73–96.

Government Publications and Documents

Annual Reports of the War Department, vol. 1. United States War Department, 1882–1883.
Baronett Bridge. Reports of the Department of the Interior, Fiscal Year Ended June 30, 1920. Washington, DC: Government Printing Office, 1920.
Baronett Bridge. *The Statutes at Large of the United States*, vol. 30, chap. 314. Washington, DC: Government Printing Office, 1899.
Black Hills. *United States v. Sioux Nation of Indians* (Ct. Cl. 1979), 601 F.2d 1157, 1161; 19 Stat. 176, chapter 289.
Culpin, Mary Shivers. *The History of the Construction of the Road System in Yellowstone, 1872–1966*. Historic Resource Study, vol. 1. Selections from the Division of Cultural Resources, no. 5. National Park Service, 1994.
Harris, Capt. Moses. "Superintendent's Annual Report, 1887." Washington, DC: Government Printing Office, 1887.
Jones, William A. "Report upon the Reconnaissance of Northwestern Wyoming." Washington, DC: Government Printing Office, 1875.
"Lamar River Bridge." *Yellowstone Roads and Bridges*. HAER No. WY-12 (1968).
Ludlow, Capt. William. *Report of a Reconnaissance from Carroll, Montana Territory, on the Upper Missouri, to the Yellowstone National Park and Return, Made in the Summer of 1875*. Washington, DC: Government Printing Office, 1876.

BIBLIOGRAPHY

Norris, P. W. "Fifth Annual Report of the Superintendent of Yellowstone National Park." Washington, DC: Government Printing Office, 1881.

———. "Report upon the Yellowstone National Park to the Secretary of Interior, 1878." Washington, DC. Montana Memory, https://www.mtmemory.org/nodes/view/104718.

"Report of Capt. Moses Harris, First Cavalry, Acting Superintendent, Yellowstone National Park: Office of Superintendent." Mammoth Hot Springs, WY, October 4, 1886.

"Report of the Superintendent of the Yellowstone National Park to the Secretary of Interior, 1888." Washington, DC: Government Printing Office, 1888.

NEWSPAPERS

Anaconda Standard (Anaconda, MT)
    "Gold in the River," May 18, 1896, p. 9.
    "Jail Breaker Holmes, Convicted of Murder, Two Days Ahead," October 6, 1897, p. 2.
    "That Was in the Early Days," January 30, 1895.

Billings Gazette (Billings, MT)
    February 7, 1887, p. 2.
    "Jack Baronett, Early Day Scout Was Builder of Initial Span," January 17, 1932, p. 11.

Billings Herald (Billings, MT)
    "Town Talk," August 2, 1884, p. 3.

Black Hills Weekly Pioneer (Deadwood, SD)
    "Centennial," July 8, 1876, p. 4.

Bozeman Avant Courier (Bozeman, MT)
    "Gallatin County News," September 5, 1872, p. 8.
    February 28, 1873, p. 3.
    "From the Yellowstone," April 4, 1873, p. 3.
    "For Clark's Fork," June 20, 1873, p. 3.
    "The District Fair," October 24, 1873, p. 3.
    "The National Park," December 31, 1875, p. 3.
    "Yellowstone Park," February 18, 1876.
    "The News," April 5, 1877, p. 2.
    "Hurrah for Norris," September 12, 1878, p. 2.
    "Sandwiches," June 24, 1880, p. 3.
    "New Town at Clark's Fork Mines," March 27, 1884, p. 3.

Bozeman Courier (Bozeman, MT)
    "Accidently Strychnined," March 13, 1890, p. 3.

Bozeman Times (Bozeman, MT)
    June 6, 1878, p. 2.

Bozeman Weekly Avant Courier
    "The Shortcomings of Col. Baronett's Guide," March 27, 1884, p. 3.
    "Richest in America," July 30, 1884, p. 3.

"Good News from Cooke," July 31, 1884, p. 3.
"Local Miscellany," April 2, 1885, p. 3.
"Local Layout," May 16, 1885, p. 3.
"Divorces," October 10, 1888.
Bozeman Weekly Chronicle (Bozeman, MT)
January 30, 1884, p. 2.
"Summons," March 12, 1884, p. 4.
"Wedding Bells," March 19, 1884, p. 4.
"Richest in America," July 30, 1884, p. 3.
"Baronett's Bridge," September 30, 1885, p. 3.
Bozeman Weekly Gazette (Bozeman, MT)
"May Be a Hanging," July 9, 1897.
Bridger Free Press (Bridger, MT)
"Scout's Varied Experience," May 15, 1903, p. 2.
Burlington Free Press (Burlington, VT)
"The Yellowstone National Park," September 20, 1882, p. 2.
Butte Miner (Butte, MT)
"The Scout," February 21, 1882, p. 1.
"An Old Scout's Story," February 22, 1882, p. 1.
"Territorial News," April 5, 1882, p. 8.
"Madisonian," March 26, 1884, p. 2.
Cheyenne Daily Leader (Cheyenne, WY)
"Field Notes," June 30, 1875, p. 2.
"Castle Creek," November 30, 1876, p. 5.
"Iron Creek," February 22, 1877, p. 4.
Chicago Tribune (Chicago, IL)
"Yellowstone Expedition," October 4, 1871, p. 2.
Cincinnati Enquirer (OH)
"Jack Baronett, the Scout," January 28, 1882, p. 12.
Deadwood Pioneer (South Dakota)
"Estrella Del Norte," June 15, 1882, p. 4.
Dodge City Times (Dodge City, KS)
"Burying the Brave," July 21, 1877, p. 5.
Gardiner Wonderland (Gardiner, MT)
"A Bit of Early History," June 5, 1902, p. 3.
May 7, 1903, p. 2.
Great Falls Tribune (Great Falls, MT)
"Mrs. Elizabeth Wickes, 88, Came to Montana in 1879," October 16, 1936, p. 12.
Harper's Weekly (New York, NY)
"The Surrender of Joseph," November 17, 1877, p. 906.
Helena Daily Miner (Helena, MT)
"Montana Mélange," October 13, 1883, p. 4.
Helena Independent (Helena, MT)
"Territorial News," April 14, 1876, p. 3.
"The New Eldorado Humbug," April 25, 1876, p. 3.

BIBLIOGRAPHY

"Crevice Gulch and Clark's Fork," May 3, 1879, p. 3.
"Montana Matters," September 14, 1883, p. 7.
"Montana Matters," February 1, 1884, p. 7.
"Jumping the National Park," February 27, 1884, p. 7.
"Court House Notes," August 22, 1890, p. 8.

Helena Weekly Herald (Helena, MT)
"The Long Lost Found," October 27, 1870, p. 7.
"The Finding of Hon. T. C. Everts," October 27, 1870, p. 8.
"Personal," July 18, 1872, p. 7.
"Sad News—Sudden Death of Wife of Sir William Blackmore," July 25, 1872, p. 8.
"Wonderland," September 18, 1873, pp. 3, 8.
"Crystal Specimens," October 9, 1873, p. 3.
"Horse Thieves," November 18, 1875, p. 7.
"The Battle of Clark's Fork," September 19, 1878, p. 4.
"The Sheridan Geyser," September 15, 1881, p. 8.
"Virginia City Items," March 9, 1882, p. 6.
"Town Talk," April 27, 1882, p. 7.
"Territorial," July 20, 1882, p. 6.
"English Tourists," February 27, 1897, p. 1.

Indiana Democrat (Indiana, PA)
P. W. Norris, "The Field of Death," August 26, 1877.

Livingston Daily Enterprise (Livingston, MT)
"By Telegraph," August 30, 1883, p. 1.
"Local Layout," January 12, 1884, p. 3.

Livingston Enterprise (Livingston, MT)
"The Park Arrests," December 20, 1884, p. 3.
"Personal Points," August 13, 1887, p. 3.
"Personal Points," February 7, 1885, p. 3.
"Personal Points," May 31, 1890, p. 3.
"Local Layout," January 7, 1893, p. 5.
"Cooke Letter," June 8, 1895, p. 1.
"Capt. Baronette," April 20, 1901, p. 1.
"County Business," June 18, 1904, p. 1.
"Death of an Old Timer," December 1, 1906, p. 3.
"A Friend's Tribute," December 8, 1906, p. 1.

Livingston Post (Livingston, MT)
"Local Matters," July 18, 1889, p. 3.
Belle Vinnedge Drake, "Uncle Billy Langston," February 12, 1891, p. 2.
"Local Matters," May 31, 1894, p. 3.
"Some Interesting Early History," January 30, 1895, p. 1.
"How Mullery Was Found," May 20, 1896, p. 3.
"Local News," April 22, 1897, p. 3.
"Horn Miller in Town," April 16, 1903, p. 1.
"Local News," May 7, 1903, p. 5.

The Madisonian (Virginia City, MT)
"Horse Thieves," November 13, 1875, p. 2.
"Montana Melange," February 11, 1882, p. 2.
"Montana Mélange," February 24, 1883, p. 2.
"Trouble in the National Park," December 20, 1884, p. 3.
Minneapolis Journal (Minneapolis, MN)
"A Scout for Superintendent," February 1, 1884, p. 2.
Montana Post (Virginia City, MT)
"Stampede to the Yellowstone," September 24, 1864, p. 3.
"The Very Latest," May 11, 1867, p. 8.
"The Upper Yellowstone," August 31, 1867, p. 2.
Montana Record-Herald (Helena, MT)
"The Lost and Found," October 28, 1870, p. 1.
"From Clark's Fork," October 4, 1883, p. 3.
Mower County Transcript (Austin, MN)
"An Englishman's Tour," July 4, 1872, p. 2.
New Idea (Red Lodge, MT)
"A Splendid Assay," July 18, 1895, p. 1.
The New North-West (Deer Lodge, MT)
"Indians Near Bozeman Again," August 15, 1874, p. 3.
"Territorial Items," February 11, 1876, p. 3.
"Life with the Nez Perces," September 14, 1877, p. 2.
"Personal," July 26, 1878, p. 3.
"Gallatin County," July 25, 1879, p. 3.
"Territorial Items," September 2, 1881, p. 3.
Philadelphia Times (Philadelphia, PA)
"Elwood Hofer, The Yellowstone," April 14, 1887, p. 1.
Picket Journal (Red Lodge, MT)
"Along the Belt," December 5, 1891, p. 1.
Pittsburgh Daily Post (Pittsburgh, PA)
"The Deadwood Case," April 18, 1879, p. 4; May 31, 1879, p. 6.
The Province (Victoria, BC)
March 13, 1901, p. 7.
Red Lodge Picket (Red Lodge, MT)
"County News," March 19, 1892, p. 1.
"News from Telluride District," April 16, 1892, p. 3.
"Mining Matters," November 12, 1892, p. 3.
"Local Brevities," December 4, 1897, p. 3.
Salt Lake Herald (Salt Lake City, UT)
"Schwatka a Dude," February 13, 1887, p. 9.
San Francisco Call (San Francisco, CA)
"Gold from the Yukon River," July 15, 1897, p. 8.
San Francisco Examiner (San Francisco, CA)
"Like News of the Old West," July 17, 1897.

BIBLIOGRAPHY

The Searchlight (Redding, CA)
"No Trace Here of Missing Heir," April 17, 1901, p. 6.
Sioux City Journal (Sioux City, IA)
"The National Park," January 30, 1886, p. 2.
St. Paul Globe (St. Paul, MN)
"In Yellowstone Park," September 26, 1885, p. 4.
Tacoma Daily Ledger (Tacoma, WA)
"Heir to a Title Lost in Tacoma," April 13, 1901, p. 5.
"For Thanksgiving," November 19, 1901, p. 5.
Tacoma News Tribune (Tacoma, WA)
"The Gold Fever," July 17, 1897, p. 1.
Victoria Daily Times (Victoria, BC)
March 24, 1901, p. 7.
Weekly Oregon Statesman (Salem, OR)
"Calamity Jane," September 15, 1876, p. 2.
Western Home Journal (Lawrence, KS)
"From Our Special Correspondent," August 18, 1872, p. 2.
"The Wonders of the Yellowstone," September 12, 1872, p. 2.

Archival Resources

Anderson to Dept. of Interior. Letter of October 27, 1893. Army Files, February 1895. Yellowstone National Park (YNP) Archives.

Baronett, Jack. Vertical Files, Biography, US Army Civilian Employment Records. National Archives, RG 92, File 1886-635 and 1887-634. YNP Archives.

Baronett, Jack. Files. "Petition for J. C. Baronett for Superintendent." RG 48, No. 62, Roll 4, 1884. National Archives, copy from YNP Archives.

Baronett, Jack. Hand-written Note Cards. Aubrey L. Haines Collection No. 2231, MtBC, us, Montana State University Special Collections, Bozeman, MT.

Baronett and Ponsford to Secretary of Interior. Letter of November 22, 1884. RG 48, No. 62, Roll 2, Letters Rec'd Interior, 1883–84. YNP Archives.

Baronett to Capt. Anderson. Letter of November 23, 1894. Army Files, LB2, Item 4, Doc. 788. YNP Archives. See also Documents #789–792, 1152, and 2321–2324.

Baronett to Capt. Anderson. Letter of February 19, 1895. Doc. #2324, Army Files. YNP Archives.

Baronett to Sanders. Letter of December 8, 1890. Wilber Fisk Sanders Papers, 1856–1905, MC53, Box 2, Folder 3. Montana Historical Society, Helena, MT.

Blackmore, William H. "1872 Yellowstone Trip, Diary #6." William Blackmore Collection, AC018, Box 3, Folder 6. Fray Angelico Chavez History Library, Santa Fe, NM.

Boutelle to Baronett. Letter of November 10, 1890. Bound Vol. 215. Vol. 111, Letters Sent, 1890. YNP Archives.

Crookes to Goode. Letter of September 10, 1900. Army Files, Letter Box 8, Item 15, Doc. 3700. YNP Archives.

Doane, Lt. to Yellowstone Command. Letter of June 13, 1877. Collection 2211—Doane Papers, 1860–1939, Series 2: Military papers, 1864–1893, Box 2, Folder 8. Montana State University Special Collections, Bozeman, MT.

Dysart, Dick. "Park County People Who Went to Alaska." September 24, 2001. Yellowstone Gateway Museum, Livingston, MT.

Flather, Robert. "Bridges." MSC007_04.01. YNP Archives.

———. "Cooke City Miner's Road." Catalog No. 210545, Box 3, Files 03.02, 03.03, 04.01. YNP Archives.

Farrar, J. S. to P. W. Norris. Letter, February 26, 1877. P. W. Norris Collection, Henry E. Huntington Library, San Marino, CA.

Haines, Aubrey L. "Baronett's Cabin." Haines Papers, Series 4, Box 33, Place Names Data, pp. 31–60. Montana State University Special Collections, Bozeman, MT.

Henderson, A. Bart. *Narrative of a Prospecting Expedition to the East Fork & Clarks Fork of Yellowstone, 1870.* July 2–15, 1870. Yellowstone Vertical Files, Yellowstone Library, Gardiner, MT.

Henderson, G. L. *Bound Volume 141.* Manuscripts, YNP Archives.

Kearns, W. E. "A Nez Perce Chief Re-Visits Yellowstone." *Yellowstone Nature Notes* 7, nos. 7–8 (June-July 1935). YNP Archives.

Letter to *Cheyenne Daily Leader* newspaper. November 30, 1876, WPA Subject 31— Black Hills Mining. Wyoming State Archives, Cheyenne, WY.

Mitchell, Silas Weir. S. W. Mitchell Papers. MSS 2/241–03, Series 5, Folder 7, Item 1, p. 44. Library of the College of Physicians of Philadelphia.

New World Mining District. *Ledger Book 1*, #2350. Montana State University Special Collections, Bozeman, MT.

New World Mining District. *Record Book A, 1879–1880.* Donna and Larry Teeter Private Collection.

Ponsford and Sanborn to Secretary of Interior. Letter of February 5, 1884, RG 48, No. 62, Roll 2, Letters Rec'd Interior 1883–84. YNP Archives.

Ponsford and Sanborn to Carpenter, Letter of November 22, 1884, RG 48, No. 62, Roll 2, Letters Rec'd Interior 1883–84, YNP Archives.

Sturgis, Col. to 1st Lt. Doane. Letter of September 2, 1877, Collection 2211-Bo2-F11. Doane Papers. Montana State University Special Collections, Bozeman, MT.

Teeter Collection. New World Mining District record books. Donna and Larry Teeter Private Collection. Personal Correspondence.

WEBSITES

Baronett. Marriage Certificate. Montana County Marriages 1865–1950. Familysearch.org.

Blust, Dick, Jr. "The President Arthur Expedition: The Fishing Trip That Helped Save Yellowstone." Accessed September 19, 2022. https://www.wyohistory.org/encyclopedia/president-arthur-expedition-fishing-trip-helped-save-yellowstone.

"How the US Cavalry Saved Our National Parks." In *The Early Years in Yellowstone*, chap. 4. https://www.nps.gov/parkhistory/online_books/hampton/chap4.htm.

National Park Service. "Chronology of the Ranger Story." http://npshistory.com/publications/ranger/ranger-story-chronology.pdf.

BIBLIOGRAPHY

New World Mining District Report. US Forest Service. Accessed July 15, 2023. https://www.fs.usda.gov/Internet/FSE_DOCUMENTS/stelprdb5127407.pdf.

Open Parks Network.org. Yellowstone Photo Album 29, page 28 #10306–1. https://openparksnetwork.org/single-item-view/?oid=OPN_NS:671CB4C1E05F982216D36016D16EC0FA.

"Park County Poor Farm Records Index 1896–1924." Accessed July 14, 2023. https://sites.rootsweb.com/~mtpcgs/media/Park%20County%20Poor%20Farm%20Records%20Index%201896–1924.pdf.

Patterson, Allie. "Nez Perce and Bannock Flight Through Yellowstone National Park." Accessed June 20, 2022. www.intermountainhistories.org.

Redington to Miller. Letter of March 16, 1887. Accessed May 18, 2022. https://www.colorado-west.com/cooke/hornletter2.jpg.

Rubinstein, Paul. "Early Explorers in Yellowstone." The Yellowstone Backcountry Page. Accessed July 14, 2022. https://www.yellowstonestereoviews.com/backcountry/explorers.html.

"Shipwreck Online Exhibit." Alaska State Library. Accessed May 5, 2022. https://library.alaska.gov/hist/exhibits/shipwrecks.html.

"Turtle Island Storyteller Rosa Yearout." *Wisdom Blogger*. Accessed October 12, 2022. https://wisdomoftheelders.org/turtle-island-storyteller-rosa-yearout/.

ABOUT THE AUTHOR

Robert V. Goss dedicated over thirty-five years to working in and around Yellowstone National Park, thirty of those for Yellowstone Park Co. and its successors, before retiring from Xanterra Parks & Resorts. An avid historian, he has studied Yellowstone history and self-published seven books, primarily focusing on the early concessioners and pioneers. Robert has authored or coauthored twenty-three articles and been featured in publications such as *Yellowstone History Journal*, *Yellowstone Science*, *Annals of Wyoming*, *Motor Coach Age*, *Points West*, *Montana Pioneer*, and other local publications. He also coauthored *Images of America: Livingston, Montana*.

While living in Gardiner, Montana, Robert was a purchasing agent for the Mineral Hill gold mine at Jardine, a town known as Bear Gulch in the 1870s–1890s. He became familiar with the local mining history, as well as the chronicles of the Cooke City surrounding areas. Now residing in southwest Utah, he continues his research while maintaining the Geyser Bob website of Yellowstone history. He is currently researching and writing a book about Yellowstone's stage drivers.

www.ingramcontent.com/pod-product-compliance
Lightning Source LLC
Chambersburg PA
CBHW020410080526
44584CB00014B/1256